BIRNBAUM GUIDES

2014

Disneyland®
RESORT

Expert Advice from the Inside Source

Wendy Lefkon EDITORIAL DIRECTOR

Jill Safro EDITOR

Jessica Ward CONTRIBUTING EDITOR

Pam Brandon CONTRIBUTING EDITOR

Clark Wakabayashi DESIGNER

Alexandra Mayes Birnbaum CONSULTING EDITOR

THE OFFICIAL GUIDE

Stephen Birnbaum FOUNDING EDITOR

DISNEY EDITIONS
NEW YORK • LOS ANGELES

For Steve, who merely made this all possible.

Other 2014 Birnbaum's Official Disney Guides:

Disney Cruise Line
Walt Disney World
Walt Disney World Dining
Walt Disney World For Kids
Walt Disney World Pocket Parks Guide

SUSTAINABLE FORESTRY INITIATIVE   Certified Sourcing
www.sfiprogram.org
SFI-00993
This Label Applies to Text Stock Only

Contents

What's New?

To spotlight shops, attractions, shows, and restaurants making their debut, some listings are marked with the stamp shown here. Look for it throughout the book. Here are a few highlights:

A Word from the Editor

Walt Disney, the man who pioneered the realm of family entertainment, was at once an artist, entrepreneur, and creative visionary. He was also a dad. And, like many of the folks who visit Disneyland each year, Walt treasured the time he spent with his children. In fact, while his two daughters were growing up, Walt accompanied them to carnivals, zoos, and local amusement parks. It was something of a Saturday tradition for the Disney family. During these outings he would often make the same observation: The youngsters were happily entertained, but the adults didn't have much to do. It didn't seem right that he'd be stuck sitting on a bench while the kids had all the fun. To his way of thinking, a park should appeal to the sense of wonder and exploration in guests of all ages. His bold vision became a reality on July 17, 1955, when Disneyland opened in Anaheim, California.

Now, more than 59 years later, Walt's original park is as beloved as ever. While Disneyland Park is wonderfully familiar to us—practically a second home—Disney California Adventure is a newer playing ground, and finding the best ways to take it in has been an adventure in itself. Attractions such as California Screamin', Tower of Terror, and Toy Story Mania! helped put this place on the map, but they're just the tip of the iceberg. The park has completed a *billion-dollar expansion*. Guests are being treated to a slew of new theme park attractions and entertainment bearing that distinctive Disney stamp. Among them: World of Color, Red Car Trolley, and The Little Mermaid—Ariel's Undersea Adventure, plus a whole "land" featuring the four-wheeled residents of *Cars'* Radiator Springs.

When Steve Birnbaum launched this guide, he made it clear what was expected of anyone who worked on it. The book would be meticulously revised each year, leaving no attraction untested, no meal untasted, no hotel untried. First-hand experiences like these, accumulated over the years, make this book the most authoritative guide to the Disneyland Resort. Our expertise, however, was not achieved by being escorted through back doors of attractions. Instead, we've waited in lines with everyone else, always hoping to have a Disney experience like any other guest.

Of course, there's more to the Disneyland Resort than the theme parks. There's also a dining, shopping, and entertainment district known as Downtown Disney, and three Disney hotels. It all adds up to a total that is truly greater than the sum of its parts. And, though it has more than a half century of history under its belt, this is just the beginning—as per its founder's wishes: "Disneyland will never be completed. It will continue to grow as long as there is imagination left in the world."

Take Our Advice

In creating this book, we have considered every possible aspect of your trip, from planning it to plotting day-to-day activities. We realize that even the most meticulous vacation planner needs detailed, accurate, and objective information to prepare a successful itinerary. To achieve that goal, we encourage the submission of factual information and insight from Disneyland staffers—but the decision to use or lose such information is entirely at the discretion of the editor.

We have also packaged handy bits of advice in the form of "Hot Tips" throughout the book. These helpful hints come directly from the copious notes we've taken during our countless trips to the Disneyland Resort and the surrounding Anaheim area. We've also used our "Birnbaum's Best" stamp of approval wherever we deemed it appropriate, highlighting our favorite attractions and restaurants—the crowd-pleasers we feel stand head, shoulders, and ears above the rest.

You, the reader, benefit from the combination of years of experience—and access to up-to-date inside information from the Disneyland staff—that makes this guide unique. We like to think it's indispensable, but you be the judge of that 130 pages from now.

Credit Where Credit Is Due

We hope we are not omitting any names in thanking Matt Gray, Michelle Harker, Karen McClintock, Gina Siebert, Kevin Gidden, Claudia Erdogan, Jennifer Bellman, Susan Leonetti, Kevin Valentine, Frank Reifsnyder, Connie Chen, Chris Won, Andrae Rivas, Christian Dhyne, George Savvas, Laura Schaeffell, Darla Bozter-Nash, Kathy Crummey, and Chris Ostrander for helping us ensure the factual accuracy of *Birnbaum's Official Guide to Disneyland 2014.*

Kudos to Michelle Olveira for her outstanding fact-checking, and to copy editor extraordinaire Erika Nein. We'd also like to tip our hats to Jennifer Eastwood, Jerry Gonzalez, Mike Carroll, Carolyn Brunetto, Tracey Randinelli, and Christina Fontana for their editorial support and production panache.

Of course, no list of acknowledgments would be complete without mentioning our founding editor, Steve Birnbaum, whose spirit, wisdom, and humor still infuse these pages, as well as Alexandra Mayes Birnbaum, who continues to be a guiding light—to say nothing of a careful reader of every word.

The Last Word

Finally, it's important to remember that every worthwhile travel guide is a living enterprise; the book you hold in your hands is our best effort at explaining how to enjoy the Disneyland Resort at the moment, but its text is no way etched in stone. Disneyland is always changing and growing, and in each annual edition we refine and expand our material to serve your needs better. Just before the grand opening of Disneyland, Walt Disney remarked that the main attraction was still missing—people. That's where you come in.

Have a wonderful time!

—Jill Safro, Editor

DON'T FORGET TO WRITE!

No contribution is of greater value to us in preparing the next edition of this book than your comments on its usefulness and your own experiences at the Disneyland Resort. Drop us a postcard or send a letter to the address on the right.

Official Disney Guides
Birnbaum's Disneyland 2014
Disney Editions
1133 Sixth Avenue, 33rd Floor
New York, NY 10036

Getting Ready to Go

A nyone who visited the Anaheim area during the past decade was sure to see evidence of the Disney Imagineers at work. Behind closed gates, construction went on day and night, and finally, the results were unveiled—a 500-acre Disneyland Resort, with Walt Disney's original theme park, Disneyland (although many Disney-philes may still refer to it fondly as the "Magic Kingdom"), at its heart. Besides this "Happiest Place on Earth," guests will find the Disney California Adventure theme park, the Downtown Disney District, and Disney's Grand Californian Hotel & Spa, which completes the trio of Disney's on-property hotels. Of course, you'll want to do and see it all, but where should you start? When should you go? And then there are the all-important questions of how to get there and where to stay. Maybe you want to extend your vacation—perhaps you'll include a visit to (or a stay at) the beach or one of the other nearby attractions.

That's a lot to think about. But don't worry: By the time you've read through this chapter, you'll have all the information you need to make smart decisions. So read on, and remember—a little advance planning goes a long way.

When to Go

When you weigh the best times to visit the Disneyland Resort, the most obvious possibilities seem to be Christmas, Easter, and summer vacation—particularly if there are children in the family. But there are a few good reasons to avoid these periods—the major one being that almost everybody else wants to go then, too. (The pedestrian traffic at Disney California Adventure is occasionally lighter than it is at Disneyland Park, but it is much busier than it used to be.)

If you can only visit during one of these busy times and worry that the crowds might spoil your fun, there are some tactics for making optimum use of every minute and avoiding the longest of lines—notably, go to the park early to get a jump on the day (and on the crowds), use the free Fastpass system whenever possible, and remember that Disney keeps the parks open later during busy seasons. Note that "early entry" (aka "Extra Magic Hour" or Magic Mornings") is offered on select days to guests staying at Disneyland hotels, Walt Disney Travel Company guests, and day guests with a pre-purchased 3-day (or more) Park Hopper.

On the other hand, choosing to visit when the parks are least crowded may mean that you miss some of the most entertaining parades and special events. For instance, Disneyland Park's Fantasmic! show and the fireworks might not be on the entertainment schedule, and certain attractions may be closed for annual refurbishment.

A lovely time to visit Disneyland—when it's not too crowded but everything is still open—is the period between Thanksgiving until about a week before Christmas, when the Christmas parade takes place and carolers add festive music to the mix. Other good times to visit are the periods after summer—September through early October—and after New Year's Day.

When Not to Go: If crowds make you queasy, keep in mind that Saturday is the busiest day year-round. In summer, Sunday, Monday, and Friday are the next busiest. If you decide to visit Disneyland Park during a weekend, opt for Sunday. And remember that the week before Christmas through New Year's Day, Easter week, and the period from early July through Labor Day are packed.

Crowd Patterns

Least Crowded
- Second week in January to Presidents' week
- Two weeks after Easter Sunday to Memorial Day week
- End of Labor Day week to Columbus Day
- End of Thanksgiving weekend to mid-December

Average Attendance
- Period just after Presidents' week until about two weeks before Easter
- Sundays in spring, autumn, and winter, except holiday weekends
- Memorial Day week to beginning of summer vacation
- Week after Labor Day weekend
- Columbus Day to day before Thanksgiving

Most Crowded
- Any Saturday
- Sundays during summer and holiday weekends
- Presidents' week
- Weeks before through weeks after Easter Sunday
- Beginning of summer through Labor Day weekend
- Thanksgiving weekend (Thursday through Sunday)
- Week before Christmas through first week of January

Keeping Disney Hours

Operating hours tend to fluctuate according to the season, so call 714-781-4565 or 714-781-7290, or visit *www.disneyland.com* for updates.

DISNEYLAND PARK: This park is typically open from about 10 A.M. to 8 P.M. Monday–Thursday, 9 A.M. to 10 P.M. on Friday and Sunday, and 8 A.M. to 11 P.M. on Saturday. Hours are often extended in the summer and during holiday seasons. "Extra Magic" hour is offered on Tuesday, Thursday, and Saturday. This allows guests staying at Disneyland Resort hotels to enter the park one hour early. Those bearing multi-day park passes that include Magic Mornings (it is stated on the ticket) may enter the park one hour early on Tuesday, Thursday, and Saturday mornings.

DISNEY CALIFORNIA ADVENTURE: The park generally opens at 9 or 10 A.M. and closes at about 9 or 10 P.M. on weekdays, sometimes later on weekends and during the summer. Call 714-781-4565 for specifics. Disneyland Resort hotel guests may enter the park one hour early on Extra Magic days: Sunday, Monday, Wednesday, and Friday.

DOWNTOWN DISNEY: Some spots in this shopping, dining, and entertainment district open as early as the theme parks do, but most stick to the following hours: 10 A.M. to 11 P.M. Sunday–Thursday, 10 A.M. to midnight on Friday and Saturday.

TRANSPORTATION: The monorail begins making its 2.5 mile loop about the time Disneyland opens (for early entry Magic Mornings), and runs until about 15 minutes before the park closes. Trams transporting guests between parking lots and the parks begin picking up guests about an hour before the first park opens, and continue transporting guests back to parking areas until about an hour or so after the last park closes. If you miss the last tram, ask a cast member about alternate transportation to the Mickey and Friends parking structure (usually in the form of a van).

Disneyland Weather

If dry, sunny weather is your ideal, Anaheim may seem like a dream come true. Rainy days are few and far between and generally occur between the months of November and April, which is also the coolest time of year. During this season, Santa Ana winds sometimes produce short periods of dry, warm desert weather and sparkling-clear skies that unveil distant mountains usually hidden by smog. In summer, thin, low morning clouds make it prudent to plan expeditions to the beach for the afternoon, when the haze burns off and the mercury rises. Mornings and nights are generally cool. The average daytime year-round temperature is about 73 degrees.

	Temperature AVERAGE		Rainfall AVERAGE
	HIGH	LOW	(INCHES)
January	71	48	2.86
February	71	48	3.18
March	73	51	1.90
April	76	53	0.80
May	78	57	0.28
June	81	61	0.10
July	87	65	0.03
August	89	65	0.01
September	87	63	0.25
October	82	58	0.72
November	76	52	1.38
December	70	47	2.02

Holidays & Special Events

The Disneyland Resort sponsors special events during the year. Here are a few highlights. Find out about specific events by calling 714-781-7290 or visiting *www.disneyland.com*.

JANUARY–FEBRUARY

Valentine's Day: Sweethearts will swoon over the romantic backdrop that Disneyland Park provides on this love-struck holiday.

Mardi Gras: With its Cajun and Creole cuisine and boutiques, Disneyland's New Orleans Square offers the most traditional Mardi Gras setting. Expect Ralph Brennan's Jazz Kitchen, in Downtown Disney, to be hopping, too.

MARCH–MAY

Easter: The parks remain open late the week before and the week after Easter, making this a popular time to visit. At the Disneyland Hotel, guests may feast at an Easter Sunday buffet presented in the grand ballroom. The event is hosted by Disney characters. Reservations are available 60 days in advance (714-781-3463). Seating is limited.

Mother's Day: Disney characters honor Mom during a special buffet in the Disneyland Hotel's grand ballroom. Reserve 60 days ahead (714-781-3463). Seating is limited.

JUNE–AUGUST

All-American College Band: Disney's All-American College Band performs for nine weeks during the summer (usually beginning in mid-June), Tuesday through Sunday. Performances take place throughout the park.

Fourth of July: This is one of the busiest days of the year—and one to avoid if you're easily overwhelmed by crowds. The more-patriotic-than-usual day features exceptionally festive fireworks at Disneyland Park.

LATE SEPTEMBER–OCTOBER

Halloween Festivities: At Disneyland, Halloween Time Carnival lets guests celebrate in not-so-scary ways. In addition to the fall color decor, the Disneyland Band and Dapper Dans celebrate with seasonal tunes, while other performers kick up their heels at Halloween Round-up at Big Thunder Ranch. The Haunted Mansion holiday transformation gives this spooky spot a *Nightmare Before Christmas* motif—inside and out. Jack Skellington hosts

a Halloween-themed fireworks show, too—as part of the special-ticket event known as Mickey's Halloween Party. At that Disneyland soiree, trick-or-treating is encouraged on select September and October evenings.

NOVEMBER–DECEMBER

Thanksgiving Weekend: The four days of this holiday weekend are filled with musical entertainment and the early installments of Disneyland's Christmas Fantasy Parade and It's a Small World Holiday, and the holiday transformations of Cars Land and Buena Vista Street, all of which kick off in mid-November. The parks observe extended hours. At the Disneyland Hotel, the characters host A Disney Family Thanksgiving buffet in the grand ballroom. Reserve up to two months in advance (714-781-3463)—seating is limited and in high demand for this perennial favorite.

Christmas Festivities: By early November, Main Street in Disneyland Park is festooned with greenery and poinsettias, while more than 200,000 lights create a holiday wonderland that glistens from the Town Square Christmas Tree to Sleeping Beauty's Winter Castle. On select evenings in December, a massive choir walks down Main Street in a Candlelight Ceremony and Procession. It features a live orchestra and guest narrator who reads the story of the Nativity. There is also a special, holiday-themed fireworks show, Believe In Holiday Magic. It is not to be missed.

In Fantasyland, It's a Small World is transformed into a world of holiday magic and music. A Christmas Fantasy Parade also takes place. Haunted Mansion Holiday extends through the Christmas festivities.

The weeks leading up to Christmas are among the best to visit the Disneyland Resort. However, the two weeks straddling the holiday are among the busiest, so plan accordingly.

Magical Milestones

Walt Disney once said, "Disneyland will never be completed. It will continue to grow as long as there is imagination left in the world." Truer words were never spoken. Here's a sampling of major milestones and important dates in Disney history.

1901

Walter Elias Disney is born on December 5 in Chicago, Illinois. He spends part of his childhood in Marceline, Missouri.

1922

Walt and collaborator Ub Iwerks start Laugh-O-Gram Films, an animation studio located in Kansas City, Missouri. (The business lasts one year.)

1923

Walt and his brother Roy open the Disney Bros. Studio in Hollywood, California.

1928

Disney's studio introduces the world to the immortal Mickey Mouse with *Steamboat Willie*, the world's first cartoon with a synchronized soundtrack. (Walt Disney himself provides the voice for Mickey.)

1932

Flowers and Trees wins the Disney Studio its first Academy Award.

1937

Disney releases *Snow White and the Seven Dwarfs*, the world's first feature-length animated movie.

1940

Great works of classical music meet Disney animation with the release of *Fantasia*.

1955

Disneyland opens its doors in Anaheim, while television's original *Mickey Mouse Club* begins a four-year run.

1967

Disneyland debuts Pirates of the Caribbean—one of the most popular and beloved attractions of all time.

1971

Walt Disney World opens near Orlando, Florida.

1989

Disney animation experiences a renaissance of sorts with the release of the Studio's 28th animated film, *The Little Mermaid*. (It later becomes a hit Broadway musical.)

1992

A bit of Disney magic travels overseas with the opening of Disneyland Paris.

2001

For the first time since its opening, the Disneyland Resort gets a new theme park: Disney California Adventure.

2003

The Many Adventures of Winnie the Pooh makes its debut in Disneyland Park.

2004

The Twilight Zone™ Tower of Terror starts shaking up guests at Disney California Adventure.

2006

Captain Jack Sparrow joins the merry marauders in the Pirates of the Caribbean.

2008

Toy Story Mania! opens at Disney California Adventure—and becomes an instant classic.

2011

The Little Mermaid—Ariel's Undersea Adventure makes a splashy debut.

2012

Cars Land races onto the scene with three new attractions: Radiator Springs Racers, Mater's Junkyard Jamboree, and Luigi's Flying Tires.

Weddings & Celebrations

The Disneyland Resort's customized Fairy Tale Weddings program lets brides and grooms create an affair to remember at one of the three Disneyland Resort hotels—either indoors or out. Couples may go the traditional route or plan a themed event with invitations, decorations, souvenirs, napkins, and thank-you notes emblazoned with their favorite Disney character couples, including Cinderella and her Prince, and Mickey and Minnie Mouse.

One spot for tying the knot is the rose garden gazebo at the Disneyland Hotel, in a picturesque garden setting where the bride or couple may arrive in Cinderella's crystal coach. Another choice is the courtyard area at Disney's Grand Californian. A fantasy reception may follow (in any of these hotels), at which the fanfare of trumpets greet the happy couple. Mickey Mouse and Minnie Mouse may arrive to help the newlyweds with the cake-cutting moment.

A Disney wedding coordinator assists with the arrangements for the wedding and reception—everything, that is, except providing a guest's very own Prince or Princess Charming.

The bridal salon (at the Disneyland Resort Center, between the Disneyland Hotel and Paradise Pier Hotel) helps guests through the planning and preparation stages, and even through those pre-ceremony jitters.

For more information about creating a happy occasion in a happy location, contact the Disneyland Fairy Tale Weddings department, which coordinates events at all three hotels and in Disneyland: 714-956-6527. To learn more about Disneyland honeymoons, contact Disneyland Resort Travel Sales at 800-854-3104.

Quinceañeras

Along with the wedding program, the Disneyland Resort also offers customized Quinceañera celebrations for young ladies who are coming of age. These family-oriented milestone events invite the birthday girl to become a "princess for a day" and step into the fairy-tale realms of Cinderella or Beauty and the Beast. Held in a ballroom, the celebration features dinner, dancing, and time-honored Quinceañera traditions. For more information, call 714-520-7079.

GETTING READY TO GO

Planning Ahead

Collect as much information as you can about the attractions you're interested in from the sources listed below (and this book, of course!). Then consider all the possibilities before making definite travel plans.

Information

For up-to-the-minute information about special events and performance times, the latest ticket prices, operating hours, rides under refurbishment, and other Disneyland Resort specifics, contact:

Disneyland Resort Guest Relations; Box 3232, Anaheim, CA 92803; 714-781-4565 (for recorded information) or 714-781-7290 (to speak directly with a Disney employee); *www.disneyland.com.*

If you are staying at one of the Disneyland Resort hotels (see the *Accommodations* chapter), contact Guest Services at the hotel for help in planning your visit to both the parks and the surrounding area.

www.disneyland.com

For up-to-date Disneyland information, visit *www.disneyland.com*, the official Disneyland Resort Website. Using the handy Trip Wizard, you can plan your vacation, learn about the Disneyland Resort hotels, book travel packages, and order park tickets, plus check park hours and show schedules. You can also book your Disneyland Resort vacation through *www.disneytravel.com.*

Fun on the Run

The Disneyland Half Marathon Weekend, which usually takes place in early September, features races and games for the whole family. Events include the half marathon, a 5K Family Fun Run, kids races (including the ever-popular "Diaper Dash"), and a Health and Fitness Expo. For details or to register for an event, call 714-781-7290 or visit *http://espnwwos.disney.go.com/events/endurance/disneyland-half-marathon/.* Entrance fees range from about $20–$200. Half Marathon Weekend is popular—register as early as possible.

Inside the Disneyland Resort: Cast members (the folks who work at Disneyland) can answer many questions. Information stations in Disneyland Park include City Hall in Town Square and the Information Board on the west side of Central Plaza, at the far end of Main Street. In Disney California Adventure, the Chamber of Commerce is on the east side of the Entry Plaza, and the Information Board is at the far end of Buena Vista Street, adjacent to the Red Car Trolley stop. At any Disneyland Resort hotel, visit the lobby for assistance.

For other area information, contact these bureaus of tourism:

Anaheim/Orange County Visitor & Convention Bureau; Visit them at *www.anaheimoc.org*, or call 714-765-8888 during business hours to reach a representative. You can visit them in the Convention Center at 800 W. Katella Ave., Anaheim, CA 92803.

Long Beach Area Convention & Visitors Bureau; 301 E. Ocean Blvd., Ste. 1900, Long Beach, CA 90802; 562-436-3645 or 800-452-7829; *www.visitlongbeach.com.*

Los Angeles Convention & Visitors Bureau; There are two walk-in Visitor Information Centers: Union Station, 800 N. Alameda St., Los Angeles, CA 90012; and 6801 Hollywood Blvd., Hollywood, CA 90028; 323-467-6412; *www.discoverlosangeles.com.*

Orange Chamber of Commerce; 307 E. Chapman Ave., Orange, CA 92866; 714-538-3581; *www.orangechamber.com.*

Reservations

With the Disneyland Resort's recent expansion, advance planning has become utterly essential. To get your choice of accommodations, especially for visits during the busy spring and summer seasons, make lodging reservations as far in advance as possible—at least six months ahead, if you can, since area hotels fill up rather quickly during these months. For visits at other times of the year, check with the Anaheim/Orange County Visitor & Convention Bureau (714-765-8888) to see if any conventions are scheduled when you want to travel. Some of these events can crowd facilities enough to warrant altering your travel plans.

Travel Packages

The biggest advantage to purchasing a travel package is that it almost always saves you money over what you'd pay separately for the individual elements of your vacation, or it offers special options not available if you simply buy a ticket at the ticket booth. This is especially true the longer you stay. And there is the convenience of having all the details arranged in advance by someone else.

Finding the best package for yourself means deciding what sort of vacation you want and studying what's available. Don't choose a package that includes elements that don't interest you—remember, you're paying for them. And if it's Disney theming and "extras" you want, consider a Walt Disney Travel Company package.

The Walt Disney Travel Company offers packages that include a stay at a Disney hotel and a Park Hopper ticket. It's possible to add extras, such as a character breakfast in the park or a guided tour of Disneyland, as well as admission to another Southern California attraction, such as Sea World or Universal Studios Hollywood. Purchase extras separately.

Besides booking guests into an official Disneyland Resort hotel, the Walt Disney Travel Company also works closely with dozens of Good Neighbor hotels and motels (see pages 45–50 for details), and they are included in its packages as well. To book a vacation package at the Disneyland Resort, contact a travel agent, or call the Walt Disney Travel Company at 714-520-5060.

The Disneyland Resort is also featured in a wide variety of non-Disney-run package tours, including those sponsored by individual hotels, airlines (United Vacations, Alaska Airlines Vacations, and American Airlines offer packages, for instance), and organizations. AAA Vacations (888-874-7222) offers travel packages to the public, with special benefits for AAA members.

This book's selective guide to Anaheim-area hotels and motels can help you decide initially which property best suits your travel style, needs, and budget (refer to the *Accommodations* chapter). Pick one, then contact a travel agent or the desired hotel directly to make a reservation or book a Disneyland Resort package. Be sure to inquire about deposit requirements, cancellation policies, and trip insurance. Happy hunting!

What to Pack

Southern California isn't so laid-back that you only need to pack a few pairs of shorts and a T-shirt. Nor is it a place that demands formal attire. Casual wear will suffice in all but the fanciest restaurants, and, even there, men can usually wear sports jackets without ties. Bathing suits are an obvious must if you plan to take advantage of your hotel's swimming pool or go for a walk on a long, surf-pounded Pacific beach. It's also a good idea to bring along a bathing suit cover-up and sunglasses (and don't forget the sunscreen). Tennis togs or golf gear may be necessary if you plan to hit the courts or the course. The weather in summer can be quite warm, but because Southern California air-conditioning is extremely efficient, you should take a light-weight sweater or jacket to wear indoors.

In winter, warm clothing is a must for evening; during nighttime visits to the parks, a heavy jacket may be a godsend. Whatever the time of year, come prepared for the unexpected: Pack an umbrella, a light shirt, and a jacket—just in case.

Making a Budget

Vacation expenses tend to fall into five major categories: (1) transportation (which may include costs for airfare, airport transfers, train tickets, car rental, gas, parking, and taxi service); (2) lodging; (3) theme park tickets; (4) meals; and (5) miscellaneous (recreational activities, souvenirs, toiletries, forgotten items, and expenses such as pet boarding, etc.).

When budgeting, first consider what level of service suits your needs. Some prefer to spend fewer days at the Disneyland Resort, but stay at a deluxe hotel like the Grand Californian or dine at pricier restaurants. Others want a longer vacation with a value-priced Good

Neighbor hotel and less expensive meals. The choice is up to you. (Having said that, we do feel that a great deal of the Disney experience comes from staying on-property and recommend at least making room in your budget for accommodations at the somewhat more moderately priced Disneyland or Paradise Pier hotel.)

Once you've established your spending priorities, it's time to determine your price limit. Then make sure you don't exceed it when approximating your expenses—without a ballpark figure to work around, it's easy to get carried away.

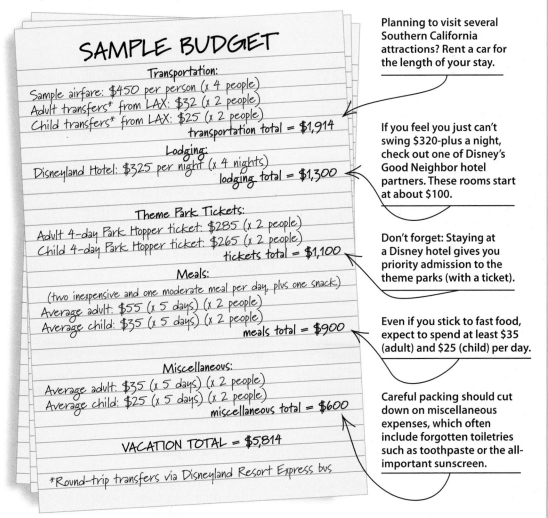

SAMPLE BUDGET

Transportation:
Sample airfare: $450 per person (x 4 people)
Adult transfers* from LAX: $32 (x 2 people)
Child transfers* from LAX: $25 (x 2 people)
transportation total = $1,914

Lodging:
Disneyland Hotel: $325 per night (x 4 nights)
lodging total = $1,300

Theme Park Tickets:
Adult 4-day Park Hopper ticket: $285 (x 2 people)
Child 4-day Park Hopper ticket: $265 (x 2 people)
tickets total = $1,100

Meals:
(two inexpensive and one moderate meal per day, plus one snack)
Average adult: $55 (x 5 days) (x 2 people)
Average child: $35 (x 5 days) (x 2 people)
meals total = $900

Miscellaneous:
Average adult: $35 (x 5 days) (x 2 people)
Average child: $25 (x 5 days) (x 2 people)
miscellaneous total = $600

VACATION TOTAL = $5,814

*Round-trip transfers via Disneyland Resort Express bus

Planning to visit several Southern California attractions? Rent a car for the length of your stay.

If you feel you just can't swing $320-plus a night, check out one of Disney's Good Neighbor hotel partners. These rooms start at about $100.

Don't forget: Staying at a Disney hotel gives you priority admission to the theme parks (with a ticket).

Even if you stick to fast food, expect to spend at least $35 (adult) and $25 (child) per day.

Careful packing should cut down on miscellaneous expenses, which often include forgotten toiletries such as toothpaste or the all-important sunscreen.

This is an example of a moderately priced budget for a family of four (two adults and two kids staying at the Disneyland Resort for four nights and five days during "off-peak" times). Theme park admission prices are likely to increase in 2014.

Money-Saving Strategies

Cost-Cutting Tips

LODGING: The most important rule is not to pay for more than you need. Budget chains don't offer many frills, but they are usually clean and provide the essentials; many even have a swimming pool, albeit a small one.

You can also save by checking the cutoff age at which children can no longer share their parents' room for free. Many of the hotels and motels in the Anaheim area allow children under age 18 to stay free. A few places have a cutoff age of 15 or 17, so it's good to find out before making a reservation. And ask about special rates or discounts, especially if you are a California resident, a member of AAA or AARP, or are in the military.

Bed-and-breakfasts sometimes represent an excellent buy. While B&Bs are scarce in Anaheim proper, there are some on the coast, within an hour of the Disneyland Resort.

Hostels and RV parks also offer lower-priced lodging alternatives. Contact the Anaheim/Orange County Visitor & Convention Bureau at 714-765-8888 for a listing of those areas closest to the Disneyland Resort.

FOOD: The budget-minded (and who isn't?) should plan to have meals in coffee shops or fast-food restaurants, or save your splurges for the buffets to get your fill and your money's worth. If you want to try an upscale place, go for lunch; the entrées are often the same as those at dinnertime, but usually cost less.

Pack a picnic and enjoy meals outside. There's a small picnic area just to the left of Disneyland's entrance. (It's surrounded by trees—so it's easy to miss—but last we checked it was still there.) Vending machines dispense soft drinks. Snacks may be brought into the parks, but not glass bottles, knives, or beverages containing alcohol. You can also save on meals by choosing lodging with kitchen facilities and opting to eat in some of the time. The savings on food may more than cover the additional cost of accommodations. Don't forget to pack snack items, too—especially if you are traveling with kids.

In the Anaheim area, a number of places offer refrigerators or full kitchen facilities (look for suite hotels); some also provide complimentary breakfast.

TRANSPORTATION: When calculating the cost of driving to the Disneyland Resort, consider your car's gas mileage, the price of gasoline, and the expense of the accommodations and food en route. If you are thinking of traveling by plane, don't forget about the cost of getting from your home to the airport and later to your hotel. Also factor in the cost of renting a car at your destination, if that's part of your plan. Remember to ask if your hotel charges for parking (the rates tend to vary) or shuttle transportation to the Disneyland Resort—these daily charges can tack quite a bit on to a family's room bill.

Disney Discounts

ANNUAL PASSPORT: Annual Pass-bearers may net savings on Disneyland hotel accommodations (based on availability), Disneyland restaurants, select merchandise throughout the theme parks and Downtown Disney, and select guided tours. For an additional $129, Deluxe Annual Passholders may purchase parking privileges. Premium and Premier Annual Passholders are entitled to free parking for the theme parks.

DISNEY VISA: Members who pay for their purchases with the Disney Rewards Visa card earn points that can be redeemed for various discounts and Disney items throughout the year. Note that purchases do not have to be made at Disneyland, and all purchases count. Details are subject to change.

AUTOMOBILE ASSOCIATION OF AMERICA (AAA): Auto Club members can order special vacation packages through local AAA offices. Contact your local AAA office for details.

DISCOUNT FOR SENIORS: Senior citizens get a $2 discount on 1-day, 1-park tickets.

Theme Park Tickets

Most admission media (with the exception of annual passes) are now called "tickets" rather than "passports." A one-day park ticket lets you visit just that: one park. Park Hopper tickets allow you unlimited park-hopping between Disneyland Park and Disney California Adventure. Admission tickets include use of all attractions (except arcades) once inside.

Ticket Options

One- through Five-Day Tickets without the park-hopping feature allow admission to one Disneyland Resort theme park per day, while One-to-Six-Day Park Hopper tickets allow admission to both parks and allow you to "hop" between the two parks. Theme park tickets generally expire 13 days after first use.

The two main types of annual passports are known as the Deluxe and Premium versions. The Premium affords the bearer shopping and dining discounts, as well as park-hopping—that is, visiting both theme parks on the same day. The Deluxe pass has the same privileges with the exception of shopping discounts.

The Premium Annual Passport is valid for a full year and includes parking (it has no block-out periods). The Deluxe Annual Passport is valid many days of the year but has block-out periods, such as each Saturday from March through June (passholders may enter the park on a blocked-out day by paying about $70). A one-time parking fee, currently $129, is available to Deluxe Annual Passholders. Premium and Premier Passholders park free.

Annual passes are sold at the ticket booths and via *www.disneyland.com* and processed in Disneyland Park.

There are usually special passes available for purchase by Southern California residents. Offers change from time to time, so be sure to inquire before you visit. Call 714-781-4565, or visit *www.disneyland.com* for details.

Purchasing Tickets

Long lines have been known to form at the Disney ticket booths—especially in the morning. Avoid the wait by buying your tickets ahead of time. If that's not incentive enough, consider the possibility of saving a little money by purchasing tickets prior to your arrival.

Where to Buy Tickets: All tickets are sold at park ticket booths. Some Disney Stores sell tickets, too (they do not offer one-day tickets). Call or visit your local store for specifics.

Tickets by Mail: Send check or money order and ticket request (plus a $10 fee for orders over $200) to Disneyland Ticket Mail Order Services, Box 61061, Anaheim, CA 92803. It's also possible to order by calling Ticketing & Reservations at 714-781-4400 (up to 30 days ahead). Allow 10 business days for processing.

Tickets Online: Select tickets are available at *www.disneyland.com*. (You can print them yourself, have them mailed to your home, or pick them up at Will Call. The latter two options come with a fee.) There are often special offers—be sure to inquire.

Tickets by Phone: Call 714-781-4565 and have a credit card handy. Allow five days for delivery, ten during busy times of the year.

How to Pay for Tickets: Cash, traveler's checks, personal checks, Disney gift cards, Disney dollars, American Express, Visa, MasterCard, JCB Card, and Discover Card are accepted. Personal checks must be imprinted with name and address, and accompanied by a valid government-issued photo ID.

Note that ticket structure and pricing are apt to change. For the latest information, visit *www.disneyland.com*.

Ticket Prices

Although prices are likely to change, the following should give you an idea of what you'll pay for tickets in 2014. (Prices do not include tax.) For updates, call 714-781-4565, or visit *www.disneyland.com*.

	ADULTS	CHILDREN*
One-Day Ticket (one park)	$92	$86
One-Day Ticket (hopper)	$137	$131
Two-Day Ticket (hopper)	$210	$197
Three-Day Ticket (hopper)	$260	$244
Four-Day Ticket (hopper)	$285	$265
Five-Day Ticket (hopper)	$300	$279
Two-Park Deluxe Annual Passport		$499
Two-Park Premium Annual Passport		$669
Premier Annual Passport		$979

*3 through 9 years of age; children under 3 free
Note that there is a single price (for adults and children) for each tier of annual passport.

Traveling with Children

When you tell your kids that a Disney vacation is in the works, the challenge is keeping them relatively calm until you actually arrive at the Disneyland Resort!

PLANNING: Get youngsters involved in plotting the trip from the outset, putting each child in charge of a small part of the vacation preparation—such as visiting *www.disneyland.com*, choosing which attractions to see and in what order to see them, and investigating which other activities to include in your Southern California visit.

EN ROUTE: Certain resources can stave off the "Are we there yet?" chorus, such as travel games, books and magazines, and snacks to quiet rumbling stomachs. If you drive, take plenty of breaks along the way. If you fly, try to time your departure and return flights for off-peak hours and during the off-season, when chances are better that an empty seat or two will be available. During takeoffs and landings, encourage toddlers to suck on bottles and pacifiers to keep ears clear, and supply older kids with gum or water.

IN THE HOTELS: During the summer and select periods, several hotels offer special kids' programs. Some offer babysitting services or babysitting referrals year-round. Pinocchio's Workshop at Disney's Grand Californian is available to take requests for "day of" child activity services for hotel guests. There is a charge for these services.

IN THE THEME PARKS: The smiles that light up your kids' faces as they enter a Disney theme park will repay you a thousandfold for any fuss en route. No place in the world is more aware of the needs of children—or their parents—than this one.

Favorite Attractions: Fantasyland and Mickey's Toontown in Disneyland Park are great places to start with small kids, who delight in the bright colors and familiar characters. In Disney California Adventure, A Bug's Land, Cars Land, Disney Junior— Live on Stage!, and Monsters, Inc.—Mike and Sulley to the Rescue! have big kid appeal. If you have children of different ages in your party, you may have to do some juggling or split the group up for a few hours so that older kids won't have to spend their whole vacation waiting in line for Dumbo. Some rides, like Snow White's Scary Adventures, may be too scary for some youngsters. If they're afraid of the witch, skip the attraction.

Strollers: They can be rented for $15 ($25 for two) at the Stroller Shop, located to the right of the main entrance of Disneyland Park. This is the only place to rent a stroller for either park. If you leave the parks, but plan to return later that day, keep the receipt and get another stroller at no additional charge.

Baby Care: Baby Care Centers feature toddler-size flush toilets that are quite cute— and completely functional. In addition, there are changing tables, a limited selection of formulas, strained baby foods, and diapers for sale, plus facilities for warming baby bottles (you can wash out your bottles here, too). A special room with comfortable chairs is available for nursing mothers.

The decor is soothing, and a stop here for diaper changing or feeding is a tranquil break for parent and child alike. The Baby Care Centers are located in Central Plaza, at the Castle end of Main Street in Disneyland, and near the Lucky Fortune Cookery inside Disney California Adventure.

Changing tables and diaper machines are also available in many restrooms.

Note: Parents of toddlers should pack a supply of swim diapers. They'll come in handy for children who want to spend time splashing in the parks' interactive fountains.

Where to Buy Baby Care Items: Besides being at the Baby Care Centers, disposable diapers and baby bottles are sold at select shops throughout the parks.

Lost Children: When a child gets separated from his or her family or fails to show up on time, it's reassuring to know that the Disneyland Resort's security force and cast members are carefully trained to follow specific procedures when they encounter a lost child.

Up to age 10, a youngster may be taken to Child Services, adjacent to First Aid, where Disney movies and books provide temporary amusement. The child's name is registered in the lost children's logbook there. Kids 11 and older may leave messages and check in often at City Hall in Disneyland Park, or Guest Relations in the entrance area of Disney California Adventure.

Traveling Without Children

Disneyland is as enjoyable for solo travelers and couples as it is for families for several reasons: Its ambience encourages interaction, and the attractions are naturally shared events.

PLANNING: Read Disney literature carefully before you arrive to familiarize yourself with the resort's layout and activities. Also, request tourist information from other places in Southern California that you intend to visit.

Food for Thought: Sightseeing takes lots of energy, and only healthy meals can provide it at a consistent level. Don't attempt to save money by skipping meals. Prices at the parks (particularly at Disneyland) and nearby "off-property" eateries are relatively reasonable, and there are healthful options, even in the fast-food restaurants. And don't forget to stay well-hydrated—running around theme parks all day is a lot of work.

Health Matters: If you visit in summer, avoid getting overheated; August in particular can be sweltering. Protect yourself from the sun with a hat and plenty of sunscreen, rest in the shade often, and beat the mid-afternoon heat with a cold drink or a snack in an air-conditioned spot.

If you feel ill, speak to a Disney cast member or go to First Aid and lie down for a while. Above all, don't take unnecessary risks. If you have a back problem, heart condition, or other physical ailment, suffer from motion sickness, or are pregnant, you should steer clear of rough rides. Any restrictions are noted at the entrance to each ride in the park, as well as in the listings in this book's theme park chapters.

Lost Companions: Traveling companions do occasionally get separated. If someone in your party wanders off or fails to show up at an appointed meeting spot, head for City Hall in Disneyland or Guest Relations in California Adventure. Here you will find a book in which guests can leave and receive messages for one another during the day.

MEETING OTHER ADULTS: Downtown Disney, with its mix of restaurants and clubs, is a good spot to mingle. While each of Disney's hotels has lounges worth visiting, Trader Sam's at the Disneyland Hotel is one of the most socially engaging. As far as the parks go, Disney California Adventure tends to attract a few more grown-ups than does Disneyland Park.

Travelers with Disabilities

The Disneyland Resort is quite accessible to guests with disabilities, and, as a result, it makes a good choice as a vacation destination. But planning is still essential.

GETTING TO ANAHEIM

Probably the most effective means of ensuring a smooth trip is to make as many advance contacts as possible for every phase of your journey. It's important to make phone calls regarding transportation well before your departure date to arrange for any special facilities or services you may need en route.

The Society for Accessible Travel & Hospitality (SATH, 347 Fifth Ave., Suite 605, New York, NY 10016; 212-447-7284; *www.sath.org*) has member travel agents who book trips for travelers with disabilities, keeping special needs in mind. Membership costs $49, or $29 for students and seniors age 63 and older.

Height Ho!

At attractions with age and/or height restrictions, a parent who waits with a child too young or too small to ride while the other parent goes on the attraction may stay at the front of the line and take a turn as soon as the first parent comes off. This is called the "rider switch" policy, and if lines are long, it can save a lot of time. Be sure to ask the attendant, and he or she will explain what to do.

The following agencies specialize in booking trips for travelers with physical disabilities: Accessible Journeys (35 W. Sellers Ave., Ridley Park, PA 19078; *www.accessiblejourneys.com*; 610-521-0339 or 800-846-4537), and Flying Wheels Travel (143 W. Bridge St., Owatonna, MN 55060; 877-451-5006 or 507-451-5005; *www.flyingwheelstravel.com*).

Hertz (800-654-3131), Alamo (800-651-1223), and National (888-273-5262) rent hand-controlled cars at the airports in Southern California. Order your car at least 48 hours in advance and confirm it before you arrive.

Though less convenient, it is also possible to access the area by public transportation. All buses operated by Anaheim Resort Transportation (call 714-563-5287, or visit *www.rideart*.org), and the Orange County Transportation Authority (714-560-6282 or *www.octa.net*), the public bus company that serves Orange County, are outfitted with lifts so that travelers using wheelchairs can board them easily. Many of the routes pass by the Disneyland resort.

Sightseeing tour buses are another option. Though only a few of them are wheelchair accessible, all have storage facilities for collapsible chairs, making this a possibility for travelers who have a companion to help them on and off the bus. Coach USA is wheelchair accessible. It offers tours to many Disneyland-area attractions. Make reservations (at least 48 hours ahead if a wheelchair lift will be needed) by calling 714-978-8855 or 800-828-6699; *www.graylineanaheim.com*.

Scootaround rents standard and electric wheelchairs, as well as scooters. Pick-up and delivery is available to all hotels in the Disneyland Resort area. Call 888-441-7575, or visit *www.scootaround.com*. Wheelchair Getaways of California rents wheelchair accessible vans and has pick-up and delivery options for most hotels in the area. Call 800-642-2042, or visit *www.wheelchairgetaways.com*.

LODGING

Most hotels and motels in Orange County have rooms equipped for guests with disabilities, with extra-wide doorways, grab bars in the bathroom for shower or bath and toilet, and sinks at wheelchair height, along with ramps at curbs and steps to allow wheelchair access. Unless otherwise indicated, all the lodging described in the *Accommodations* chapter (page 39) provide rooms for travelers with disabilities.

INSIDE THE DISNEYLAND RESORT

Cars displaying a "disability" placard will be directed to a section of each Disney parking lot, next to the tram pick-up and drop-off area.

Wheelchairs and Electric Conveyance Vehicles (ECVs) can be rented at the Stroller Shop just outside the main entrance at Disneyland Park. This is the only rental location for both theme parks. The rental price is $12 per day for wheelchairs, and $50 for ECVs, plus a refundable deposit of $20. A small number of wheelchairs may be available to rent from Disney's three hotels; inquire at the front desk. We recommend you bring your own wheelchair whenever possible.

Most waiting areas are accessible, though some attractions have auxiliary entrances for guests using wheelchairs or other mobility devices; guests may be accompanied by up to five other party members using the special entry point. The Main Street train station is not wheelchair accessible. However, guests using wheelchairs may access the train in New Orleans Square, Mickey's Toontown, or Tomorrowland.

Accessibility information is provided in special brochures (see Park Resources below). In all cases, guests with mobility disabilities should be escorted by someone in their party who can assist as needed.

In some attractions, guests may remain in their wheelchair or ECV; in others, they must be able to transfer in and out of their wheelchair or ECV. In a few attractions, they must be able to leave their wheelchair or ECV and remain ambulatory during the majority of the attraction experience.

All the shops and food locations in the theme parks are designed to be completely accessible to guests in wheelchairs.

Park Resources

Contact Guest Relations at 714-781-7290 for information on *Services for Guests with Visual Disabilities*, *Services for Guests with Hearing Disabilities*, *Services for Guests with Service Animals*, and *Attraction Access for Guests Using Wheelchairs and Electric Conveyance Vehicles (ECVs)*. Information is also available at *www.disneyland.com* and at City Hall inside Disneyland and at Guest Relations in Disney California Adventure.

For Guests with Visual Disabilities:

An audio tour, along with the *Braille Guidebook*, are available upon request at City Hall in Disneyland and at Guest Relations in California Adventure. Both are free, but require a $100 and $20 refundable deposit, respectively.

Service animals are permitted almost everywhere, except on attractions that involve a great deal of motion. In such instances, the service animal waits with a Disney cast member while the guest goes on the ride.

For Guests with Hearing Disabilities:

Several dozen attractions provide a written story line for guests to follow while they experience the attraction. Check at City Hall in Disneyland Park and Guest Relations in California Adventure for more information.

Closed captioning is available in the pre-show areas of select attractions—inquire at the attraction entrance; contact Guest Relations for the use of a handheld closed-captioning unit (available for free with a refundable deposit). Reflective captioning and audio descriptions are available at several shows as well; inquire at each attraction. Quantities are limited—be sure to reserve in advance and confirm before you leave home.

Text typewriters (TTYs) are located in between the main entrance to Disneyland and the kennel, and at the pay phones near the exit from Space Mountain. In Disney California Adventure, TTYs can be found in the area beside King Triton's Carousel and inside the Guest Relations Lobby.

Sign language interpretation is available for select shows and attractions in both Disneyland Resort theme parks. Reservations must be made at least seven days in advance. To make this arrangement, contact Resort Tour Services at 714-817-2229.

Volume-control telephones are located in the theme parks. Audio tours, assistive listening devices, and closed-captioning devices may be borrowed at City Hall and the Guest Relations Lobby (with a refundable deposit).

DISNEYLAND RESORT TOURS

The following "behind-the-scenes" tours provide guests with an opportunity to explore Disneyland and Disney California Adventure in entertaining and informative ways. Annual Passholders, AAA members, and Disney's Visa cardholders receive a 20 percent discount. For more information, call 714-781-4565 or visit *www.disneyland.com*.

- *Cruzin' Disney California Adventure* (Daily; 7:30 A.M.): This 3-hour guided, behind-the-scenes tour allows guests a chance to view the park from a special perspective—a Segway personal transporter. Guests must be at least 16 years old (those under 18 must be accompanied by an adult), weigh between 100 and 250 pounds, and be able to safely step on and off the Segway. (It's not as easy as it looks! Guests should be in good physical condition to participate.) Instruction is provided. Cost is about $99 per person. Park admission is not included or required.

- *Welcome to Disneyland* (Daily): A 2½-hour journey that takes you through Disneyland Park and Disney California Adventure, with stops at several attractions, shows, and interactive experiences. It includes VIP viewing for select shows and priority seating for some restaurants. It costs about $25 per person. Park admission is required, but not included.

- *A Walk in Walt's Footsteps* (Daily): Led by a knowledgeable guide, the tour covers the whole park. If you already have a park ticket, you pay an extra $64 (per person, all ages) for the 3½-hour tour. It includes lunch, a pin, a peek at the exclusive Club 33, and a special visit to a classic Disneyland attraction, focusing on Audio-Animatronic technology.

- *Discover the Magic* (Friday–Sunday): This family tour promises a unique experience for the whole family, while promoting the idea that Disneyland is a community where Disney characters live and play. The tour lasts approximately 3 hours and is recommended for families with kids ages 5 to 9. Strollers are discouraged, and kids under age 18 must be accompanied by an adult. Cost is $59 for the first two tickets, $49 for each extra ticket. Park admission is required, but not included.

- *Holiday Time at Disneyland* (Daily during the run of the Christmas parade): This tour is designed for families or groups looking for a unique way to celebrate the holidays together, or guests looking for a personalized experience. The tour, which makes everyone feel like a VIP, shares the history of Disneyland's holiday traditions, includes visits to attractions that have had special holiday makeovers, and offers special seating for A Christmas Fantasy, Disneyland's holiday parade. Tours may be booked up to 30 days in advance. Availability is limited for all tours. Cost is $68 per person. For more information or to book a tour, call 714-781-4400. Park admission is required.

How to Get There

Most visitors to the Disneyland Resort arrive by car. Many of those who live nearby own an annual pass and drive down frequently to spend a day or weekend at the resort. But for those traveling any significant distance, it tends to cost less to fly than to drive, and certainly saves time. During your days at the Disneyland Resort, you won't need a vehicle. Rent a car for the days you plan to venture off-property, or rely on local tours to see the area sights. If you prefer to leave the driving to someone else altogether, traveling to Disneyland by bus or train are alternatives.

> **HOT TIP!**
> Driving to Disneyland and looking for an address for the GPS? Look no further: 1313 S. Harbor Blvd., Anaheim, CA 92802.

By Car

SOUTHERN CALIFORNIA FREEWAYS: Driving almost anywhere in Orange County, or farther afield, requires negotiating a combination of freeways and surface streets. But once you familiarize yourself with a few names and numbers, navigating becomes much more manageable.

The freeways are well marked and fast, barring (common) traffic snags. That said, they can be rather frenetic. Major thoroughfares may merge with little or no notice. Monstrous traffic jams are common during morning and evening rush hours. And proper names of most roads change, depending on where you are. I-5, for instance, is called the Santa Ana Freeway in Orange County; in the Los Angeles area, it becomes the Golden State Freeway; to the south, it's the San Diego Freeway. It's a good idea to learn both the name and the route

number of any freeway on which you plan to travel. Exit signs list a route number and either a direction or city name (but not always both).

It's also useful to have an idea of the overall layout of the freeways. Several run parallel to the Pacific coast and are intersected by others running east and west. While this scheme is fairly straightforward, it is complicated by a couple of freeways that squiggle across the map.

CALIFORNIA DRIVING LAWS: Under state law, seat belts are required for *all* passengers; right turns at red lights are legal unless otherwise posted, as are U-turns at intersections; and pedestrians have the right-of-way at crosswalks. By law, kids must be in car or booster seats until they reach the age of 8 or a height of 4 feet, 9 inches. And keep that phone in your pocket—it is illegal to use it while driving in California.

AUTOMOBILE CLUBS: Any one of the nation's leading automobile clubs will come to your aid in the event of a breakdown en route (be sure to bring your membership card with you), as well as provide insurance covering accidents, arrest, bail bond, lawyers' fees for defense of contested traffic cases, and personal injury. They also offer trip-planning services—not merely advice, but also complimentary maps and route-mapping assistance.

MAPS: Many car rental agencies provide GPS systems and maps, but it's still wise to familiarize yourself with the route. Or drop by a visitor information office; it can usually provide useful maps. Routes can also be plotted in advance through *http://maps.yahoo.com*; *www.mapquest.com*; or *http://maps.google.com*.

By Air

Anaheim lies about 45 to 90 minutes southeast of Los Angeles by car. Most Disneyland Resort guests who arrive by plane disembark at Los Angeles International Airport (LAX), one of the world's busiest. It handles approximately 1,500 departures and arrivals daily of more than 75 commercial airlines. Major carriers serving Los Angeles include American, Delta, and United airlines.

Much closer to Anaheim, Orange County's John Wayne Airport, in Santa Ana, is less than a half-hour drive from Disney and is served by 9 commercial airlines and more than 250 flights a day. It is sometimes possible to find the same fare to John Wayne/Orange County Airport (SNA) as to LAX, and if it's a nonstop flight, so much the better. There aren't as many direct flights available, but given the proximity to the Disneyland Resort, it's worth considering. Another airport vying for attention is the Long Beach Airport (LGB). It is also near Anaheim, but few airlines serve it on a nonstop basis.

HOW TO GET THE BEST AIRFARE: These days, airfares are constantly in flux, changing from day to day, seemingly hour to hour. That makes it important to shop around—or have your travel agent do so. It pays (literally) to keep these suggestions in mind:

• Find out the names of all the airlines serving your destination, and then check them all. See if you can get a lower fare by slightly altering the dates of your trip, the hour of departure, or the duration of your stay—or, if you live halfway between two airports, by leaving from one rather than the other or by flying into a different area airport.

• Fly weekends on routes heavily used by business travelers, or midweek on routes more commonly patronized by vacationers.

• Purchase your tickets online. Airlines often offer lower fares or bonus frequent flier miles for tickets purchased through their Websites.

• Keep an eye on Websites and newspapers for advertisements announcing new or special promotional fares.

AIRPORT TRANSPORTATION: Frequent scheduled bus service is offered by Disneyland Resort Express (call 714-978-8855 or 800-828-6699, or visit *www.graylineanaheim.com*). It not only goes to the Disneyland Resort hotels and the properties in Anaheim, but also several hotels in Buena Park (seven miles away). The bus stops at each LAX airline terminal, outside the baggage claim area; look for the green bus stop signs on the center island and for DISNEYLAND RESORT EXPRESS in the windshield (of course, the elaborate Disney theming makes the buses pretty easy to spot!).

Those who fly into John Wayne Airport (named after one of Orange County's most famous residents), 16 miles from Disneyland, have an easier time of it. The ride into town takes half the time than from LAX. From baggage claim, head to the Ground Transportation Center. The coaches pick up from the ticket booth located to the left. Look for the full-size motor coach that has DISNEYLAND RESORT EXPRESS displayed in the windshield.

SuperShuttle (call 800-258-3826, or visit *www.supershuttle.com*) also serves area airports. At Los Angeles International Airport, claim your luggage, then head to the SHARED RIDE VAN sign on the outer island and contact a blue-uniformed guest service rep for details. A van should arrive within 15 to 30 minutes.

At John Wayne, proceed to the transportation center across the street and look for the island marked VAN SHUTTLE SERVICE. A van should arrive within 15 to 30 minutes. Advance reservations are required for pick-up at Long

To Anaheim from the Airports

	Disneyland Resort Express Bus	SuperShuttle
Los Angeles Int'l Airport	$22 ($32 round-trip) per adult $19 ($25 round-trip) per child 3–11	$18 per person (one way)
John Wayne Airport	$17 ($27 round-trip) per adult $14 ($18 round-trip) per child 3–11	$12 per person (one way)
Long Beach Airport	Resort Express service is not available, but it's possible to take a Yellow Cab for about $52–$60 each way.	$37 for the first guest in the party, about $9 for each additional guest.

Children under 3 ride free. Prices were accurate at press time, but are subject to change. SuperShuttle customers net a small discount if they book round-trip fares online: www.supershuttle.com.

Beach. Here, vans collect passengers across from the main terminal in the car rental return lot. To return to any airport without an existing reservation, check with your hotel front desk the day before the departure for bus schedules and reservation information.

CAR RENTALS: Several major car rental agencies have locations at LAX, John Wayne, and Long Beach airports; in Union Station; at many hotels; and elsewhere in Anaheim. Expect to pay between $170 and $210 a week for a midsize car, and $105 to $120 for a three-day weekend, with unlimited mileage. Some rental companies to choose from are Avis (800-331-1212), Budget (800-527-0700), Dollar (800-800-3665), Hertz (800-654-3131), Alamo (800-651-1223), and National (888-273-5262).

It pays to call all the agencies and check Websites to get the best available deals. Be sure to ask about any special promotions or discounts. Loss Damage Waiver (LDW) coverage is essential for your protection in case of an accident, but it can add a lot to your bill (usually at least $9 a day). Most packages that include a rental car do not include LDW. If you have your own car insurance, check with your carrier to see what is covered.

An increasing number of credit card companies offer free collision damage coverage for charging the rental to their card, and some may provide primary coverage. That means your credit card company may deal with the rental company directly in the event of an accident, rather than compensate you after your insurance has kicked in. It's worth a phone call to find out.

If you're renting a car at Los Angeles International Airport (LAX), the drive to the Disneyland Resort is only 31 miles, but it will take at least 45 minutes with no traffic, or up to two hours if the roads are congested. From John Wayne Airport (SNA), the drive takes about 25 minutes (without traffic). Expect a drive of about a half hour from Long Beach Airport (LGB)—again, that estimate does not factor in that tricky wild card known as Los Angeles traffic.

PHOTO BY JILL SAFRO

By Train

It's possible to get to Anaheim by rail from L.A.'s Union Station using Amtrak's Pacific Surfliner train (*www.amtrak.com*; 800-872-7245) or L.A.'s Metrolink Orange County light rail (*www.metrolinktrains.com*; 800-371-5465). Union Station is in downtown Los Angeles and is served by trains from all over the country.

You can get to Union Station from L.A. International Airport (LAX) by cab, by bus (LAX FlyAway Bus; *www.lawa.org/flyaway*; 866-435-9529), or by L.A.'s Metro subway (323-466-3876; *www.metro.net*. The system also serves Long Beach Airport.). Hertz and Budget rental agencies have counters at Union Station; call companies directly for rates and hours.

The Anaheim train station is adjacent to Angel Stadium in Anaheim, which is about two miles from the Disneyland Resort. Yellow Cabs can be called from the station (714-535-2211). In addition, Hertz and Budget car rental agencies will pick up customers from the Anaheim train station; contact the companies directly for rates and hours.

By Bus

Buses make sense if you're traveling a short distance, if you have plenty of time to spend in transit, if there are only two or three people in your party, and/or if cost-control is key.

Buses make the trip from Los Angeles and San Diego, though they usually make a few stops along the way. Travel from most other destinations usually requires a change of vehicle in L.A. Transfers are usually made at 1716 E. 7th St. at Alameda in downtown L.A.

The Anaheim Greyhound bus terminal is at 100 W. Winston Rd., about one mile east of Disneyland; *www.greyhound.com*; 800-231-2222. Yellow Cabs can get you to Disneyland from the bus terminal for about $8; 714-535-2211.

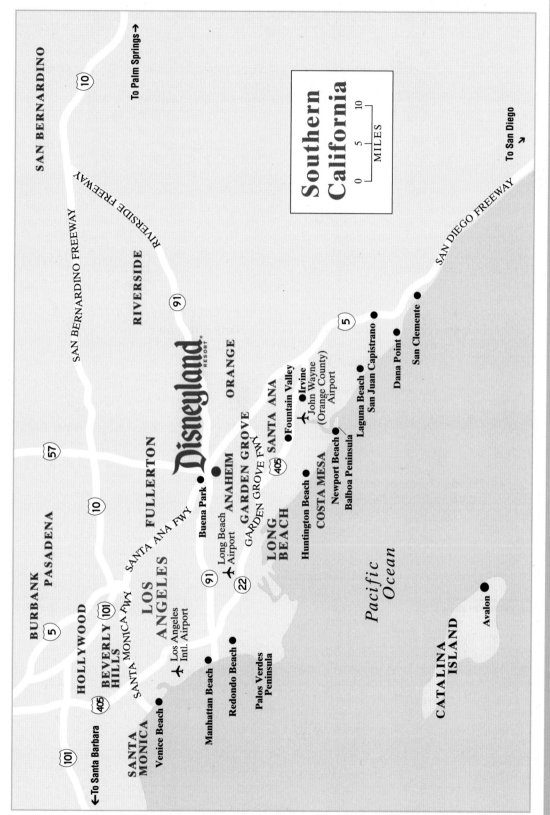

Southern California

0 5 10
MILES

SAN BERNARDINO

To Palm Springs →

RIVERSIDE FREEWAY

SAN BERNARDINO FREEWAY

RIVERSIDE

10

91

ORANGE

Disneyland RESORT

FULLERTON

57

PASADENA

BURBANK

HOLLYWOOD

BEVERLY HILLS

LOS ANGELES

SANTA MONICA FWY

SANTA ANA FWY

Los Angeles Intl. Airport

Venice Beach

Manhattan Beach

Redondo Beach

Palos Verdes Peninsula

SANTA MONICA

101

← To Santa Barbara

Buena Park

ANAHEIM

GARDEN GROVE

GARDEN GROVE FWY

Long Beach Airport

LONG BEACH

SANTA ANA

Fountain Valley

Irvine

John Wayne (Orange County) Airport

Huntington Beach

COSTA MESA

Newport Beach

Balboa Peninsula

Laguna Beach

San Juan Capistrano

Dana Point

San Clemente

5

SAN DIEGO FREEWAY

To San Diego ↗

Pacific Ocean

CATALINA ISLAND

Avalon

Santa Ana

John Wayne

5

91

22

405

405

10

405

101

5

Getting Oriented

Southern California's patchwork of small communities has undeniably blurred borders. The Disneyland Resort is in Anaheim, but you might not know if you were in that city or one of its immediate neighbors except for the signs. Buena Park lies to the northwest, Garden Grove to the south, Santa Ana to the southeast, and Orange to the east.

Farther south—in Huntington Beach, Newport Beach, Laguna Beach, and San Juan Capistrano—there's a bit more breathing room between communities. Heading northwest from Anaheim, you'll come to Los Angeles International Airport.

Continuing northwest into L.A., you'll find Santa Monica to the west, and, to the east, Beverly Hills, West Hollywood, and Holly-wood. On the beach farther north and west is Malibu, and inland to the east are Burbank (home of the Walt Disney Studios) and Glendale. The San Fernando Valley lies farther north and a bit inland from Los Angeles proper, while Santa Barbara, Southern California's northern boundary, is on the coast, about two hours to the north.

North–South Freeways: There are two. I-5 (the Santa Ana Freeway in the Anaheim area) runs from Vancouver, Canada, to San Diego, and is the main inland route in Southern California, linking Los Angeles and San Diego. I-405 (the San Diego Freeway) sprouts from I-5 north of Hollywood, veers south toward the coast, then rejoins I-5 at Irvine, a bit south of Anaheim.

East–West Freeways: Of the roads that intersect the two principal north-south arteries, one of the closest to the Disneyland Resort is Route 22, also known as the Garden Grove Freeway; it begins near the ocean in Long Beach and runs beyond the southern border of Anaheim. Route 91, called the Artesia Freeway on the west side of I-5 and the Riverside Freeway on the east, lies about eight miles north of Route 22.

Farther north you'll reach I-10, called the Santa Monica Freeway from its beginning point near the Pacific shore in Santa Monica to just east of downtown Los Angeles. At this juncture, it jogs north and then turns east again, becoming the San Bernardino Freeway. I-10 is located approximately 12 miles north of Route 91.

North of I-10 (anywhere from two to eight miles, depending on your location) is U.S. 101, which heads south from Ventura and then due east, crossing I-405. It is known as the Ventura Freeway until a few miles east of I-405, at which point it angles south and becomes the Hollywood Freeway, and eventually merges into I-5.

HOW TO GET THERE: Disneyland Resort is on Harbor Boulevard between Katella Avenue, Disneyland Drive, and Ball Road,

Travel Times

To/From the Resort	Approx. Distance	Drive Time
Balboa	30 miles	40 min.
Buena Park	7 miles	12 min.
Carlsbad	50 miles	60 min.
Costa Mesa	20 miles	30 min.
Dana Point	30 miles	40 min.
Garden Grove	5 miles	10 min.
Huntington Beach	15 miles	25 min.
John Wayne Airport	16 miles	25 min.
Laguna Beach	30 miles	45 min.
Las Vegas	280 miles	5–6 hrs.
Long Beach	20 miles	30 min.
Los Angeles (downtown and airport)	31 miles	45–90 min.
Newport Beach	20 miles	30 min.
Palm Springs	180 miles	3–4 hrs.
San Diego	87 miles	90 min.
San Juan Capistrano	32 miles	45 min.
San Simeon	270 miles	5–6 hrs.
Santa Ana	5 miles	10 min.
Santa Barbara	110 miles	2–3 hrs.

Drive times are under optimal conditions; rain or rush-hour traffic could increase or even double the time.

31 miles south of downtown Los Angeles and 87 miles north of San Diego. Many visitors drive to Disneyland from elsewhere in Southern California, while those who come from farther away fly into one of the area airports, rent a car, and drive from there. Once at their hotel, guests may prefer to use the hotel's shuttle or Anaheim Resort Transit (ART) to and from Disneyland.

Southbound I-5 Exit: To get to Disneyland, southbound I-5 (the Santa Ana Freeway) travelers should exit at Disneyland Drive, turn left, cross Ball Road, and follow signs to the most convenient parking area.

Northbound I-5 Exit: Northbound travelers should exit I-5 at Katella Ave., proceed straight to Disney Way, and then follow signs to the most convenient parking area.

From John Wayne/Orange County Airport: Take I-405 north to CA-55 north to I-5 north. Watch carefully for highway signs once out of the airport. Exit at Katella Ave., head straight to Disney Way, then follow signs to the most convenient parking area.

From Los Angeles International Airport: Take I-105 east to I-605 north to I-5 south. Take Disneyland Drive exit toward Ball Road. Merge onto Disneyland Drive, and proceed to the most convenient parking area.

Exit off Orange Freeway: Travelers on the 57 freeway should exit on Katella Ave. and proceed west. Turn right on Harbor Blvd., and follow signs to the parking area.

ANAHEIM SURFACE STREETS: Disneyland is in the center of the Anaheim Resort, a 1,100-acre district. Disneyland is bounded by Harbor Boulevard on the east, Disneyland Drive (a segment of West Street) on the west, Ball Road on the north, and Katella Avenue on the south.

Harbor Boulevard, near Ball Road, is the most convenient place to pick up I-5 (Santa Ana Freeway) going north to Los Angeles. Katella Avenue, past Anaheim Boulevard, is the most convenient entrance to southbound I-5 going to Newport Beach and points south.

Note: Be sure to park in a designated lot, or feed the parking meter often: Parking fines can run between $32 and $282 in Anaheim.

LOCAL TRANSPORTATION: The Orange County Transportation Authority (OCTA; 714-636-7433; *www.octa.net*) provides daily bus service throughout the area, with limited weekend service. Several different lines stop

at the Disneyland Resort, but know that public transportation can involve considerable waiting and transferring. At press time, the fare was $1.50 one way or $5 for a one-day unlimited pass. Seniors (age 65 and older) and people with disabilities pay 60 cents one way or $1.25 for a one-day pass. Exact change is required; pennies are not accepted.

If you have wanderlust but lack wheels, your best bet is to sign up for a bus tour, such as one of those offered by Gray Line of Anaheim (*www.graylineanaheim.com*; 800-828-6699). Hotel and motel desks provide information on tour schedules and prices, and even arrange to have you picked up at the hotel.

Anaheim Resort Transit (*www.rideart.org*; 714-563-5287) is a multi-route guest transit system serving the Anaheim Resort area. Passes may be purchased from many area hotels, public sales outlets, and various kiosk locations. Drivers do not sell passes. Adult fares are $5 for a one-day pass, $12 for three days, and $20 for a five-day pass. Kids ages 3–9 pay $2 for one day, $3 for three days, and $5 for five-day passes. There is no charge for baby passengers.

The Met serves L.A. County and the major attractions of Orange County (323-466-3876; *www.metro.net*). Cost is about $1.50 each way (55 cents for seniors). Exact change or a token is required. Tokens may be bought in bags of ten ($15) at locations throughout the L.A. area.

TAXIS: The only licensed taxi company officially authorized to serve the Disneyland Resort is Anaheim Yellow Cab Company (714-535-2211). Cab fare to John Wayne Airport from the Disneyland Hotel runs about $40, plus tip; if you're going to LAX, figure at least $90 (or more, depending on the traffic); Long Beach Airport runs about $52–$60, plus gratuity. Prices for town cars are slightly higher. Taxis can be called to pick you up at train and bus stations.

Planning Your Itinerary

For those lucky enough to live in the Los Angeles/Orange County area, the Disneyland Resort offers the opportunity to return frequently. Seasoned visitors and first-timers alike will do well to plan each step of their visit far in advance—make the travel arrangements as soon as vacation dates are set (refer to the Trip Planning Timeline below to make sure you don't miss any crucial steps), and then study the following chapters of this book to decide how you'd like to spend each day of the trip.

How many days should you spend with the Mouse? Well, that's up to you, but to experience the Disneyland Resort at its best, we recommend a stay of at least four full days—you will have enough time to see every attraction, parade, and show (plus revisit all of your favorites), lounge by your hotel's pool, enjoy a character meal, shop for souvenirs, and dance the night away. If you'd like to visit other area attractions, add on one day for each excursion. But don't try to cram too much into one visit; this is a vacation, after all.

Once you've decided how many days you're going to dedicate to Disney, it's time to decide how you'll split up your time on-property. We suggest that you begin with a day at Disneyland Park (for the original and quintessential Disney experience), followed by a visit to Disney California Adventure (to sample the attractions and shows). On the third day, return to Disneyland and hit the park's highlights, plus any attractions you missed on the first day, and save time for souvenir shopping. Day four should be dedicated to your preferred park and some downtime by the pool or in Downtown Disney's shopping plaza. Evenings can be spent in the park, if it's open late, or in Downtown Disney's clubs, lounges, and movie theaters. The options are plentiful.

On the next four pages, we've provided full-day schedules to guide you through four days in the theme parks (with special tips for families with young children and priorities for days when the lines are at their longest). The schedules are meant to be flexible and fun (not Disney boot camp), so take them at your own pace and plan breaks to relax: Have a Mickey Mouse ice cream bar, browse through the shops, feed the ducks, or just pick a bench and watch the crowds rush by.

Trip Planning Timeline

First Things First

★ Make hotel and transportation reservations as far ahead as possible. Call 714-520-5050 to purchase theme park tickets and to book Disney hotel accommodations (see page 39 for details); remember that a deposit must be paid within 21 days of the reservation. Log all confirmation numbers in a notebook, and call to confirm before you leave home.

★ Decide where you will be on each day of your vacation, and create a simple schedule.

6 Months

★ Unless you opted for a vacation package that includes theme park admission, it's time to purchase your Disney park tickets (see page 17 for ticket options and ordering methods).

Up to 2 Months

★ Find out park hours, the attraction refurbishment schedule, and details on any special events by calling 714-781-4565 or by visiting www.disneyland.com; add this information to your day-by-day schedule.

★ Make dining reservations (they're necessary at certain table-service Disney restaurants; call 714-781-3463), and add the information to your day-by-day schedule. Refer to the *Good Meals, Great Times* chapter for details on Disneyland Resort eateries.

2 Weeks

★ Airline confirmation and travel vouchers should have arrived by now. Contact your travel agent or the travel company if they haven't shown up yet.

1 Week

★ Reconfirm all reservations and finalize your day-by-day vacation schedule.

★ Add all your important telephone numbers (doctor, family members, house sitter) to your trip planning notebook, and be sure to bring it and your day-by-day schedule with you.

1 Day

★ Place any tickets you may have purchased (and a valid, government-issued photo ID) into a carry-on bag.

Disneyland Park

One-Day Schedule

❤ Disneyland's breakfast options have expanded of late. If you don't nosh at the hotel, consider eating at River Belle Terrace, Plaza Inn, or Carnation Cafe.

❤ Take in the sights as you walk down Main Street, but don't stop to shop or snack now (you'll have time for that later). Instead, head straight to Adventureland's Indiana Jones* and Jungle Cruise before making your way to Splash Mountain* and The Many Adventures of Winnie the Pooh in Critter Country. (If you plan to dine at the Blue Bayou, be sure to make a reservation in advance by calling 714-781-3463.)

❤ Backtrack to New Orleans Square, and visit the Haunted Mansion and Pirates of the Caribbean before breaking for an early lunch.

❤ Next, see the classic show at the Golden Horseshoe Saloon, take a relaxing river cruise on the *Mark Twain*, or raft over to Pirate's Lair on Tom Sawyer Island before tackling Big Thunder Mountain* in Frontierland.

❤ Explore Fantasy Faire. Then walk through the Castle into Fantasyland and visit Snow White, Pinocchio, Peter Pan, and Mr. Toad. Be sure to see Alice, the Mad Tea Party, the Matterhorn, and It's a Small World, too.

❤ Keep an eye on the time and try to fit the afternoon parade into your schedule.

❤ Make your way to Mickey's Toontown and see as many of this land's attractions as you can, making Roger Rabbit's Car Toon Spin* a top priority.

* Fastpass is available for this ride. Retrieve your time-saving Fastpass before visiting the land's remaining attractions. To learn how the system works, see page 58.

Continued on page 30 . . .

LINE BUSTERS

When the park is packed, head to the Disneyland Railroad, Enchanted Tiki Room, Pirates of the Caribbean, Innoventions, Haunted Mansion, and The Disneyland Story—Presenting Great Moments with Mr. Lincoln.

IF YOU HAVE YOUNG CHILDREN

- First, head to Fantasyland and visit each area attraction (note that some are scary for small children) before heading to Mickey's Toontown. Then visit Critter Country to enjoy The Many Adventures of Winnie the Pooh.

- Scope out a spot on a Main Street curb at least an hour before the parade. For smaller crowds, watch the parade from the viewing area near It's a Small World.

- Take tykes for a 'round the park ride on the Disneyland Railroad and then visit It's a Small World. If you need cooling off, backtrack to Toontown and splash around at Donald's Boat.

- Ride the Jungle Cruise, then sing with the Tiki Birds in Adventureland and climb Tarzan's Treehouse before returning to your favorite rides.

DISNEYLAND DELIGHTS

These attractions form the quintessential Disneyland experience:

Indiana Jones Adventure	**Star Tours—The Adventures Continue**
Pirates of the Caribbean	**Jungle Cruise**
Haunted Mansion	**The Many Adventures of Winnie the Pooh**
Big Thunder Mountain Railroad	**Buzz Lightyear Astro Blasters**
Splash Mountain	**Space Mountain**
Peter Pan's Flight	**Finding Nemo Submarine Voyage**
Matterhorn Bobsleds	
It's a Small World	**Mr. Toad's Wild Ride**

Disneyland Park

One-Day Schedule

. . . Continued from page 29

MEET THE CHARACTERS

There are lots of places to mix and mingle with Disney characters in this park. Some of the best spots include Toontown (Mickey, Minnie, Donald, Goofy, and more), Critter Country (Pooh and pals), and Fantasyland's Fantasy Faire (princesses). Check a park Times Guide for the schedule. And don't forget your camera!

TOP SHOPS

Whether you're browsing or buying, Disneyland is a shopper's paradise. Here are a few of the spots where wallets get a workout:

Candy Palace

Emporium Market House

The Disney Gallery

Main Street Magic Shop

Pieces of Eight

Pioneer Mercantile

The Star Trader

South Seas Traders

🔴 Hop on the Disneyland Railroad and disembark in Tomorrowland. Hit the Finding Nemo Submarine Voyage, Buzz Lightyear Astro Blasters, and Space Mountain* before heading to dinner.

Note: If the park is open late, you can board the monorail in Tomorrowland and dine in Downtown Disney before returning to the park.

🔴 After dinner, catch a screening of *Captain EO* (if it's operating) before riding Autopia*, Star Tours—The Adventures Continue, and/or Astro Orbitor.

🔴 Take little ones back to Mickey's Toontown before it closes for the day—it closes earlier than the rest of the park when there is a fireworks presentation (generally one hour before the show starts).

🔴 On nights when Fantasmic! is presented, make a point of getting to New Orleans Square and the Rivers of America in plenty of time to see it. (Check a park Times Guide for the schedule.) If there is more than one performance scheduled, the later one is usually less crowded.

🔴 Stroll back to Main Street. Shop, stop for dessert, see the Disneyland Story, and watch the fireworks burst over the Castle.

🔴 If there's time, take a second spin on your favorite attractions.

* Fastpass is available for this ride. Retrieve your free time-saving Fastpass before visiting the land's remaining attractions.

HOT TIP!

If you'd like to meet Mickey Mouse, make a beeline for his Toontown house—the big cheese greets guests in the movie barn out back. For the shortest wait, get there as soon as Toontown opens.

Disney California Adventure

One-Day Schedule

❤ Begin your California adventure by snagging a Fastpass for a high-flying ride on Soarin' Over California* (it tends to run out of Fastpass assignments early, as do Tower of Terror and Radiator Springs Racers). Then head directly to Toy Story Mania! followed by The Little Mermaid—Ariel's Undersea Adventure. If you plan to stay until the park closes, get a Fastpass for World of Color*.

❤ Depart from Paradise Pier and head to Cars Land. Do not miss Radiator Springs Racers*! If possible, visit Mater's Junkyard Jamboree before moving on to Hollywood Land. Enjoy a thrilling trip at the Twilight Zone™ Tower of Terror*. Refer to a park guidemap for the next showtime for Aladdin—A Musical Spectacular, and plan to arrive at the theater at least 20 minutes before the show. In the meantime, enjoy Monsters, Inc.—Mike & Sulley to the Rescue!, Muppet•Vision 3-D, and Disney Animation (be sure to see Turtle Talk with Crush). Take toddlers to the interactive Disney Junior—Live on Stage show.

❤ Head to A Bug's Land and don your insect eyes for a creepy-crawly screening of It's Tough to be a Bug! (though it may scare little ones).

Fastpass is available for this ride. Retrieve your free time-saving Fastpass before visiting the land's remaining attractions.

Continued on page 32 . . .

IF YOU HAVE YOUNG CHILDREN

- Head straight to the Hollywood Land section of the park. Stop in to see the Muppets before experiencing Monsters, Inc.—Mike & Sulley to the Rescue! Head over to Animation for Turtle Talk and Sorcerer's Workshop. Next, pay a visit to Disney Junior—Live on Stage. Then maneuver young water lovers through the sprinkler maze and rides in A Bug's Land. Note that It's Tough to be a Bug! often frightens young children.

- Try the kid-friendly obstacle course on the Redwood Creek Challenge Trail and visit Russell and Dug (from the film *Up*).

- Take a spin on the carousel and go to Toy Story Mania! before hitting The Little Mermaid—Ariel's Undersea Adventure.

- Finally, treat night-owl tots to the World of Color water show. (The noisy water jets might spook some.) Warn kids that they might get a little wet.

MEET THE CHARACTERS

Guests have plenty of opportunities to catch up with favorite Disney characters at Disney California Adventure. Among the best spots are Buena Vista Street (Mickey, Minnie, Goofy, Donald, Chip, and Dale), Cars Land (Mater, McQueen, and Big Red), Redwood Creek Challenge Trail (Russell and Dug), Paradise Pier (Duffy, the Disney Bear, Woody, Buzz, Jessie, and more). Check a park Times Guide for the schedule. And don't forget your camera.

Disney California Adventure

One-Day Schedule

. . . Continued from page 31

ADVENTURE ACES

If you're short on time, be sure to catch as many of the following four-star attractions at Disney California Adventure as possible:

Turtle Talk with Crush	California Screamin'
Radiator Springs Racers	Monsters, Inc. —Mike & Sulley to the Rescue!
Muppet•Vision 3-D	
Mater's Junkyard Jamboree	The Twilight Zone™ Tower of Terror
World of Color	Aladdin— A Musical Spectacular
Soarin' Over California	
Toy Story Mania!	The Little Mermaid— Ariel's Undersea Adventure
It's Tough to be a Bug!	

🐭 Make your way over to Grizzly Peak, and get set to get wet on the drenching Grizzly River Run* white-water raft ride. If you're up for it (and properly shoed), then visit the Redwood Creek Challenge Trail.

🐭 Pick up some wine-pairing tips or sample California's finest at the Golden Vine Winery.

🐭 Explore the Pacific Wharf area before proceeding on to Paradise Pier's daredevil rides (don't ride on a full stomach!).

🐭 Work your way around Paradise Bay, making sure California Screamin'* and The Little Mermaid—Ariel's Undersea Adventure are top priorities.

🐭 Be sure to catch the delightful nighttime extravaganza World of Color*. Line up for a waterside viewing spot at least 45 minutes before showtime—and know that you might get a little wet if you are up close.

* Fastpass is available for this ride. Retrieve your free, time-saving Fastpass before visiting the park's remaining attractions.

TOP SHOPS

Shopping at this park can be an adventure in and of itself! These are some of the spots that belong in the spotlight:

Big Top Toys

Elias & Co.

Rushin' River Outfitters

Off the Page

Sarge's Surplus Hut

Tower Hotel Gifts

Trolley Treats

LINE BUSTERS

When lines abound at Disney California Adventure, we suggest heading to the following: Redwood Creek Challenge Trail, Disney Animation, Muppet•Vision 3-D, King Triton's Carousel, and Monsters, Inc.—Mike & Sulley to the Rescue!

A Second Day in
Disneyland Park

Returning for a second or third day in each of the theme parks means more time to savor the atmosphere, try any attractions you missed the first day, and revisit all the old and new favorites. Knowing that there will be a second day to play also makes for a much less harried pace on day one.

♥ Start the morning with a character breakfast at the Plaza Inn (you can also share a morning meal with the characters outside the park at Goofy's Kitchen in the Disneyland Hotel, the Grand Californian's Storytellers Cafe, or PCH Grill in Disney's Paradise Pier Hotel).

♥ Head to Tomorrowland and ride Space Mountain*, Star Tours*, Buzz Lightyear Astro Blasters, and other favorite attractions.

♥ Hop on the Disneyland Railroad to Mickey's Toontown. See the sights, and spend some time mingling with resident Disney characters.

♥ Visit It's a Small World and the nearby character greeting area, and then tour Fantasyland.

♥ Stroll, shop, and stop for lunch on Main Street, U.S.A.

♥ Watch the afternoon parade from the Main Street Railroad depot, or secure a curbside spot.

♥ Ride a Main Street Vehicle up to Town Square and continue on foot toward Adventureland.

* Fastpass is available for this ride.

♥ Stop at the Enchanted Tiki Room and Tarzan's Treehouse before heading on to New Orleans Square. Here the priorities are the Haunted Mansion and Pirates of the Caribbean. Visit them and move on to Splash Mountain* in Critter Country.

♥ Meander through the shops of New Orleans Square, and then stop for a leisurely dinner at a nearby eatery. River Belle Terrace, the French Market, and the full-service Blue Bayou and Cafe Orleans are all excellent options.

♥ Select a riverside spot about 45 minutes ahead for the evening's performance of Fantasmic! (if it is scheduled).

♥ Wait for the crowds to disperse at show's end and make your way to Big Thunder Mountain Railroad* for one last ride before the park closes.

A Second Day in
Disney California Adventure

🐭 If you don't have a reservation for Ariel's Princess Celebration Breakfast at Ariel's Grotto, grab breakfast at Fifer, Fiddler, and Practical Cafe (aka Starbucks).

🐭 Cut through Hollywood Land and head straight for the Twilight Zone™ Tower of Terror*. Then move over to Cars Land, followed by Paradise Pier.

🐭 Thrill-seekers will flip for California Screamin'*, and gamers will swoon over Toy Story Mania!

🐭 Take a lunch break at Award Wieners, Cocina Cucamonga, or Pacific Wharf Cafe; or, if the park is open late, head back to your hotel to relax or splash in the pool (get your hand stamped before exiting, so that you can return later in the day). Another option is to spend the afternoon in Downtown Disney—the restaurants and shops open by noon.

🐭 Your California adventure picks up again with Soarin' Over California*, followed by a trip to It's Tough to be a Bug!, a visit to The Little Mermaid—Ariel's Undersea Adventure, then on to Grizzly River Run* (if you don't mind the possibility of getting soaked).

🐭 Stop for the parade if you haven't seen it already, and then make your way over toward Hollywood Land.

🐭 Wander through the backlot, enjoying the impromptu entertainment, take in Turtle Talk with Crush and the Toy Story Zoetrope inside Disney Animation, and catch Muppet•Vision 3-D. Take little ones to Monsters, Inc.—Mike and Sulley to the Rescue!

🐭 Line up about 20 minutes early for one of the evening's performances of Aladdin—A Musical Spectacular at the Hyperion Theater.

🐭 If time permits after the show, revisit some of your favorite attractions or search for last-minute souvenirs at the large shops on Buena Vista Street.

🐭 Don't miss World of Color*—it's an extremely popular show. (Guests up front may get spritzed.)

* Fastpass is available for this ride.

Fingertip Reference Guide

BARBERS AND SALONS

Hair may be cut or coiffed at Marika's Hair Salon at the Hilton Anaheim (777 Convention Way; 714-703-1367), or at Bella Hair Salon & Spa at the Annabella Hotel (1030 W. Katella Ave.; 714-535-2659).

CAR CARE

The Anaheim office of the Automobile Club of Southern California is located at 420 N. Euclid Street; 714-774-2392; *www.aaa-calif.com*. For emergency roadside service, call 800-400-4222.

DRINKING POLICIES

While there's a strict no-alcohol policy at Disneyland Park, drinking is an option at many of the dining spots at Disney California Adventure and at Downtown Disney, as well as at all three Disneyland Resort hotels. Alcohol may also be purchased in the lounges and restaurants of the three Disney hotels. The legal drinking age in California is 21.

LOCKERS

Lockers of various sizes are available just outside the main entrance of the parks, (our preferred location), inside Disneyland on Main Street (behind the Market House), and inside Disney California Adventure (DCA) across from Guest Relations. Prices are $7, $10, $12, or $15 per day, depending on the locker's size. These storage facilities make it convenient to intersperse frolicking on the attractions with shopping; just make your purchases and stash them in a locker. Availability is limited, and during busy periods all the space can be taken well before noon. Disney California Adventure guests may stash items in lockers for free while they ride Grizzly River Run. The lockers are off to the side of the attraction's entrance.

> ## HOT TIP!
> To avoid the sometimes maddening congestion at the Main Street locker location, consider stowing your stuff at the lockers near the picnic area, just outside Disneyland Park's turnstiles.

LOST AND FOUND

At any given time, a survey of the shelves of Lost and Found might turn up cameras, umbrellas, strollers, handbags, lens caps, sunglasses, radios, jewelry, and even a few crutches, false teeth, and hubcaps. Once, a wallet containing $1,700 in cash was turned in. The Disneyland Resort will return lost items to guests who fill out a report.

If you find a lost item, you'll be asked to fill out a card with your name and address; if the object isn't claimed within 60 days, you have the option of keeping it. This system encourages honesty, so if you lose something in the parks, check at Lost and Found. If you lose something at a hotel, contact the front desk.

MAIL

Postcards are sold in gift shops throughout Anaheim, in many shops and souvenir stands on Disney property, and at the three Disneyland Resort hotels. Stamps are sold in both theme parks and at all Disney hotels.

Cards that are deposited in the mailboxes in the Disney theme parks are picked up and delivered to the U.S. Post Office once a day, early in the morning. All items are postmarked Anaheim, not Disneyland. (By the way, don't forget to arrange for your own mail to be held by the post office or picked up by a neighbor while you're on vacation.) Due to the heavy volume, expect delivery to take a bit longer than usual. (There's a lot to write home about in these parts!)

Post Office: The U.S. Post Office closest to Disneyland is Holiday Station, a half-mile away (1180 W. Ball Rd., Anaheim; 714-533-8182). It's open from 9 A.M. to 5 P.M. weekdays only.

MEDICAL MATTERS

Blisters are the most common complaint received by Disney's First Aid departments, located at the north end of Main Street, next to Lost Children in Disneyland, and by Ghirardelli Soda Fountain & Chocolate Shop in the Pacific Wharf area of Disney California Adventure. So be forewarned, and wear comfortable, broken-in shoes (bring a back-up pair, too)—and pack Band-Aids, just in case.

If you have a serious medical problem while on-property, contact any Disney cast member (aka employee). He or she will get in touch with First Aid to make further arrangements. First Aid, staffed with registered nurses, will supply breathing machines and crutches for guests. It will not dispense medication to anyone under 18 without the consent of a parent or chaperone.

It's a good idea to carry an insurance card and any other pertinent medical information. Those with chronic health problems should carry copies of all their prescriptions, along with their doctor's telephone number.

Prescriptions: The pharmacy at CVS, about a mile from Disneyland, is open daily from 7 A.M. to 10 P.M. (1676 W. Katella Ave. at Euclid, Anaheim; 714-956-5920). Also on Katella near Euclid Street is a Walgreens, with a drive-thru pharmacy that is open Monday through Friday from about 8 A.M. until about 10 P.M., Saturdays from 9 A.M. to 6 P.M., and Sundays from 10 A.M. until 6 P.M. (10840 Katella Ave., Anaheim; 714-808-0126).

Refrigerator Facilities: In the parks, insulin and antibiotics that must be refrigerated can be stored for the day at First Aid. (It does not store breast milk for nursing mothers.) Outside the parks, there are refrigerators in many of the area's hotels and motels. If your room doesn't have one, a fridge can usually be supplied for a nominal charge, or the hotel or motel may be able to store insulin in its own refrigerator. Inquire in advance.

MONEY

Cash, traveler's checks, Disney Dollars, American Express, Visa, MasterCard, Disney gift cards, Disney dollars, Disney Rewards Visa, and the Discover Card are accepted as payment for admission to the theme parks, for merchandise purchased in shops, and for meals (except at souvenir and food carts, where it's strictly cash or Disney Dollars). Personal checks may be used to pay for park admission. Checks must be imprinted with the guest's name and address, drawn on a U.S. bank, and accompanied by proper ID—that is, a valid driver's license or passport. Department store charge cards are not acceptable identification

for check-writing purposes. Disney hotel guests who have left a credit card number at check-in can charge most expenses in the parks to their hotel bill.

Disney Dollars: Accepted as cash throughout the parks, Disney Dollars are the exact equivalent in value of U.S. dollars. They are sold at the main entrances of the parks, as well as at City Hall in Disneyland, at select shops on property, and at Disney resort hotels. They also make good gifts and souvenirs, and may be accepted as cash at Disney Store locations.

Disney Gift Cards: Available for purchase at many merchandise locations, these may be redeemed throughout the Disneyland Resort (though there are some exceptions at Downtown Disney and vendors not equipped to accept credit cards).

Financial Services: Automated Teller Machines (ATMs) are located at each park's main entrance; in Disneyland at The Disney Gallery on Main Street, by the Fantasyland Theatre, by the Frontierland Stockade, and in Tomorrowland's Starcade; in California Adventure at the Entry Plaza, in the Pacific Wharf region, at the restrooms near Goofy's Sky School, and by Embarcadero Gifts; in Downtown Disney by Häagen-Dazs; and in all Disneyland Resort hotels. For details, inquire at Guest Relations.

Personal checks made out to Disneyland (for up to $100) may be cashed at the main entrance to each park or Disneyland's City Hall; proper ID is required. The ATMs at the main entrance accept credit cards for cash advances. Note that the presence of a bank on Main Street is a tad deceiving: The bank offers no financial services.

American Express Cardmember Services:
Cardholders can purchase American Express Travelers Cheques, American Express Gift Cheques, and American Express gift cards, and exchange foreign currency (for a fee) at the Altour/American Express Travel Representative Office: 240 Newport Centre Dr., Suite 116, Newport Beach, CA; 714-541-3318. This office is open Monday through Friday from 9 A.M. to 6 P.M. and on Saturday from 9 A.M. to 4 P.M.

Many Anaheim banks sell American Express traveler's checks, usually for a one-percent fee.

Foreign Currency Exchange: In addition to the American Express office mentioned above, foreign currencies can be exchanged (for a fee) at the Travelex office in Downtown Disney (near Compass Books); 714-502-0811. Paper currency only (no coins).

PETS

Except for service animals, pets are not allowed in Disneyland or Disney California Adventure. However, nonpoisonous creatures may be boarded in the Disneyland Pet Care Kennel, which is located by the entrance to Disneyland Park. Reservations are not necessary (the kennel rarely reaches capacity). Pets may be boarded for the day (no overnight stays). In addition to proof of rabies and distemper vaccinations, guests have to show proof of hepatitis and leptospirosis vaccinations for dogs over four months of age. Without proof of all four vaccinations, the dog will not be permitted entrance to the kennel. At press time, it cost about $20 per day, per pet. Cash or Disney

HOT TIP!
Craving more Disneyland Resort news? Disneyland offers (free) monthly podcasts for your listening pleasure. Go to *www.disneyland.com/podcast* to download the informative "behind-the-magic" shows.

Dollars only. To inquire about the kennel rates during your visit, call 714-781-7290.

Disney personnel do not handle the animals, so the pet owners themselves must put their animals into the cages and take them out again. Guests are encouraged to drop by to visit with and walk their pets several times a day. Kennel attendants are not responsible for walking any animals in their care.

Note: During busy seasons, there may be a morning rush, starting about 30 minutes before the theme parks open, so you may encounter some delay in arranging your pet's stay.

Outside the Disneyland Resort: If you want to board your pet nearby, contact Animal Inns of America, 10852 Garden Grove Blvd., Garden Grove, CA 92843; 714-636-4455; *www.animalinns.com.*

Some hotels and motels in the Disneyland area accept well-behaved (preferably small) pets, but most do not allow guests to leave animals in the room unattended.

To find out about other possibilities for pets, contact the Anaheim/Orange County Visitor & Convention Bureau; 714-765-8888; or search "pets" at *www.anaheimoc.org.*

PHOTOGRAPHIC NEEDS

The Main Street Photo Supply Co. inside Disneyland can answer questions and recharge most batteries (or you can bring your own charger and plug it in there). Disney California Adventure offers similar services. For anything more serious, rent a camera and have a factory-authorized shop do the work on your camera when you return home. If you've lost your lens cover, it's worth checking at Lost and Found (see page 35); they may not have your cap, but they often have extras.

Try not to take your camera on wet, rough, or bumpy rides. Stash it in a locker or with a non-riding member of your party.

RELIGIOUS SERVICES

Catholic: St. Justin Martyr; 2050 W. Ball Rd., Anaheim, about two miles from Disneyland; *www.saintjustin.org*; 714-774-2595. Masses are in English and Spanish; call or check the Website for times.

Episcopal: St. Michael's Episcopal Church; 311 W. South St., Anaheim; 714-535-4654; *http://stmichaels.ladiocese.org*; about seven blocks from Disneyland. Sunday services are at 7:30 A.M. and 11 A.M. (English), and at 8:45 A.M. and 1 P.M. (Spanish).

Jewish: Temple Beth Emet; 1770 W. Cerritos Ave., Anaheim; 714-772-4720; *www.tbe-anaheimoc.org*; a few blocks from Disneyland. Services are held on Fridays at 6:30 P.M., the fourth Friday of each month at 8 P.M., and 9 A.M. Saturdays.

Lutheran: Prince of Peace Lutheran Church; 1421 W. Ball Rd., Anaheim; 714-774-0993; *www.princeofpeaceanaheim.org*; about one mile from the Disneyland Resort. Sunday services are at 8:30 A.M. (traditional), 10 A.M. (contemporary), and noon (Korean).

Non-denominational: The Kindred Community Church; 8712 E. Santa Ana Canyon Rd., Anaheim; 714-282-9941. Services are held on Sundays at 8:45 A.M. and 10:30 A.M. The church is about 11 miles from Disneyland; *www.kindredchurch.org*.

United Methodist: West Anaheim United Methodist Church; 2045 W. Ball Rd., Anaheim; 714-772-6030; Sunday morning services are held at 10:30 A.M.; approximately two miles from Disneyland.

SHOPPING FOR NECESSITIES

It's a rare vacationer who doesn't leave some essential at home or run out of it mid-trip. Gift shops in almost all the hotels stock items no traveler should be without, but they usually cost more than in conventional retail shops. One good source is CVS Pharmacy, about a mile from the Disneyland Resort: 1676 W. Katella Ave. at Euclid; 714-956-5920.

Inside the theme parks, aspirin, bandages, suntan lotions, and other sundries are sold at a variety of shops; just ask a cast member to direct you to the closest one. Some items are also available at each park's First Aid location and Baby Care Center.

SMOKING POLICIES

State law bans smoking anywhere inside restaurants, bars, and cocktail lounges, but most establishments provide patios for puffing and often heat them on chilly evenings. At the Disney theme parks, smoking is allowed in designated smoking areas. Check a park guidemap for exact locations. All hotels at the Disneyland Resort are completely smoke-free.

TELEPHONES

If you don't have your wireless phone handy, know that local calls from most pay phones in Southern California cost 50 cents. Most hotels in the area charge an average of a dollar or more for local, toll-free, and credit-card calls made from your room.

For long-distance calls, policies vary from hotel to hotel, but charges are always higher than they would be for direct-dial calls made from a pay phone. It makes the most sense to use a calling card when dialing long-distance from a room phone.

Phone Cards: Disney offers AT&T prepaid phone cards in values of $10 and $20. They can be purchased from machines in Disneyland Park and at select locations at the Disneyland resort hotels.

Weather Hotlines: For weather information, call 800-555-8355; *www.weather.gov; www. weather.com; or www.underground.com*.

Wireless Phones: To ensure a dose of uninterrupted magic for you and those around you, stick to texting while visiting the parks. You'll be glad you did.

TIPPING

The standard gratuities around Anaheim are about the same as in any other city of its size. Expect to tip bellhops about $1 per bag. Generally, tip cabdrivers 15 percent; outstanding shuttle or tour bus drivers, $1. Valets usually get $1–$2 when you pick up the car. In restaurants, a 15 to 20 percent gratuity is the norm. If you are pleased with the condition of your room, it is customary to leave a gratuity of $2–$5 per day for the housekeeper (leave a note with the tip to avoid confusion). Note that room service bills often include a gratuity.

Accommodations

The welcome sign is always out at the three Disneyland Resort hotels, where themed meals, amenities, and decor are definitely in character and add to the fun of a Disneyland vacation. And the resort's Disneyland Hotel and Grand Californian Hotel & Spa take staying at Disneyland to a lovely level of luxury.

In addition to the three hotels within the Disneyland Resort, there are dozens of properties in Orange County, known as Disneyland Good Neighbor hotels, that the Walt Disney Travel Company has handpicked to round out the Disney lodging options. We've selected a bunch of these recommended hotels, based on services and proximity to Disneyland, to highlight in this chapter.

If the sole purpose of your trip is to visit Disney, plan to stay in Anaheim, either on Disneyland property or at one of the surrounding hotels. Once you arrive and check in, you won't need your car again until you leave. Transportation to and from the parks is provided by monorails and trams serving the Disneyland Resort, and by buses serving neighboring hotels, motels, and inns. If struck with a bit of wanderlust, know that Anaheim is within range of a host of Southern California destinations, including movie studios, museums, beaches, and more. Whatever your vacation goals, we've provided a variety of options in Anaheim, from old-fashioned to contemporary, simple to sublime.

Disneyland Resort Hotels

Fans of the Disneyland Resort are faced with a difficult decision. It isn't whether or not to stay on-property (that's recommended if it's within the budget), but which of the three hotels to choose. Some factors to consider:

The whimsical new pool area and character meals make the classic Disneyland Hotel appeal to the kids in the family (and the kid in us all).

Meanwhile, Disney's Paradise Pier Hotel boasts a sunny facade to complement Disney California Adventure. Inside, Disney's influence is subtle, but it is possible to dine with characters.

The design team has really outdone itself with the Grand Californian Hotel & Spa. Located inside Disney California Adventure, the hotel's theming and style touch every detail, right down to the floorboards.

Whichever hotel you choose, one thing is certain—a stay on-property is sure to complete the overall Disney experience. From a resort information TV channel to wake-up calls from Mickey Mouse himself, every detail reminds you that you're in Disney's land.

Exclusive Benefits: Some perks are reserved for guests staying at a Disneyland Resort Hotel. Perhaps the most significant of these is "Extra Magic Hour," which allows early entry

HOT TIP!

Rooms equipped for guests with disabilities are available at the three Disney hotels, all of which are completely non-smoking. No exceptions.

into the parks (at no extra cost) on each morning of their stay (with a ticket). There's also preferred admission (with ticket) to a park if it reaches capacity.

One of the most convenient perks is the ability to charge almost any expense incurred at a Disney theme park back to the hotel room, if a credit card imprint was taken at check-in. Purchases can be charged to the room from the time of check-in until 11 A.M. on the day of departure.

Shoppers may also enjoy the benefit of having purchases delivered to their hotel's Bell Services Desk, where they can pick up their packages the next day—rather than having to carry them through the parks all day.

Other on-property perks include in-lobby screenings of Disney's animated classics (at all Disneyland Resort hotels) in-room light shows (Disneyland Hotel, only) and wake-up calls from Mickey. Courtesy pick-up is available for guests with disabilities to and from Paradise Pier in Disney California Adventure park.

Check-in and Check-out: Check-in begins at 3 P.M. (4 P.M. for the villas at Disney's Grand Californian), but guests who arrive early can check in, store their luggage at the Bell Desk, and go have fun. A photo ID is required at check-in. Check-out is at 11 A.M., and, again, bags can be stored until guests are ready to depart. Express check-out is available by leaving a credit card imprint at check-in.

Prices: Rates for standard guestrooms range from about $240 to $535. They vary based on hotel, view, and season. Note that Disney resorts no longer charge a daily resort fee. Local calls, weekday newspaper, fitness center access, and unlimited high-speed wireless Internet access are now available to all hotel guests.

Deposit Requirements: A deposit equal to one night's lodging (plus tax) is required at time of booking when making a "room only" reservation. Packages require a $200 deposit, due within 38 days of booking. Final payment is due 45 days prior to arrival. Packages booked within 30 days prior to final payment due date (45 days before arrival) don't require a deposit. If you prefer not to use a credit card to pay the deposit, call 714-520-5050.

Cancellation Policy: For a room-only booking, the deposit will be refunded if the reservation is canceled at least 5 days before the scheduled arrival. If you need to cancel a package, expect to be charged a $200 cancel fee plus insurance cost (where applicable) if the package is canceled 29 days or less prior to arrival.

Additional Costs: Sleeping bags and cribs are free. Self-parking costs $15 per day, while valet parking is available for $22 per day. Note that there is no longer an additional fee for extra guests (up to room capacity).

Discounts: Annual Pass-bearers may net many special rates and discounts throughout the Disneyland Resort. There may be discounts available to Southern California residents, members of the military, and teachers, too—be sure to ask when you make your reservation. Disney's Visa cardholders can redeem reward dollars at Disneyland, Walt Disney World, and Disney Cruise Line. If you are not a Disney Visa cardholder and would like to become one, flip to the back of this book. Our coupon can help you get a special bonus.

Packages: The Walt Disney Travel Company offers packages that feature a stay at one of the Disneyland hotels. Call 714-520-5050.

PHOTO BY MIKE CARROLL

DISNEYLAND HOTEL: This fanciful resort adjacent to the Downtown Disney District was the first hotel erected at Disneyland Resort— way back in 1955. It has had many looks over the years, and the newest one proves the old adage: Everything old is new again! While the new motif is a tribute to yesteryear and highlights the original mid-20th-century style of the hotel, there are some decidedly 21st-century touches, such as fiber-optic "fireworks" on many guestroom headboards.

Some of the most noticeable changes have taken place in the pool area. With a nod to iconic park signage, "Disneyland" is spelled out in familiar blocks atop a platform supporting two new water slides. Reminiscent of the original monorail station at the Disneyland Hotel, at each slide's entrance sits a replica monorail car that guests glide through as they twist and turn toward the water below. The largest of the slides sits 26 feet high and stretches 187 feet. The area also has a two-lane, mini slide for younger guests, as well as bubble jets in which to play. There are two hot tub spas and six poolside cabanas, too (there's a fee for cabana use).

The hotel has nearly 1,000 rooms, including 60 or so suites, located in three towers. Most tower rooms have two queen beds, and many rooms can accommodate up to five people (one of them on a daybed). The 11-story Adventure Tower looks toward Downtown

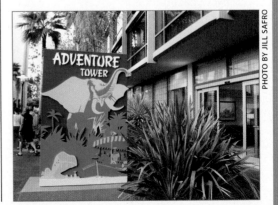

PHOTO BY JILL SAFRO

Disney and Disney California Adventure on one side and the main pool on the other. The 11-story Fantasy Tower offers rooms with pool views, but only on one side; guests on the other side look out over city rooftops, with Disneyland to the right, and the best view of the fireworks. The 14-story Frontier Tower's rooms provide city and courtyard views.

A monorail stop is a short walk away in neighboring Downtown Disney, which means extremely easy access to Disneyland (it drops guests off in Tomorrowland)—a nice convenience for guests who relish a break in their park-going with a trip to one of the hotel pools, the Mandara Spa, or the Fitness Center (a gym that features weight machines and aerobic exercise equipment). The workout room may be used by all resort guests and is accessed with a room key.

In the lobby of the Fantasy Tower, a large shop called Fantasia sells Disney souvenirs. Goofy's Kitchen, hosted by Chef Goofy and his Disney pals, is an extremely popular buffet open for brunch and dinner; Steakhouse 55 offers breakfast and dinner in an elegant setting; The Coffee House provides snacks and quick meals for guests on the go. Room service is available; and Tangaroa Terrace, a tiki-inspired casual dining spot serves up three meals a day with a South Seas flare, as well as "grab and go" items. The adjoining bar, Trader Sam's, is a nice spot for drinks and appetizers. (For more information about dining, see *Good Meals, Great Times*, beginning on page 109.)

The convention and meetings area, adjacent to Goofy's Kitchen and linked to the lobby via a photo-lined passageway, deserves a look for its Disney-related artwork, including a floor-to-ceiling collage of Disney collectibles

and milestones. Created entirely from old toys, souvenirs, name tags, and other assorted memorabilia, it commemorates the colorful and unique history of Disneyland.

The hotel can provide safe-deposit boxes, currency exchange, and child-care referrals. An ATM is on the premises. Airport buses bound for Orange County and Los Angeles airports stop at the nearby Disneyland Resort transportation area on Harbor Boulevard (aka West Shuttle Area), as do tour buses, city, and county buses.

Standard room rates run from about $305 to $443, depending on the view and season; no charge for rollaways or cribs. Concierge-level rooms start at $535. Suites range from $630 to $3,939. (The higher amount is for the Pirates of the Caribbean Suite and Mickey Mouse Penthouse Suite.)

Self-parking costs $15 per day; valet parking runs $22 a day. Non-resort guests visiting the hotel pay $6 per hour, with a $30 maximum for 24 hours. High-speed Internet access is included, too. Note that all prices were correct at press time, but are likely to change in 2014.

Disneyland Hotel, 1150 Magic Way, Anaheim, CA 92802; 714-956-6425 (to make reservations) or 714-778-6600 (front desk); *www.disneyland.com*.

DISNEY'S GRAND CALIFORNIAN HOTEL & SPA: This hotel is in a prime location—right in the middle of the Disneyland Resort. And, thanks to the Disney Vacation Club, the resort includes about 200 new rooms, 44 suites, 50 villas, and a swimming pool. The resort has its own private entrance to Disney California Adventure park and easy access to the Downtown Disney District.

A border of trees surrounds the six-story hotel, built as a tribute to the American Craftsman tradition of the early 1900s. Cedar and redwood paneling decorates the cavernous lobby, where display cabinets filled with original art and reproductions introduce guests to that rich period of art. The lobby's great hearth has a perennially lit fire. Furnishings throughout the hotel have warm colors and intricate textures.

Each deluxe guestroom and suite features a 32-inch flat-panel TV, DVD player, small safe, 24-hour room service, desk with two-line telephone, high-speed Internet access (no charge), iron, and small (unstocked) refrigerator. The bathroom has a makeup mirror and hair dryer.

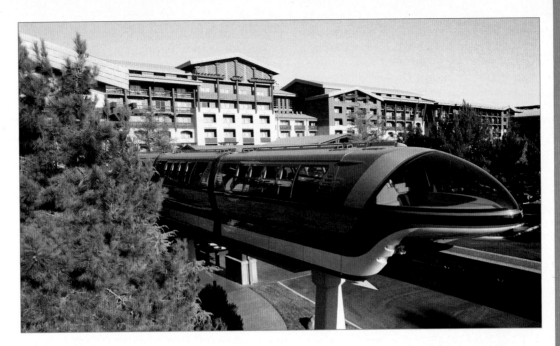

Most of the guestrooms in the hotel feature two queen beds, though 80 have a king bed, and 160 have one queen bed plus a bunk bed with a trundle (these rooms sleep five). The carved wooden headboards are designed to resemble vines on a trellis, and Bambi appears subtly in the shower curtain pattern.

The Disney Vacation Club villas reflect the same design as the hotel and are available to all guests when not occupied by DVC members. Each studio has a queen-size bed and queen-size sleeper sofa, plus a kitchenette with microwave, coffeemaker, and mini fridge. Larger (one-, two-, and three-bedroom) villas sleep 5 to 12 and offer dining areas, kitchens, laundry facilities, master baths with hot tub spas, and DVD players. They include a king-size bed in the master bedroom, a living room with queen-size sleeper sofa (and a sleeper chair in the one- and two-bedroom villas), and either two queen-size beds or a queen bed and a double sleeper sofa in extra bedrooms.

Guest services include 24-hour room service, laundry and dry cleaning, and a full-service business center. The concierge level offers upgraded amenities and services. Guests can relax at the Fountain Pool or frolic in the Redwood Pool (the two are adjacent); or they can enjoy the kids' pool, gift shop, and a licensed child-care center known as Pinocchio's Workshop. (Guests staying at the Paradise Pier and Disneyland Hotels may also use this service.) The luxurious Mandara Spa features treatment rooms and a couples suite accented with Balinese-inspired art and textiles. The spa includes a modern fitness center, steam rooms, and a nail salon.

Among the dining options are the award-winning Napa Rose, which features California cuisine and wines, and Storytellers Cafe, open for three meals in an Old California setting and the backdrop for a character-hosted breakfast. A quick-service eatery, Whitewater Snacks, supplies coffee, fast food, and baked goods; the poolside bar is good for a quick meal or snack. The Hearthstone Lounge doubles as a breakfast spot, dispensing coffee and pastries to guests heading into the park.

The hotel can provide safe-deposit boxes and currency exchange. An ATM is on the premises. Airport buses bound for Orange

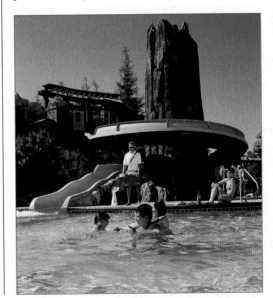

County and Los Angeles airports stop at the hotel's main entrance, as do tour buses, and city and county buses. City and County buses stop at the nearby Disneyland Resort transportation center (aka East Shuttle Area).

Rates for standard rooms run about $359 to $549, depending on the view and season. Concierge rooms start at about $627; presidential suites start at about $3,606. There are no rollaway beds, but a themed sleeping bag with a pad can be supplied; no charge for cribs. Self-parking costs $15 a day; valet parking is $22.

Disney's Grand Californian, 1600 S. Disneyland Drive, Anaheim, CA 92803; 714-956-6425 (for reservations) or 714-635-2300 (front desk); *www.disneyland.com*.

PHOTO BY KEITH GROSHANS

DISNEY'S PARADISE PIER HOTEL: This property's facade reflects the ambience and breezy, carefree California style of the Paradise Pier district of the park, which it overlooks. The smallest of the Disneyland Resort hotels, Paradise Pier is popular with business people and families alike.

The hotel's two high-rise towers—one 15 stories, the other 14 stories—are juxtaposed to create a central atrium, which cradles the lobby and a larger-than-life character sculpture. Mickey's familiar silhouette shows up in subtle ways in the hotel's beachy decor. We absolutely love the playful beachball pillows in the resort rooms.

Each of the 481 rooms, including 20 suites, features Disney-themed furnishings, one king-size bed or two queen beds, plus a twin daybed in the sitting area (a particular convenience

for families). The rooms on the cabana level open onto a large recreation area that includes a sundeck, swimming pool, slide, hot tub spa, children's play area, and snack bar. If you plan to spend a lot of time in or beside the pool, consider a concierge-level room on the third floor for direct access.

The spacious and well-stocked Mickey in Paradise shop, a coffee bar, and a restaurant are on the ground level of the hotel. Disney's PCH Grill offers dishes inspired by board-walk-style favorites and a popular character breakfast, Surf's Up Breakfast with Mickey and Friends (refer to the *Good Meals, Great Times* chapter). Room service offers PCH Grill specialties. The hotel also has an exercise room, guest laundry service, a small concierge lounge, and an ATM. A glass-enclosed eleva-tor provides a bird's-eye view of the lobby and Disney California Adventure.

Guests at the hotel have exclusive access to the hotel guest entrance from the Grand Californian Hotel & Spa into Disney Califor-nia Adventure. The hotel is also connected to the Disneyland Resort and Downtown Disney by a landscaped walkway. Guests can also get to Disneyland by taking the monorail from the Downtown Disney station. Both Disneyland and Disney California Adventure theme parks are within a 10- to 15-minute walk.

Standard room rates run from about $240 to $321, depending on the view and the season (no charge for kids under 18 sharing their parents' room); no charge for rollaways or cribs. Concierge rooms start at about $325. Suites range from about $595 to $2,114. Self-parking costs $15 a day; valet parking is $22.

Disney's Paradise Pier Hotel, 1717 S. Disneyland Dr., Anaheim, CA 92802; 714-956-6425 (reservations) or 714-999-0990 (front desk); *www.disneyland.com*.

Disneyland Good Neighbor Hotels

With fewer than 2,500 rooms available at the Disneyland Resort and tens of thousands of guests pouring through the parks each day, it's no wonder that a majority of visitors stay off Disney property. To make it easier for guests to narrow down their off-property choices, the folks at Disney have selected local hotels and motels that meet their standards and anointed them Disneyland Good Neighbor properties. Before receiving the Disney seal of approval, hotels are reportedly graded on amenities, services, decor, guest satisfaction, price, and location. Note that all Good Neighbor properties sell Disneyland park tickets.

Ranging from national chains to smaller operations, the Good Neighbor hotels proliferate along Harbor Boulevard, which flanks the resort on the east. From Harbor, it's easy to walk to the Disneyland Resort. A few properties are on Ball Road, the resort's northern boundary. Below Katella Avenue, which borders the resort to the south, side streets lead to the Anaheim Convention Center and the city's major convention hotels. Divided into the categories of Suite, Superior, Moderate, and Economy, there are more than 40 Good Neighbor hotels in all. In the following pages, we describe some of our favorites. For the Good Neighbor properties not described here, see The Rest of the Best on page 50.

Prices: Expect to pay $99 to $299, or more, per night for a hotel room for two adults and two children (kids usually stay in their parents' room for free), $69 to $262 for a motel room, and $40 to $70 for tent or RV camping. Prices drop a bit in winter; they are highest in the summer and over holidays. The room tax in Anaheim is 15 percent.

Additional Costs: When comparing accommodation costs, consider hidden zingers, like parking. Big hotels usually charge for it ($14 to $24 a day; more for valet service). Many also charge an additional fee when more than four people occupy a room. Inquire about telephone rates when you check in—hotel surcharges are notoriously huge.

Savings: You can save money by staying in a hotel that offers complimentary breakfast and shuttle service to Disneyland. Discounts are sometimes offered to those who belong to an automobile or retirement association.

Individual Needs: What's essential for one vacationer—and worth the extra cost—might seem frivolous to another guest: room service, on-site restaurants, live music, a suite, a kitchen, concierge service and amenities, large swimming pool, exercise room, or a place that accepts pets.

Packages: The Walt Disney Travel Company offers packages in conjunction with each of the Good Neighbor hotels—representing potentially big savings for travelers. For details or to book a package, contact the Walt Disney Travel Company directly at 714-520-5060.

Note: The following recommended establishments accept major credit cards and offer rooms for travelers with disabilities, unless otherwise indicated. Call the properties directly to inquire about deposit requirements and cancellation policies. Rates given were correct at press time, but are subject to change and should always be confirmed by phone.

Suite Hotels

RESIDENCE INN BY MARRIOTT ANAHEIM MAINGATE: At first glance, the buildings with tile roofs could easily be mistaken for a condominium complex. The well-maintained grounds are landscaped with hibiscus, bougainvillea, lemon, sweetgum, and pepper trees, plus park-style benches and, we're convinced, the only remaining orange tree still standing in the city of Anaheim.

Inside the inn, the living room-like lobby is inviting, with chairs, cocktail tables, fireplace, and television. Facilities include a fitness center, a swimming pool that's open 24 hours, a kids' pool, a whirlpool, and a single court that can be adapted for tennis, basketball, or volleyball. There is also a guest laundry, a small market, and a barbecue patio.

The suites are spacious, and they all feature a 32-inch television, pay-per-view movies, and Nintendo; and a fully equipped kitchen with a dishwasher, stove, microwave, refrigerator, and cooking utensils. Several room configurations are available.

Complimentary services include a full, daily breakfast buffet, business center with free Internet access, grocery delivery (guests must pay for the actual groceries), housekeeping, and a social hour Monday, Wednesday, and every other Friday from 5 P.M. to 7 P.M. The hotel will accept pets for a flat charge of $100. Anaheim Resort Transit provides bus transportation for a fee.

There are five levels of suites available. Each comes with either one or two queen beds and/or a king bed, and all have sofa beds. Rates range from $139 for a studio to $329 for the multi-room Penthouse Family Suite. Lower, long-term rates are also available. There is no extra charge for use of cribs. Rollaway beds are not available.

Residence Inn by Marriott Anaheim Maingate, 1700 S. Clementine St., Anaheim, CA 92802; 714-533-3555 or 800-331-3131; or *www.marriott.com/SNAAH*.

Superior Hotels

ANAHEIM MARRIOTT: Next to the Anaheim Convention Center, the Marriott is a favorite among conventioneers. Most of the 1,030 rooms, located in two towers and two four-story wings, have balconies. Each has one king-size bed or two doubles and HDTV. The hotel restaurants—JW's Steakhouse and Cafe Del Sol—are quite popular (especially at traditional mealtimes). For a quick bite, drop

PHOTO BY KEITH GROSHANS

by the Pizza Hut, Degrees Wine & Patio Bar, or Starbucks Marketplace, all on the premises. There is a partially covered pool surrounded by lounge chairs, as well as a whirlpool and a health club. Guests enjoy poolside and lobby bars, and concierge services.

The hotel is a couple of long blocks from the Disneyland Resort—for some, it is not within walking distance. Shuttle service to the Disney theme parks is provided by Anaheim Rapid Transit for a fee; transportation to area airports may also be arranged.

Room rates for two start at $139 (there is no charge for children under age 18 sharing their parents' room); suites start at about $149; $20 per additional adult. Rollaway beds are $20 per stay, and cribs are free. Special packages are available. Self-parking costs $24 per day; valet parking is $28 per day. Note that pets are no longer accepted at this hotel.

Anaheim Marriott, 700 W. Convention Way, Anaheim, CA 92802; visit the hotel's Website at *www.marriottanaheimhotel.com*, or call 714-750-8000 or 800-228-9290.

HILTON ANAHEIM: The 14-story glass exterior of this property reflects the Anaheim Convention Center, just steps away, and the lobby invites the outdoors (and swarms of conventioneers) inside. The Hilton has 1,572 rooms, including 93 suites, decorated in contrasting dark wood tones, with crisp white linens, and warm wall coverings.

The hotel's outdoor recreation center, on the fifth floor, features a heated swimming pool, two whirlpools, and a family-friendly water play area. There is a Starbucks Marketplace on the premises. Other dining options include Mix Restaurant, featuring three meals a day in a contemporary (yet casual) setting, and the Gazebo for outdoor dining (seasonal). Don't overlook Baja Fresh, Mix Lounge, Sbarro, Just Grillin, or Submarina (sandwich options). Note that restaurants tend to be especially crowded at lunchtime and during convention breaks.

Add to that a business center, several shops, and a fitness center. The 25,000-square-foot Health Club at Hilton has exercise equipment, an indoor saltwater pool, basketball court, whirlpool, steam room, sauna, exercise classes, spa facials, body treatments, and massage.

Rates for a room with two queen beds range from $119 to $309 (there is no charge for kids under 18 when sharing their parents' room with existing bedding); suites run a bit higher. Ask about packages. There's no extra charge for cribs, but rollaway beds cost $20 a night. Self-parking costs $16 per day; valet parking, $22. Pets are permitted for a fee.

Hilton Anaheim, 777 Convention Way, Anaheim, CA 92802; 714-750-4321 or 800-445-8667; *www.hiltonanaheimhotel.com*.

HYATT REGENCY ORANGE COUNTY: The hotel, located in Garden Grove, is one mile south of Disneyland Resort. Its dramatic, 17-story atrium encloses palm trees and greenery and houses the Tusca restaurant, Starbucks, a gift shop, Citris Grove Deli, and OC Brewhouse. Each of the 653 guestrooms features either a king-size bed or two queen beds, and modern interior design.

Amenities include coffeemaker, hair dryer, iron with board, plus an iPod docking station. The one- and two-bedroom suites also have a living room, refrigerator, and microwave. Suites can accommodate up to 8 people.

Kids' Suites include a room for the little ones, complete with bunk beds and a flatscreen TV. The parents' room has a king bed, TV, fridge, and microwave.

The hotel's impressive recreational facilities, located on the South Tower's third-story roof, include a heated swimming pool, a whirlpool, a fitness center, basketball court, and tennis courts. Another outdoor pool and whirlpool are on the ground floor of the North Tower. Transportation to the Disneyland Resort is provided (for $5), and airport shuttle service is available.

Room rates run $109 to $264 (no charge for children under age 18 occupying their parents' room), plus $25 for each additional adult; $139 to $334 for suites. There is no charge for cribs. Self-parking is $16 per day; valet parking, $22.

Hyatt Regency Orange County, 11999 Harbor Boulevard, Garden Grove, CA 92840; *www.orangecounty.hyatt.com*; 714-750-1234 or 800-233-1234.

SHERATON ANAHEIM HOTEL: With its turrets and Tudor design, this 489-room hotel looks more like a castle, surrounded by grounds that incorporate three peaceful courtyards, a rose garden, fountain, pond, and small waterfall. The lobby boasts an exotic fish tank and free Internet service in a comfortable, contemporary setting. The hotel also has a restaurant, cocktail lounge, and combination deli and gift shop called the California Deli. The staff gets high marks for their enthusiasm.

The hotel has 463 rooms and 26 suites— all with signature Sweet Sleeper Beds. The rooms—all large (490 square feet on average)—have two queen- or one king-size bed, cable television, in-room movies, voice mail, iron, refrigerator, hair dryer, and coffeemaker (with Starbucks coffee). Each suite has a sitting area with a sofa bed.

The hotel has an arcade, a heated pool, whirlpool, an exercise room, guest laundry, and conference rooms. It provides room service and frequent complimentary shuttle service to the Disneyland Resort. Airport transportation is available. Room rates for doubles run from $129 during off-season to $275 during peak season (no charge for children under 18 sharing their parents' room); $325 for suites; rollaways are $15; no charge for cribs. This hotel is pet-friendly. Request the best available rate when confirming prices.

Sheraton Anaheim Hotel, 900 S. Disneyland Dr., Anaheim, CA 92802; 714-778-1700 or 800-325-3535; *www.sheraton.com/anaheim*.

SHERATON PARK HOTEL AT THE ANAHEIM RESORT: This 14-story tower is easy to spot, and the 490 rooms and six suites have full or small balconies that provide a view of the pool or the Disneyland Resort (and a view of the fireworks). All rooms offer either one king or two queen beds, refrigerator, iron, coffeemaker, and hair dryer.

A large gift shop is on the premises, as is a lobby bar, coffee shop, a Southwestern-themed restaurant, snack shop, and a sports bar. The hotel also has a fitness center, large pool, whirlpool, and a poolside bar.

Shuttle service is available (provided by Anaheim Resort Transit for a fee) to the Disneyland Resort. Room rates run $129 to

$199, depending on occupancy and season; suites start at $550. Rollaways cost $15 extra; cribs are available free of charge.

Sheraton Park Hotel at the Anaheim Resort, 1855 S. Harbor Blvd., Anaheim, CA 92802; 714-750-1811 or 800-325-3535, or visit *www.sheraton.com/anaheimresort.*

Moderate Hotels

ANABELLA HOTEL: Architectural elements of this 7-acre Spanish-style property reflect the rich history of California missions. White-washed adobe walls and curved roof tiles are graced by palm trees and lush, blossoming plants. Thick arches welcome guests into public areas featuring covered walkways and a fountain. Even the shape of the outdoor whirlpool echoes this theme in its rose window design.

Standard and deluxe rooms sleep up to four; Casita Suites sleep up to four, while Mission and Kids' Suites sleep up to five with an additional sleeper sofa or bunk beds. The Hacienda Suite sleeps six. All rooms have granite baths, refrigerators, hair dryers, coffeemakers, and satellite TV service. In a separate building, the Club Anabella Concierge Rooms also come with robes and slippers, flat-panel TVs, and complimentary continental breakfast. Wireless Internet is available.

There are two pools, one for adults only. The on-site salon offers a variety of services, including pedicures, manicures, and facials. Guests can enjoy breakfast, lunch, and dinner indoors at the Tangerine Grill or outdoors on the Tangerine Patio (where cocktails are also served at the Nectarine Bar). Other amenities include a fitness center, a business center, and a guest laundry.

Rooms range from $99 to $199; suites from $149 to $299; and concierge rooms from $149 to $329. The daily charge for rollaways is $20; for cribs, $10. There is a daily fee for self-parking. Guests can walk to the Disneyland Resort in 10–15 minutes, but it is best to use Anaheim Resort Transit.

The Anabella Hotel, 1030 W. Katella Ave., Anaheim, CA 92802; 714-905-1050 or 800-863-4888; *www.anabellahotel.com.*

ANAHEIM CAMELOT INN & SUITES: Directly across the street—and a relatively short walk away—from the Disneyland Resort, this hotel, with its shingled roof, clock tower, turrets, and tidy window boxes, looks like something out of a Bavarian village. Each of the 121 rooms and suites has a microwave, refrigerator, coffeemaker, hair dryer, and an iron with board. It also has a fourth-floor terrace pool (with a view of Disneyland's Matterhorn), a whirlpool, two gift shops, and a guest laundry facility (fees apply).

Although there's no in-house restaurant, many places to eat, including Millie's Restaurant & Bakery, are within walking distance. Millie's also provides room service to all guestrooms. In-room dining is available daily from 7 A.M. to 10 P.M.

Deluxe standard rooms, most with two queen-size beds, range from $109–$159 year-round; one-bedroom suites range from $199 to $249 and accommodate up to six people, but they have only one bath. Rollaways are $20 plus tax; cribs are free. There is no hotel shuttle service, but it is possible to walk to the Disneyland Resort entrance via Harbor Boulevard. Of course, Anaheim Resort Transit provides transportation to Disneyland Resort (for a fee). There is a daily fee for parking.

Anaheim Camelot Inn & Suites, 1520 S. Harbor Blvd., Anaheim, CA 92802. Call 714-635-7275 or 800-828-4898, or visit *www.camelotinn-anaheim.com.*

FAIRFIELD INN ANAHEIM: Fronted by palms and pines, this inviting 467-room hotel is situated across from the Disneyland Resort. All of its rooms are accented with Disney artwork. The rooms are in two towers (one tower is nine stories high; the other, eight). Each room features a king-size bed or two queen beds, child-size sleeper sofa, satellite TV, an iron and board, a hair dryer, refrigerator, and coffeemaker. The hotel is served by a popular family-style eatery called Millie's Restaurant & Bakery, which also provides room service to guests.

Other facilities include a heated pool, whirlpool, gift shop, video arcade, Seattle's Best Coffee, and Pizza Hut. The rooms may be occupied by up to five people, and rates range from about $119 to $199; cribs are available.

Anaheim Fairfield Inn by Marriott, 1460 S. Harbor Blvd., Anaheim, CA 92802. Call 714-772-6777 or 800-228-2800, or visit the hotel's Website at *www.marriott.com/laxoc.*

BEST WESTERN PLUS PARK PLACE INN & MINI SUITES: This three-story, 199-room inn is located across from Disneyland Resort's pedestrian entrance. The lobby is spacious, with a high ceiling and several cozy seating areas, a fireplace, and windows looking out onto Harbor Boulevard.

A gift shop sells Disney souvenirs. Room configurations include a king-size bed and sleeper sofa, two queen-size beds and a sleeper sofa, or two double beds. All rooms are equipped with a refrigerator, microwave, iron with board, and coffeemaker (coffee is included at no additional cost).

Among the facilities are a pool with an adjacent whirlpool, and a guest laundry. Rates, which include continental breakfast at the inn or pancakes at the adjacent Captain Kidd's, run $104 to $144 for a standard room that sleeps up to four; mini suites run $124 to $164 (and sleep up to six). Rollaway beds cost $20; cribs are free.

Best Western Plus Park Place Inn & Mini Suites, 1544 S. Harbor Blvd., Anaheim, CA 92802. Call 714-776-4800 or 800-854-8175, ext. 4, or visit *www.stovallshotels.com.*

BEST WESTERN PLUS STOVALL'S INN:
This inn is known for its topiary garden. The property features 288 guestrooms, complimentary continental breakfast, fitness room, business center, and a pair of pools (one is heated), two whirlpools, a wading pool, and a gift shop. Room configurations include two queen, one king, or two double beds, and a bathroom with a separate sink and lots of counter space. Room service is available.

Refrigerators and microwaves are included (no charge). Room rates for up to five guests run $79 to $149. Rollaways are $15; cribs are free.

Best Western Plus Stovall's Inn, 1110 W. Katella Ave., Anaheim, CA 92802. Call 714-778-1880 or 800-854-8177, ext. 3, or visit *www.stovallshotels.com.*

CANDY CANE INN:
There's a lot to like about this sweet, two-story hotel—fountain out front, relaxed ambience, wrought-iron touches, and flowers everywhere. Located just down the street from the Disneyland Resort's main entrance (a manageable walk for adults and non-toddlers), the Candy Cane Inn is family-run and well-maintained.

Each of the 171 rooms, most of which face a courtyard, has a refrigerator, safe, dual-line phone with voice mail, coffeemaker, iron, hair dryer, and two queen beds with custom bedding. Add to that a guest laundry, swimming pool, gazebo-covered whirlpool, and fitness center. A complimentary continental buffet breakfast is served daily. Premium

HOT TIP!
If you stay in the 1300 to 1500 block of Harbor Boulevard, you can cross the street and walk to both theme parks. Of course, once you reach Disneyland Resort property, it's another 5- to 15-minute walk to get to the parks' turnstiles.

rooms also have robes, microwaves, free movie rentals, in-room breakfast, turndown service, and 2 P.M. check-out. Sightseeing services are available, as well as free shuttle service to and from the Disneyland Resort. Transportation to airports can be arranged. Parking is free.

Rates for a double room with two queen-size beds range from about $95 to $189, depending on the season. Rollaways, available only in deluxe and premium rooms, are $10; no charge for cribs. The inn is located across the street from a small shopping area with fast-food eateries.

Candy Cane Inn, 1747 S. Harbor Blvd., Anaheim, CA 92802. Call 714-774-5284 or 800-345-7057, or visit *www.candycaneinn.net.*

HOWARD JOHNSON ANAHEIM HOTEL AND WATER PLAYGROUND:
This property has some of the lushest landscaping of any place in Anaheim, except for the Disney hotels, and that's a major reason to stay here. Flowers and trees proliferate; a central fountain anchors the four, two-story units. The hotel is close to Disneyland Resort and local eateries. For a fee, Anaheim Resort Transit offers shuttle service to and from Disneyland.

The 303 non-smoking rooms are divided among several buildings on seven acres. Most have two queen beds, and all have a fridge, safe (fits a 17-inch laptop), and free high-speed Internet access. The rooms are relatively spacious, though bathrooms are a bit small.

There is one heated pool with a large whirlpool spa, plus Castaway Cove—a pirate playground featuring slides, water cannons, toddler pool, and fountains. Facilities include two launderettes, a gift shop, and an arcade. The hotel's partner restaurant, Mimi's Café, is next door. Rates range from $99 to $174, depending on the season. There is no charge for parking. Rollaways cost $15 per day; cribs are available for free.

Howard Johnson Anaheim Hotel and Water Playground, 1380 S. Harbor Blvd., Anaheim, CA 92802; 714-776-6120 or 800-422-4228, or visit *www.hojoanaheim.com.*

TROPICANA INN & SUITES: This establishment is across from the pedestrian crosswalk to the Disneyland Resort. Each of its 194 recently renovated rooms has a flatscreen TV, coffeemaker (with coffee), refrigerator, microwave, hair dryer, iron, and either a king-size bed or two queens. Each morning, continental breakfast is served in the hospitality room. Wireless Internet is available for a fee.

The inn has a small cafe, and a shop sells fruit, fried chicken, and breakfast items; a gift shop sells souvenirs and sundries. IHOP, Millie's Restaurant & Bakery, and other eateries are nearby. Millie's provides room service. It's about a 10-minute walk to the Disneyland Resort. Anaheim Resort Transit provides shuttle service for a fee. There is a daily fee for self-parking.

The inn has a heated outdoor Junior Olympic pool, spa, and guest laundry. Room rates are about $99 to $139. Suites sleep up to eight people. Rates for suites range from $179 to $349. Some suites have kitchens.

Tropicana Inn & Suites, 1540 S. Harbor Blvd., Anaheim, CA 92802; 714-635-4082 or 800-828-4898; *www.tropicanainn-anaheim.com.*

The Rest of the Best

Here's a roundup of the remaining Good Neighbor hotels. They have amenities and rates similar to those described in this chapter. However, some are a bit far from the Disneyland Resort.

Note: The various properties that boast Good Neighbor status are subject to change during the year; visit *www.disneyland.com* for updates.

SUPERIOR HOTELS

★ Crowne Plaza Anaheim Resort, 12021 Harbor Blvd., Garden Grove; 714-867-5555

★ Red Lion Hotel Anaheim, 1850 S. Harbor Blvd., Anaheim; 714-750-2801

MODERATE HOTELS

★ Best Western Plus Anaheim Inn, 1630 S. Harbor Blvd., Anaheim; 714-774-1050

★ Best Western Plus Pavilions, 1176 W. Katella Ave., Anaheim; 714-776-0140

★ Best Western Plus Raffles Inn & Suites, 2040 S. Harbor Blvd., Anaheim; 714-750-6100

★ Carousel Inn & Suites, 1530 S. Harbor Blvd., Anaheim; 714-758-0444

★ Clarion Hotel Anaheim Resort, 616 W. Convention Way, Anaheim; 714-750-3131

★ Cortona Inn & Suites, 2029 S. Harbor Blvd., Anaheim; 800-416-6819

★ Courtyard by Marriott Anaheim Buena Park, 7621 Beach Blvd., Buena Park; 714-670-6600

★ Hilton Garden Inn Anaheim/Garden Grove, 11777 Harbor Blvd., Garden Grove; 714-703-9100

★ Holiday Inn–Anaheim Resort, 1915 S. Manchester Ave., Anaheim; 714-748-7777

★ Holiday Inn Hotel & Suites, 1240 S. Walnut St., Anaheim; 714-535-0300

★ Hotel Menage Anaheim, 1221 S. Harbor Blvd., Anaheim; 866-599-6674

SUITE HOTELS

★ Anaheim Marriott Suites, 12015 Harbor Blvd., Garden Grove; 714-750-1000

★ Anaheim Portofino Inn & Suites, 1831 S. Harbor Blvd., Anaheim; 800-374-1623

★ DoubleTree Suites by Hilton, 2085 S. Harbor Blvd., Anaheim; 714-750-3000

★ Embassy Suites Anaheim-North, 3100 E. Frontera St., Anaheim; 714-632-1221

★ Embassy Suites Anaheim-South, 11767 Harbor Boulevard, Garden Grove; 714-539-3300

★ Homewood Suites by Hilton Anaheim–Main Gate Area, 12005 Harbor Blvd., Garden Grove; 714-740-1800

★ Residence Inn by Marriott Anaheim/Resort Area, 11931 Harbor Blvd., Garden Grove; 714-591-4000

★ Staybridge Suites, 1855 S. Manchester Ave., Anaheim; 714-748-7700

ECONOMY HOTELS

★ Jolly Roger Hotel, 640 W. Katella Ave., Anaheim; 714-782-7500

★ Motel 6 Anaheim Maingate, 100 Disney Way, Anaheim; 714-520-9696

★ Quality Inn & Suites, 1441 S. Manchester Ave., Anaheim; 714-991-8100

★ Ramada Maingate–At the Park, 1650 S. Harbor Blvd., Anaheim; 714-772-0440

Disneyland Park

When you wish upon a star, your dreams come true. So says the song, and it's always possible in Disneyland, Walt Disney's own dream come true. He envisioned "a place of warmth and nostalgia, of illusion and color and delight." The result: a place where imagination is given free reign, grins and giggles are encouraged, and everyone can see the world through a child's eyes.

The undisguised pleasure on the faces of park-goers reveals that they have fallen under the spell of a turreted pink castle; the oompah of a band marching down Main Street, U.S.A.; the sound of a train conductor's voice calling, "All aboard!"; a close-up encounter with Mickey and Minnie; and a nighttime spectacle more fantastic than the most elaborate dream.

Those who first entered Disneyland as kindergartners now return with their own children—or even grandchildren—to find the park of their memories unchanged in spirit and heart. Attractions have come and gone since the park opened in 1955, of course, and whole new "lands" have been added. But the enchantment guests experience when they walk through the portals of "The Happiest Place on Earth" remains constant. That may well be Disneyland's most enduring accomplishment.

Main Street, U.S.A.

1. Disneyland Railroad Station
2. Main Street Cinema
3. Main Street Vehicles
4. The Disneyland Story—Presenting Great Moments with Mr. Lincoln

Adventureland

5. Enchanted Tiki Room
6. Indiana Jones Adventure™
7. Jungle Cruise
8. Tarzan's Treehouse

Critter Country

9. Splash Mountain
10. The Many Adventures of Winnie the Pooh

Mickey's Toontown

11. Chip 'n Dale's Treehouse
12. Disneyland Railroad Station
13. Donald's Boat
14. Gadget's Go Coaster
15. Goofy's Playhouse
16. Mickey's House
17. Minnie's House
18. Roger Rabbit's Car Toon Spin

- - - Parade Route

Frontierland

19. Big Thunder Mountain Railroad
20. Golden Horseshoe Stage
21. Mark Twain Riverboat
22. Rafts to Tom Sawyer Island
23. Sailing Ship Columbia

New Orleans Square

24. Disneyland Railroad Station
25. Haunted Mansion
26. Pirates of the Caribbean

Tomorrowland

27. Astro Orbitor
28. Autopia
29. Disneyland Monorail
30. Disneyland Railroad Station
31. Captain EO
32. Innoventions
33. Space Mountain
34. Star Tours—The Adventures Continue
35. Buzz Lightyear Astro Blasters
36. Finding Nemo Submarine Voyage

Fantasyland

37. Alice in Wonderland
38. Casey Jr. Circus Train
39. Dumbo the Flying Elephant
40. It's a Small World
41. King Arthur Carrousel
42. Mad Tea Party
43. Matterhorn Bobsleds
44. Mr. Toad's Wild Ride
45. Peter Pan's Flight
46. Pinocchio's Daring Journey
47. Sleeping Beauty Castle
48. Snow White's Scary Adventures
49. Storybook Land Canal Boats

Getting Oriented

Disneyland Park's layout—a basic hub-and-spokes configuration—is simple, but it was quite innovative when the park opened in 1955. The design makes getting around easy, though it's not altogether effortless, since the numerous nooks, crannies, and alleyways can be a bit confusing at first.

The hub of the theme park's wheel is Central Plaza, which fronts Sleeping Beauty Castle. From it extend five spokes leading to eight "lands": Main Street, U.S.A.; Adventureland; Frontierland; New Orleans Square; Critter Country; Fantasyland; Mickey's Toontown; and Tomorrowland.

As you face Sleeping Beauty Castle, the first bridge to your left takes you to Adventureland; the next one, to Frontierland and New Orleans Square. To your right, the first walkway goes to Tomorrowland, and the next one—known as Matterhorn Way—leads directly into Fantasyland and on to Mickey's Toontown. If you cross the Castle's moat and walk through the archway, you'll also end up in Fantasyland. Critter Country occupies its own cul-de-sac extending north from New Orleans Square.

Study the map at left to familiarize yourself with the layout of Disneyland Park. When you arrive at the park, ask for a park Times Guide, which includes information about the times and locations of the day's scheduled entertainment, as well as where and when to meet your favorite Disney characters.

PARKING

Guests are directed to park in Disney's Mickey and Friends parking structure or to a parking lot: Pinocchio, on Disneyland Drive beside the Disneyland Hotel; Simba, behind and adjacent to Disney's Paradise Pier Hotel; or the *Toy Story* lot, on Harbor Boulevard. If one parking area is full, a cast member will direct you to one that isn't. Courtesy tram service transports guests from the parking deck only.

Parking areas open an hour before the park does, but getting a space can take a half hour if there's a long line of park-goers, all with the same idea of getting a head start on the day. Guests using wheelchairs will be directed to a special parking area and have access to ramps in the tram-loading area.

Parking Fees: Guests arriving in regular passenger vehicles pay $16 to park for the day. (The fee for oversize vehicles is $21, and the cost for buses and trucks with extended trailers is $26.) You may leave the lot and return later the same day at no additional charge. (Hold on to your parking stub as proof of payment.)

Lost Cars: Even if you take careful note of where you parked, you might have trouble remembering the exact spot when you return later. Hundreds more vehicles will likely be parked around yours. If this happens, contact a cast member and tell him or her approximately when you arrived. With that information, parking lot personnel can usually figure out the car's general location pretty quickly, and someone will then comb the lanes for it on a scooter.

GETTING AROUND

The Disneyland Railroad's five narrow-gauge trains make a 20-minute loop around the perimeter of the park, stopping at stations in Main Street, U.S.A.; New Orleans Square; Mickey's Toontown; and Tomorrowland. Horse-drawn streetcars, horseless carriages, and a motorized fire engine make one-way trips up and down Main Street, U.S.A.

To travel outside Disneyland Park, consider the sleek monorail, which glides between Tomorrowland and Downtown Disney. From Downtown Disney, you can walk to any of the three on-property hotels—the Disneyland Hotel, Disney's Paradise Pier Hotel, and Disney's Grand Californian Hotel & Spa.

The Grand Californian has its own entrance to Disney California Adventure and is just steps from the entrance to Disneyland (the parks require separate admission, unless you have a Park Hopper ticket; see page 55 for ticket pricing). If you plan to leave Disney property, there is an Alamo rental car location at Downtown Disney.

Park Primer

BABY FACILITIES

The Baby Care Center, on Main Street, U.S.A., by First Aid, provides changing tables, high chairs, toddlers' toilets, and a nursing area. Baby bottles can be warmed here, and baby powder, diapers, formula, and food are sold. There are no napping facilities or babysitting services.

FIRST AID

First Aid is located at the north end of Main Street, next door to the Main Street Photo Supply Co. A registered nurse is on duty during park operating hours.

GUIDED TOURS

Three behind-the-scenes tours originate from the Guided Tour Gardens, just left of City Hall. They are *Welcome to Disneyland*, *A Walk in Walt's Footsteps*, and *Discover the Magic*. There are also two seasonal tours: *Disney's Happiest Haunts* for the Halloween season, and *Holiday Time at Disneyland* during Christmastime. Park admission is required for all tours. Prices and schedules vary from tour to tour. For details, turn to page 21.

HOURS

Disneyland is open daily. Monday–Thursday hours are generally from about 10 A.M. to 8 P.M., Friday and Sunday from about 9 A.M. to 10 P.M., Saturday from 8 A.M. to 11 P.M., with extended hours during the summer months

PHOTO BY JILL SAFRO

and holiday periods. For specific Disneyland Park hours, visit *www.disneyland.com*, or call 714-781-4565.

During the busy spring break, summer, and Christmas holiday seasons, it's especially wise to arrive first thing in the morning so that you can visit the popular attractions before the lines get long. If you arrive at Disneyland too late, the parking structure and surrounding lots could be more crowded than usual; this is almost always the case in the summer months and during the last week of December.

For more timing tactics, see Hot Tips in this chapter and Crowd Patterns in the *Getting Ready to Go* chapter.

INFORMATION

Cast members at Disneyland Information Centers in City Hall and at Central Plaza can answer any questions you might have (or help plot your day so that you can make the most efficient use of your time and see what attractions truly interest you). Specifics on services and safety considerations have been compiled in Disneyland's guidemap; ask for it when you enter the park. There are also several services available for guests with disabilities.

Information Board: An invaluable resource for planning the day, the Information Board (aka Tip Board) is set up permanently at the north end of Main Street, U.S.A. Located by a grassy spot near the Plaza Pavilion and the entrance to Adventureland, it lets you know how long the waits are for most of the popular attractions, what (if anything) is not operating that day, and where and when park entertainment will take place. The board is updated every hour. Cast members who are stationed there will also answer questions and provide information about the restaurants and hotels in the Disneyland Resort. They can help guests locate favorite Disney characters, too.

LOCKERS

Storage lockers are located outside the main entrance (on the left) and on Main Street, U.S.A. (about halfway to the Castle, on the right). Fees range from $7 to $15 per day, depending on size. A small number of "charging lockers" are available for wireless devices. They cost $2 per hour, with a one-hour minimum.

MONEY MATTERS

Cash and traveler's checks are accepted at all food and merchandise locations throughout Disneyland. American Express, MasterCard, Visa, JCB Card, Disney Visa, and Discover Card are accepted at all shops, cafeterias, fast-food eateries, snack bars, and full-service establishments (cash and Disney Dollars only at some park vending carts).

Personal checks with your name and address printed on them, drawn on U.S. funds, and accompanied by a government-issued photo ID, may be accepted as payment, too.

Main Street's City Hall can assist with foreign currency exchange, as well as personal and traveler's check cashing. Disneyland Resort hotel guests may charge almost any purchase made in the theme park back to their hotel bill if they gave a credit card number at check-in. Keep in mind that this service is not available at most Downtown Disney locations.

Guests may purchase Disney gift cards (in amounts of $5–$1,500) and Disney Dollars in $1, $5, and $10 denominations from any park entrance ticket booth and City Hall. Disney Dollars and gift cards are accepted at the Disney hotels, Downtown Disney, California Adventure, and throughout Disneyland. They are also valid at Walt Disney World in Florida and at U.S. Disney Store locations.

There are several ATMs here. The first one, encountered when first entering the park, is located near the Disney Gallery. (Though one might expect the Bank on Main Street to be, well, a bank, it is not. No financial services are offered at this address.)

PACKAGE CHECK

There's no need to lug bags around. You can store bulky purchases at the Newsstand at the entrance to Disneyland (on the right as you exit the park). Stashing them in a Main Street locker is also an option (for a fee).

SAME-DAY RE-ENTRY

Guests who wish to leave the park and return later the same day may do so by getting their hand stamped upon exiting. The stamp will survive numerous hand washings. Keep in mind that you will need both your park ticket and a hand stamp for re-entry.

SMOKING POLICY

At Disneyland Park, smoking is only permitted in designated smoking areas; refer to a park guidemap for specific locations. It is prohibited inside all attractions, waiting areas, shops, and indoor and outdoor dining areas.

STROLLERS & WHEELCHAIRS

Strollers ($15) and wheelchairs ($12 with a $20 refundable deposit and a major credit card) may be rented outside the main entrance of Disneyland Park. Electric Conveyance Vehicles (ECVs) cost $50 for the day, with a $20 deposit and major credit card. Wheelchair and ECV supplies are limited. Lost strollers may be replaced at the park's main entrance and at The Star Trader shop in Tomorrowland.

SECURITY CHECK

All guests entering Disney theme parks are subject to a security check. Backpacks, purses, etc., are searched by security personnel before guests are permitted to enter.

Expect car trunks to be searched when entering Disney parking facilities.

Guests checking into Disneyland Resort hotels are asked to present a valid government-issued photo ID.

Ticket Prices

Note that prices and ticketing structure are apt to change in 2014. The following will give you an idea of what you can expect to pay. For current prices, call 714-781-4565, or visit **www.disneyland.com.***

	ADULTS	CHILDREN**
One-Day Ticket (one park)	$92	$86
One-Day Ticket (hopper)	$137	$131
Two-Day Ticket (hopper)	$210	$197
Three-Day Ticket (hopper)	$260	$244
Four-Day Ticket (hopper)	$285	$265
Five-Day Ticket (hopper)	$300	$279
Two-Park Deluxe Annual Passport		$499
Two-Park Premium Annual Passport		$669
Premier Annual Passport		$979

*Discounts may be available through the Website.
**3 through 9 years of age; children under 3 free

Main Street, U.S.A.

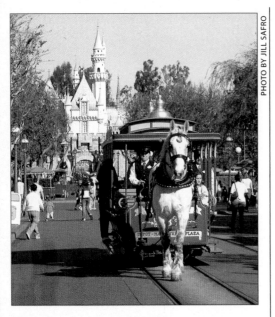

PHOTO BY JILL SAFRO

This pretty thoroughfare represents Main Street America in the early 1900s, complete with the gentle clip-clop of horses' hooves on pavement, melodic ringing of streetcar bells, and strains of nostalgic tunes such as "Bicycle Built for Two" and "Coney Island Baby."

The sounds of brass bands, a barbershop quartet, and ragtime piano fill the street. An old-fashioned steam train huffs into a handsome brick depot. Rows of picturesque buildings line the street. Authentic gaslights, which once lit up Baltimore and St. Louis, flicker at sundown in ornate lampposts lining the walkways, and the storefronts—painted in a palette of pastels—could not be more inviting. Walt Disney was a master of detail:

Birnbaum's Best

Stamps like this one indicate the attractions that we find superlative in one (and usually more) of the following ways: state-of-the-art technology, theming, beauty, novelty, thrills and spills (make that splashes), and overall whimsy. Each "Birnbaum's Best" promises to deliver a dynamite Disneyland experience!

throughout Main Street, even the doorknobs are historically correct.

To make the buildings appear taller, a set designer's technique called forced perspective was employed. The first floor is seven-eighths scale (this allows guests to enter comfortably); the second story is five-eighths scale; and the third, only half size. The dimensions of the whole are small enough for the place to seem intimate and comforting, yet the proportions appear correct. (Forced perspective was also used to make the Matterhorn and Sleeping Beauty Castle seem taller than they are.)

The shops that line Main Street, U.S.A., draw guests back repeatedly during their Disneyland visit (see the Shopping section of this chapter and you'll understand why).

The following attractions are listed in the order in which you'll encounter them while walking from the main entrance up Main Street to the Central Plaza, toward Sleeping Beauty Castle.

CITY HALL: Before strolling up Main Street, stop briefly at the Information Center at City Hall, on the west side of Town Square, to find entertainment schedules, make dining reservations, or get advice to help you plan your Disneyland day. City Hall is also a great meeting place if members of your party separate and plan to regroup later in the day.

FIRE STATION: Next door to City Hall, this was Walt Disney's home away from home during the construction of Disneyland. His apartment, on the top floor, is decorated just as he left it, but it's not open to the public. A light burns in the window in his memory. Kids love—and are welcome—to climb on the fire wagon parked inside the firehouse. It's a realistic copy of a truck from the early 1900s and provides a great photo opportunity.

THE DISNEY GALLERY: This shop has wares representing creative efforts from throughout the Walt Disney Company, often including never-before-seen art, displayed in an ever-changing exhibit area.

DISNEYLAND RAILROAD: Walt Disney loved trains so much he actually built a one-eighthscale model of one, the Lilly Belle, in the backyard of his home. So it was only natural that his first theme park include a railroad—five narrow-gauge steam trains that circle Disneyland Park in about 20 minutes, making stops in Main Street, U.S.A.; New Orleans Square; Mickey's Toontown; and Tomorrowland.

Main Street just wouldn't be Main Street without the sound of the trains chugging in and out of the station and the conductors calling, "All aboard!"

Two of the locomotives were built at the Walt Disney Studios, while three had other lives before coming to Disneyland. Guests who ride the train between Tomorrowland and Main Street, U.S.A., are in for a couple of surprises. In 1958, Walt Disney added a diorama of the Grand Canyon, depicted from its south rim on a seamless, handwoven canvas that is 306 feet long and 34 feet high, and covered with 300 gallons of paint. The fauna and foliage depict deer, a mountain lion, a golden eagle, wild turkeys, skunks, porcupines, and desert mountain sheep, surrounded by quaking aspens, piñons, and ponderosa pines, with a snowfall, a storm, a sunset, and a rainbow thrown in for good measure. The accompanying music is the "On the Trail" section of American composer Ferde Grofé's *Grand Canyon Suite.*

Adjacent to the Grand Canyon, yet eons away, the Primeval World diorama—a scene of misty swamps, deserts, rain forests, erupting volcanoes, and 46 prehistoric creatures—inspired by Disney's 1940 film *Fantasia*—opened in 1966, after an interim stop at the Ford Pavilion at the New York World's Fair.

THE DISNEYLAND STORY, PRESENTING GREAT MOMENTS WITH MR. LINCOLN: The Disneyland Opera House makes the perfect backdrop for a tribute to the "Happiest Place on Earth," and the man who created it, one Walter Elias Disney. A unique collection of art, models, and mementos—as well as a film—marks more than fifty years of Disneyland magic. After taking a walk down Disney memory lane, guests may pay a visit to the 16th President of the United States. Yes, Abraham Lincoln is back! (In realistic, Audio-Animatronics form.) After a brief presentation about the Civil War, "Mr. Lincoln" stands and delivers a stirring discourse about liberty, the American spirit, and the challenges facing the nation. It's exceptionally *au courant* for an 18th-century allocution.

MAIN STREET VEHICLES: Main Street's motorized fire wagon, horseless carriages, and horse-drawn streetcars give the thoroughfare a real touch of nostalgia, while at the same time giving guests a lift from one end of the street to the other. The fire truck is modeled after those that might have been discovered on an American Main Street in the early 1900s, except that it has seats where the hose was meant to be carried.

The horse-drawn streetcars, inspired by those in 19th-century photographs, carry 30

Save Time in Line!

For those of us who'd prefer not to waste time standing in line for theme park attractions, Disney's Fastpass is nothing short of a miracle. Basically, the free system lets guests forgo the task of waiting in an actual line for a number of theme park attractions.

How? Simply by walking up to the Fastpass booth (located near the entrance of participating attractions) and slipping their park ticket into the Fastpass machine.

In return, guests get a slip of paper with a time printed on it (in addition to the safe return of their park ticket). That time—for example, 4:05 P.M. to 5:05 P.M.—represents the "window" in which guests are invited to return to the attraction and practically walk right on—without standing in a long line! Note that latecomers will not be accommodated.

Once you use your Fastpass to enter an attraction (or the time on it has passed), you can get a new Fastpass time for another attraction. It's also possible to get a Fastpass for a second attraction two hours after the first one is issued.

For example, if one pass was issued at 2 P.M., you can get a Fastpass for another attraction at 4 P.M. Sound confusing? It won't be once you've tried it.

Disney's Fastpass service is free and available to everyone bearing a valid theme park ticket. It should be available during peak times of the day and all peak seasons. We've placed the Fastpass logo (FP) beside the listings for all of the attractions that were participating at press time. However, since more attractions are scheduled for inclusion, check a park map for an up-to-the-minute listing of Fastpass attractions.

Note that Fastpass service may be offered on a seasonal basis, and some attractions may stop offering Fastpass in 2014. For updates, call 714-781-4565, or visit *www.disneyland.com*. If Fastpass is offered during your visit, by all means, use it!

passengers each. Most of the horses that pull the cars are Belgians (characterized by white manes and tails and lightly feathered legs) and Percheron draft horses.

MAIN STREET CINEMA: This small, standing-room-only theater features classic, early Mickey Mouse cartoons.

PENNY ARCADE: This place is more of a candy shop than an arcade, but the air of nostalgia remains. Those who have frequented it in the past will be happy to find Esmeralda front and center, as before, ready as always to tell your fortune. The arcade still has Mutascopes, machines that feature hand-cranked moving pictures and require a penny to operate. Fans of the classic electrocution machine will be sad to know that it is M.I.A.

Save some change for the arcade's nine penny presses. You insert a penny (plus a few other coins to pay for the service), and the penny will be flattened and imprinted with the image of Sleeping Beauty Castle or the face of one of the Disney characters.

CENTRAL PLAZA: Main Street, U.S.A., ends at Central Plaza, the hub of the park, and four of the park's lands are directly accessible from here. At its center stands the Walt and Mickey Partners statue. It's one of the park's most popular picture spots.

One of Disneyland's two Information Centers is located here, near the entrance to Adventureland. Besides the information desk, there is a handy Information Board, updated hourly, that posts wait times for many attractions, which attractions offer Fastpass, what (if anything) is not operating that day, and where and when park entertainment will take place. They offer park guidemaps, too.

Adventureland

For someone who grew up in Marceline, Missouri, around the turn of the 20th century, as Walt Disney did, the far-flung regions of the world must have seemed most exotic and exciting. So it's not surprising that when he was planning his new park, he designated one area, called Adventureland, to represent all the (then) remote and mysterious corners of the world.

The original South Seas-island ambience all but disappeared with the opening of the Indiana Jones Adventure in 1995, and Adventureland became a 1930s jungle outpost. Today, the entrance to the Jungle Cruise is a walk-through headquarters, with old photographs and radios playing big band music interrupted by news flashes about Professor Jones's latest exploits and discoveries. Shops here sell wares that are meant to appeal to modern-day adventurers.

WALT DISNEY'S ENCHANTED TIKI ROOM: Introduced in 1963, this was the first of the park's Audio-Animatronics attractions and the precursor of more elaborate variations, such as "Great Moments with Mr. Lincoln" and the above-mentioned Dr. Jones. Housed in a vaguely Polynesian complex situated at the entrance to Adventureland, the 15-minute show was recently given a spiffy face-lift.

The stars are four feathered emcees (José, Michael, Pierre, and Fritz), backed up by a sextet of pastel-plumed, long-eyelashed parrots, and an eclectic chorus of orchids, carved wooden tiki poles, tiki drummers, singing masks, bird-of-paradise flowers, macaws, Amazon parrots, toucans, fork-tailed birds, cockatoos, and several other species.

The 225 performers all sing and drum up a tropical storm with so much animation that it's hard to resist a smile. Their repertoire includes "In the Tiki, Tiki, Tiki Room," "Let's All Sing," and "Aloha to You."

JUNGLE CRUISE: The spiel delivered by the skipper on this seven-minute river adventure has its share of corny jokes, but your navigator may turn out to be a natural comic with a funny delivery. Just remember that the silly jokes are all part of the fun.

As jungle cruises go, this one is as much like the real thing as Main Street, U.S.A., is like life in a real small town—long on loveliness and short on the visual distractions and minor annoyances that constitute the bulk of human experience. There are no mosquitoes and no Montezuma's revenge. And the Bengal tiger and king cobras at the ancient Cambodian ruins, and the great apes, gorillas, crocodiles, alligators, elephants, hippos, and lions in the water and along the shores represent no threat to passersby—though according to maintenance crews, they are almost as much trouble as real ones. Of course, there's no telling how guests will take the attraction's newest residents: a pack of peeved piranhas. Or vice versa. Good luck with that!

Movie buffs should note that Bob Mattey, who helped develop these jungle creatures, also worked on the giant squid for the Disney film *20,000 Leagues Under the Sea*, the man-eating plants in many Tarzan movies, and the menacing mechanical shark in *Jaws*.

The large-leafed upright tree in the Cambodian ruins section of the attraction is a Sacred Fig (*Ficus religiosa*), the same species of tree under which Buddha received enlightenment in India many centuries ago.

TARZAN'S TREEHOUSE: The 70-foot-high *Disneyodendron semperflorens grandis*, or "large, ever-blooming Disney tree," which cradled the Swiss Family Treehouse from 1962 to mid-1999, now embraces another lofty dwelling: Tarzan's Treehouse, inspired by the book by Edgar Rice Burroughs and Disney's 1999 animated feature *Tarzan*. Overlooking the Jungle Cruise and the Temple of the Forbidden Eye (the setting for the Indiana Jones attraction), this moss- and vine-covered "high-rise apartment" shelters Tarzan, his adoptive mom, Kala (the ape), and Jane.

An interactive play area at the base of the tree has been designed around the scientific equipment that Jane and her father brought to the jungle. (Guests are welcome to experiment with some of it.) Nearby, a makeshift wooden staircase crafted from shipwreck salvage and a weathered suspension bridge provide easy access to the treehouse itself.

Jane's drawings, displayed throughout the compound, reveal the amazing story of Tarzan's survival and coming-of-age in the wild. (But could there be trouble in paradise? That lout of a leopard, Sabor, is lurking in the tree!) By the time guests plant their feet on terra firma once more, they will have hit new heights—not unlike a certain high-flying hero himself—and gotten acquainted with some of the characters (both human and animal) who have shared in his notorious exploits.

Note: Tarzan's Treehouse requires guests to climb quite a few stairs. Just a heads-up.

BIRNBAUM'S ★BEST★ INDIANA JONES™ ADVENTURE:

Hidden deep within the dense jungles of India, the Temple of the Forbidden Eye was built long ago to honor the powerful deity Mara. According to legend, Mara could "look into your very soul" and grant the "pure of heart" one of three gifts: unlimited wealth, eternal youth, or future knowledge. But legend also issues a rather stern warning: "A terrible fate awaits those who gaze upon the eyes of Mara!" Dr. Jones would only comment, "Records indicate that many have come, but few have returned."

Now you can take an expedition through the ancient temple ruins in this attraction based on the George Lucas/Steven Spielberg film quartet. The whole experience, including the pre-show and queue area, can easily take more than an hour (without a Fastpass), though the ride itself lasts about 3½ minutes. You follow the jungle path through Dr. Jones's cluttered encampment, then enter the temple via the path marked by his original team. In the queue area, a newsreel tells of Jones's latest expedition. What it does not reveal is that he has entered the temple and disappeared.

Following in his footsteps, you will see warning signs that indicate there still may be booby traps that have not yet been disarmed. (The fun is in paying no heed to the warnings and letting the spikes fall where they may.) Inside the temple, guests board 12-passenger vehicles reminiscent of 1930s troop transports. One person takes the wheel and serves as the expedition driver, but not until all are securely fastened in their seats for the twists and turns ahead. Hold on to your hat!

The search for Indiana Jones is on, and an encounter with the fearsome Mara is unavoidable. The trip reveals a world of mummies, glowing fires, falling lava, worrisome snakes, and poisonous darts.

Surprises lurk around every bend, and escape is only temporary (just as in the movies), as you suffer an avalanche of creepy crawlies, traverse a quaking suspension bridge, and, best of all, find yourself face-to-face with a gigantic rolling ball that threatens to flatten everyone in its path. At the end of the ride, Indy himself is waiting for you, with a flippant parting remark, such as "That wasn't so bad," or "Next time you're on your own."

Thanks to the creative wizardry of Disney Imagineers, no two rides are exactly the same, so each time you enter the Temple of the Forbidden Eye, the overall experience will be slightly different.

Note: Pregnant women and guests who suffer from heart conditions, motion sickness, weak backs, and other limitations should not ride this attraction. Kids must be at least 3 years old and at least 46 inches tall to board; those under 7 must be accompanied by an adult. Spooked by snakes? There are more than a few in here. They're not real, but still rather creepy. Just a warning.

New Orleans Square

Just as Main Street, U.S.A., makes the theme park a great place to shop, New Orleans Square makes it a fine spot to spend a few relaxing hours. Those click-click sounds emanating from the railroad station are the Morse code version of the actual dedication speech Walt Disney gave on the opening day of Disneyland back in 1955.

The attractions that are described on the following pages are listed in the order in which you would encounter them while strolling from east to west in Disneyland's festive New Orleans Square.

Though New Orleans Square did not figure in the Disneyland layout until 1966, it's certainly among the park's most evocative areas. This would be true even if it were home to just the superb Haunted Mansion and Pirates of the Caribbean. But there's also its picturesque site on the shores of the Rivers of America, and its architecture, a pastiche of wrought iron, pastel stucco, French doors, and beckoning verandas.

Not to be missed are the pleasant open-air dining spots; the romantic Blue Bayou restaurant overlooking the moonlit lagoon stretch of Pirates of the Caribbean; the unique assortment of shops; and the music—lively jazz and Dixieland, performed in traditional New Orleans style.

As you sit here on a warm evening, snacking on fritters and hot chocolate, images of Disneyland-as-amusement-park evaporate.

BIRNBAUM'S BEST

PIRATES OF THE CARIBBEAN: The most swashbuckling adventure you'll find at Disneyland, this 16-minute boat ride transports guests through a series of sets portraying a rowdy pirate raid on a Caribbean village. Bursting with cannon fire, stolen loot, a gluttonous feast, and a raucous band of unruly mercenaries, Pirates of the Caribbean has entertained more people than any theme park attraction in history. It was the last attraction built under Walt Disney's direct creative supervision.

The experience begins with a short excursion through a bayou, where will-o'-the-wisps glow just above the grasses. Fireflies twinkle nearby, while stars spangle the twilight-blue sky overhead. The attention to detail nearly boggles the mind. The Audio-Animatronics cast includes plastered pigs whose legs actually twitch in their soporific contentment, singing marauders, and wily wenches. The observant will note a couple of new rapscallion residents. Yep, that beloved scallywag Captain Jack Sparrow has dropped anchor here, as has his nefarious nemesis, Captain Barbossa.

While it's by no means the most politically correct attraction on property (far from it, actually), the theme song, "Yo-Ho, Yo-Ho (A Pirate's Life for Me)" manages to transform what is actually a picture of some blatant buccaneering into a rousing time for all. A must—again and again.

BIRNBAUM'S ★BEST★ HAUNTED MANSION: FP

In a British radio interview, Walt Disney once explained how sorry he felt for those homeless ghosts whose hauntable mansions had fallen to the wrecker's ball. Feeling that these lost souls sorely needed a place of their own, he offered this Haunted Mansion, unquestionably one of Disneyland's top attractions. From its stately portico to the exit corridor, the special effects are piled on to create an eerie, but never terrifying, mood. Just frightfully funny.

Judicious applications of paint and expert lighting effects heighten the shadows that play ghoulishly on the walls outside. The jumble of trunks, chairs, dress forms, and other assorted knickknacks in the attic are left appropriately dirty, and extra cobwebs, which come in convenient liquid form, are strung with abandon. The eerie music and the slightly spooky tones of the Ghost Host often set small

children to whimpering, and soon their Mickey Mouse ears have been pulled tightly over their eyes. Still, the spirits that inhabit this house on the hill—999 in all—are a tame lot for the most part, though they are always looking for occupant number 1,000. Any volunteers?

HOT TIP!

Haunted Mansion Holiday kicks off in late September and runs through the New Year. It features Jack Skellington from Tim Burton's *The Nightmare Before Christmas*, as well as holiday decor galore. Silly, seasonal sight gags abound.

What makes the seven-minute attraction so special is the attention to, and abundance of, details—so many that it's next to impossible to take them all in during the first, or even the second or third, time around. In the Portrait Chamber—a roomful of fearsome-looking gargoyles that adjoins the chandeliered and lace-curtain-adorned foyer—it's fun to speculate on whether the ceiling moves up or the room moves down. (It's one way here and the opposite way at the mansion's counterpart at Walt Disney World's Magic Kingdom.)

Once in your Doom Buggy, look for the bats' eyes on the wallpaper, the tomb-sweet-tomb plaque, and the rattling suit of armor in the Corridor of Doors. Can you spot a Hidden Mickey in the haunted dining room?

Then there are the dead plants and flowers and broken glass in the Conservatory, where a hand reaches out of a half-open casket; the terrified cemetery watchman and his mangy mutt in the Graveyard; the ghostly teapot that pours spectral tea; the ectoplasmic king and queen on the teeter-totter; the bicycle-riding spirits; the transparent musicians; and the headless knight and his supernatural Brunhilde. Nice stuff all.

The mansion was constructed in 1963, based on studies of houses around Baltimore; the attraction itself opened in 1969. The song "Grim Grinning Ghosts" was composed especially for the Haunted Mansion attraction.

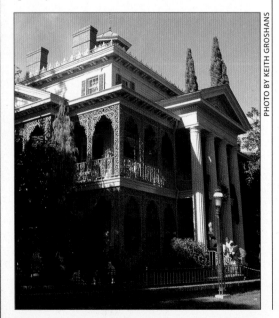

PHOTO BY KEITH GROSHANS

Frontierland

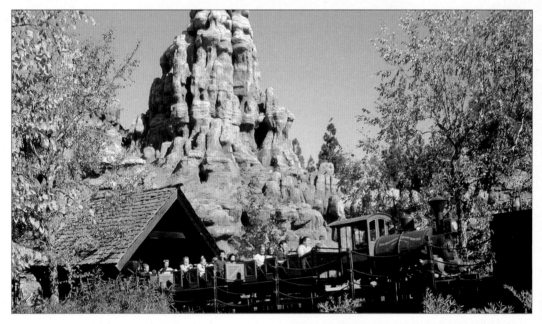

This is the America experienced by the pioneers as they pushed westward: rough wilderness outposts, dense forests, rugged mountains delineating the skyline, and rivers lapping at the shore.

The sights in Frontierland are just about as pleasant as they come in Disneyland, and the atmosphere as relaxing. That's especially true in the afternoon, when the riverboat *Mark Twain*, with its elaborate wooden lacework trim, pulls majestically away from its dock for a cruise along the Rivers of America.

The following Frontierland attractions are described in the order in which visitors encounter them while moving counter-clockwise from the Central Plaza gateway toward Big Thunder Mountain.

FRONTIERLAND SHOOTIN' EXPOSITION:

This shooting gallery, set in an 1850s town in the Southwest Territory, is completely electronic. Eighteen rifles are trained on Boothill, a mining town complete with a bank, jail, hotel, and stables. They fire infrared beams that trigger silly results whenever they strike the red, reactive targets. The most challenging target is the moving shovel, which, when struck, causes a skeleton to pop out of a grave.

Note: Disneyland tickets do not include use of the arcade. Pay about 50 cents for 20 shots—then fire away. (Price subject to change).

BIRNBAUM'S BEST ★ **BIG THUNDER MOUNTAIN RAILROAD:** FP Hold on to your hats and glasses, because this here's the wildest ride in the wilderness. Inspired by peaks in Utah's Bryce Canyon and Arizona's Sedona, Big Thunder Mountain is entirely a Disney creation. The name comes from an old Indian legend about a sacred mountain in Wyoming that thundered whenever men tried to excavate its gold. The attraction took five years of planning and two years of construction, and it cost about as much to build as the rest of the original Disneyland attractions put together.

As roller coasters go, this one is relatively tame. It's short on steep climbs and precipitous drops that put hearts in throats and make stomachs protest, but long on tight curves that provoke giggles of glee. Adding to the appeal of this thrill ride is the scenery that the runaway mine train passes along the way: a pitch-black bat cave, giant stalactites and stalagmites, a waterfall, a natural-arch bridge that affords fine views over the Big Thunder landscape, and mine walls ready to cave in.

The queue area sets the scene of the quaint mining town, with two hotels, a newspaper office, dance hall, saloon, and general store. If you listen closely, you may hear a local bar-maid flirting with a miner to the tune of "Red River Valley" or "Listen to the Mockingbird."

PHOTO BY KEITH GROSHANS

DISNEYLAND PARK

As you proceed toward the loading area, notice the brownish stone walls on each side of you. They were created from a hundred tons of real gold ore from the former mining town of Rosamond, California, which also yielded the ten-foot-tall stamp mill designated "Big Thunder Mine 1880."

For the best of both worlds, ride twice—once by day, to see the scenery, and again after dark, for the pleasure of hurtling through the cool night (you might also catch a glimpse of the Fantasmic! show).

Note: Pregnant women and guests who have heart conditions, motion sickness, weak backs, and other limitations should not ride. Children must be at least 3 years old and a minimum of 40 inches tall to board. Kids under 7 years old must be accompanied by an adult.

MARK TWAIN RIVERBOAT: One of the original Disneyland attractions and the first paddle wheeler built in the United States in half a century, this five-eighths-scale vessel circumnavigates Tom Sawyer Island. Along the way, it passes the River Belle Terrace, the Royal Street Veranda, the docks for the Tom Sawyer Island Rafts, piney Critter Country,

a waterfall, abandoned railroad tracks, and lovely dense woods full of the alders, cottonwoods, maples, and willows that might have been found along the Missouri frontier more than a century ago. Moose, elk, and (real) ducks complete the passing scene.

On a busy day, this 14-minute ride offers a pleasant respite from the crowds. And if you manage to get one of the few chairs in the bow, the *Mark Twain* also provides a rare opportunity to put your feet up.

PHOTO BY JILL SAFRO

GOLDEN HORSESHOE SALOON: Tongue-in-cheek humor and Western flair are the key ingredients in the musical and specialty acts featured at this entertainment venue. The hall itself is resplendent with chandeliers, polished floors and banisters, and a long brass railing. Walt Disney kept a private box here, just to the left of the stage, on the upper level.

Billy Hill & the Hillbillies, brothers who mix bluegrass music and wacky comedy, are

HOT TIP!

Select one member of your party to be a Fastpass representative—someone who'll gather the park tickets and get Fastpass assignments for the group.

regular performers at the Golden Horseshoe Stage (for specifics, see page 88). Performance times vary. Check the entertainment Times Guide for the schedule or drop by City Hall when you arrive at the park.

There is no assigned seating inside; all of the seats are good, though those up front or on the balcony are perhaps the best.

SAILING SHIP COLUMBIA: A full-scale replica of the ten-gun, three-masted "Gem of the Ocean," the *Columbia* operates seasonally and on higher-attendance days at Disneyland. The original ship, constructed in Plymouth, Massachusetts, in 1787 and christened the *Columbia Rediviva* ("freedom reborn"), was the first American craft to circumnavigate the globe. (Back then, that took three years to do.)

Disney's *Columbia*, dedicated in 1958 and renovated in 1984, was the first of its kind to be built in more than a century, and it circumnavigates the Rivers of America in 15 minutes. It has a steel hull, a deck planked with Douglas fir, and measures 110 feet from stem to stern, with an 84-foot mainmast. Usually moored at Fowler's Harbor, opposite the Haunted Mansion, the ship towers majestically over the treetops below.

Below Decks: The *Columbia*'s maritime museum, open only when the ship is operating, illustrates the way sailors lived on the original vessel during its later voyages, as reported in the ship's log and in letters between the captain and the owners.

PIRATE'S LAIR ON TOM SAWYER ISLAND: Yes, you read that right—there's been a pirate invasion in Frontierland! The formerly peaceful getaway that was pre-pirate Tom Sawyer Island has been transformed into a pirate-y paradise, complete with hidden treasure, creepy caves, and shipwrecks.

The only way to reach the island, which sits in the middle of the Rivers of America and was at one time the highest point in Disneyland, is by raft (which is piloted by a pirate). Once there, guests have many areas to investigate. Among them is Smuggler's Cove, which incorporates the island's beloved bridges and invites guests to man the bilge pumps in an effort to raise some sunken treasure. Then there's the Castle Rock lookout point, complete with spyglasses and peepholes (perfect for spying on scallywags or fellow theme park guests); Will Turner's Blacksmith Shop offers a glimpse at some of

his works-in-progress; Dead Man's Grotto is a dark and labyrinthine set of caves sporting some spooky-yet-snazzy special effects. Purists are pleased by the preservation of Tom and Huck's Tree House.

Small signs point to places of interest on the island, and even though the footpaths are decidedly well-trodden, any time spent here is worthwhile and could encompass some of your happiest moments at Disneyland.

Note: Tom Sawyer Island closes early to allow for Fantasmic! preparation. Check at the dock for excursion times, particularly the last departure of the day.

Disneyland Park Fastpass Attractions

Long lines got you down? Not to worry—some of the major Disneyland attractions offer Fastpass. (For an explanation of this time-saving, line-skipping system, turn to page 58.) Here's a list of those "E-ticket" crowd-pleasers. (Note that attractions listed here may change and that Fastpass may not be offered at all times throughout the year.)

ADVENTURELAND

Indiana Jones Adventure

CRITTER COUNTRY

Splash Mountain

FRONTIERLAND

Big Thunder Mountain Railroad

MICKEY'S TOONTOWN

Roger Rabbit's Car Toon Spin

NEW ORLEANS SQUARE

Haunted Mansion (late September through December only)

TOMORROWLAND

Autopia; Space Mountain;

Star Tours—The Adventures Continue

Critter Country

PHOTO BY KEITH GROSHANS

Lush, shady forests of pines, locusts, white birches, coastal redwoods, and evergreen elms surround Critter Country, one of the most pleasant corners of Disneyland. In 1972, this land debuted as Bear Country, the backwoods home of the since-departed Country Bear Playhouse. From 1956 through 1971, the area was called the Indian Village, complete with teepees and a dance circle, and was considered part of Frontierland.

In 1989, the zone welcomed foxes, frogs, geese, rabbits, crocodiles, and many of the other critters that make up the Audio-Animatronics cast of Splash Mountain. To make the new furry residents feel at home, Disney Imagineers rechristened the area Critter Country. Observant guests will spot scaled-down houses, lairs, and nests tucked into hillsides and along the river.

BIRNBAUM'S ★BEST★ SPLASH MOUNTAIN: FP The fourth peak in Disneyland's mountain range of thrill rides—along with Big Thunder Mountain, the Matterhorn, and Space Mountain—Splash Mountain is unlike the other three attractions, where passengers ride roller coaster-style cars down tubular steel tracks. In this nine-minute ride, they board hollowed-out logs and drift on

a waterborne journey through backwoods swamps and bayous, down waterfalls, and finally (here's where the speed picks up) over the top of a super-steep spillway at the peak of the mountain into a briar-laced pond five stories below.

HOT TIP!

If you want to get soaked on Splash Mountain, sit in the front of the log; the spray has less of a dampening effect in the back. Though nobody stays dry!

Splash Mountain is based on the animated sequences in Walt Disney's 1946 film *Song of the South*, and the principal characters from the movie—Brer Rabbit, Brer Fox, and Brer Bear—appear in the attraction courtesy of Audio-Animatronics technology. In fact, Splash Mountain's stars and supporting cast of 103 performers number almost as many as those in Pirates of the Caribbean, which has 119 Audio-Animatronics characters.

Comparisons to Pirates of the Caribbean are particularly apt, as Splash Mountain was consciously designed to be a "How do we top this?" response to the popular, long-running pirate adventure. Splash Mountain breaks new ground on several counts. Besides its impressive number of animated characters, it also boasts one of the world's tallest and sharpest flume drops (52½ feet at a 47-degree angle). It's one of the fastest rides ever operated at Disneyland Park.

One other twist makes Splash Mountain unique in the annals of flumedom: After hurtling down Chickapin Hill, the seven-passenger log boats hit the pond below with a giant splash—and then promptly sink underwater (or seem to), with just a trace of bubbles left in their wake.

Splash Mountain's designers didn't only borrow the attraction's characters and color-saturated settings from *Song of the South*, they also included quite a bit of the film's Academy Award-winning music. In fact, the song in the attraction's finale, "Zip-a-Dee-Doo-Dah," has become something of a Disney anthem over the years. The voice of Brer Bear is performed by none other than Nick Stewart, the same actor who spoke the part in the film when it was released in 1946.

Keep in mind: The hotter the day, the longer the lines, so go early or late.

Note: You must be at least 40 inches tall and 3 years old to ride the Splash Mountain attraction. Children under age 8 must be accompanied by an adult.

DAVY CROCKETT'S EXPLORER CANOES: Of all the boats that circle the Rivers of America, these 35-foot fiberglass craft may offer the most fun, at least for the stalwart. They are real canoes, and, no, they are definitely not on tracks. Though the helmsman and the sternman may be strong enough to handle the rowing, guests' contributions are also vital when it comes to completing the 2,400-foot voyage. It's quite the workout!

Note: This attraction operates only on certain days, and it closes at dusk. Check at the landing for excursion times.

HOT TIP!
Davy Crockett's Explorer Canoes is an attraction that operates seasonally. In other words, the canoes might not be open during your visit. To learn if the canoes will be bobbing in the Rivers of America during your trip, visit *www. disneyland.com* before you leave home.

BIRNBAUM'S BEST ★★★ THE MANY ADVENTURES OF WINNIE THE POOH:
There's a cuddly critter in town, and he goes by the name of Winnie the Pooh. In this colorful attraction, everyone's favorite honey-lovin' cub treats Disneyland guests to a wild and whimsical 3½-minute tour of his home turf.

The attraction features a most unlikely form of transportation: beehives! They whisk (and bounce) guests through the Hundred Acre Wood, where the weather's most blustery. The wind is really ruffling the feathers of one of the locals. It seems Owl's treehouse has been shaken loose and just may topple to the ground—and onto the beehives below.

Similar sight gags abound, from a bubble-blowing Heffalump (hey, this is Disneyland) to a treacherous flood that threatens to sweep Tigger, Piglet, and the rest of the gang away. When the Pooh bear saves the day, it's time to celebrate—and everyone is invited to the party.

Note that, like many of the Fantasyland attractions, this Critter Country ride has a few scenes that take place in near darkness. Some youngsters may find these moments a bit unsettling. (If they can handle the likes of Mr. Toad's Wild Ride and Pinocchio's Daring Journey, they should be fine in the Hundred Acre Wood.)

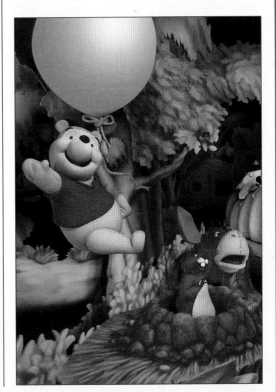

Fantasyland

Walt Disney called this a timeless land of enchantment. We couldn't agree more. The skyline, dominated by the peak of the Matterhorn, bristles with chimneys and weather vanes, turrets and towers. At the center of it all, as if deposited here by an itinerant carnival, is the regal King Arthur Carrousel.

Note: Parents of young children should be aware that many of Fantasyland's attractions have moments that take place in the dark. These include Peter Pan's Flight, Mr. Toad's Wild Ride, Alice in Wonderland, Snow White's Scary Adventures, Pinocchio's Daring Journey, and Storybook Canal Boats.

SLEEPING BEAUTY CASTLE: Rising above the treetops at the end of Main Street, U.S.A., it could be a figment of your imagination or a mirage created by Tinker Bell's pixie dust. Closer inspection proves this architectural confection is as real as the swans in the moat surrounding it. A composite of medieval European castles, primarily in the French and Bavarian styles, Sleeping Beauty Castle, the gateway to Fantasyland, is constructed of concrete, with towers that rise 77 feet above the moat. Trimmed in 22-karat gold leaf, it appears shiny even on gray days. The structure seems larger than it really is due to the use of forced perspective, down to the bricks.

From the Central Plaza, you're actually looking at the back of the castle; Walt Disney decided it was prettier that way and had the builders turn it around. The drawbridge, lowered when the park first opened in 1955, is like a real one—though it's been raised (and lowered again) only once since then. That historic event took place in 1983, at the rededication ceremony for the "new" Fantasyland.

Outside the castle, juniper is planted around the water's edge; it's one of the few green plants that the swans won't eat. One of the two graceful trees to the right of the drawbridge bears hundreds of tiny yellow flowers in spring, and the other is covered with fragile lavender flowers for several weeks in early summer.

CASTLE WALK-THROUGH: This classic Disney experience has "re-awakened" with additional scenes and enhanced special effects. The show, which features a series of dioramas, tells the story of *Sleeping Beauty*—including the magic of fairies Flora, Fauna, and Merryweather and the sinister spells of the evil Maleficent.

Guests enter the walk-through from the right, on the Fantasyland side of the castle. Note that it is rather dark inside (which may spook tots) and there are some stairs to climb. Guests who are unable to do stairs or navigate the narrow passageways of the castle may experience the walk-through "virtually" in a special room on the ground floor.

FANTASY FAIRE: Once upon a time . . . in a brand-new storybook village nestled beside Sleeping Beauty Castle, folks of all ages were invited to mix and mingle with Disney characters and enjoy two live (and lively!) stage shows. That time is now, and the guest list includes *you*. The Royal Hall and The Royal Theatre are the highlights of Fantasyland's newest neighborhood (located in the spot formerly occupied by Carnation Gardens).

THE ROYAL HALL: Behind the richly detailed facade of this regal residence, you'll find a gorgeous gothic interior fit for a princess. A rotating group of royals is always on hand to greet guests. Expect favorites such as Rapunzel, Cinderella, Ariel, Aurora, Belle, and more.

THE ROYAL THEATRE: Be sure to bring your funny bone to this theatre—the antics on stage are meant to make you chuckle. The two shows feature a madcap and original retelling of the classic and beloved tales: *Beauty and the Beast* and *Rapunzel*. The highly theatrical stories are presented by Mr. Smythe and Mr. Jones, Renaissance bards with vastly vaudevillian vigor, and a multitasking supporting cast. It's fun for the whole family. Check a park Times Guide for schedules.

PIXIE HOLLOW: Where do Disney fairies live? Right here in Pixie Hollow. Disneyland guests are invited to enter the world of Tinker Bell and her friends. As guests walk along the garden path, they feel as though they are shrinking down to fairy size as the landscape gets larger and larger. Bring a camera (or take advantage of PhotoPass) and an autograph book for youngsters. Open daily, this magical, miniature realm is extra sparkly on summer nights, when it glows with the "magic" of pixie dust. You'll find Pixie Hollow between the Castle and the entrance to Tomorrowland.

SNOW WHITE WISHING WELL & GROTTO: Tucked off Matterhorn Way, at the eastern end of the moat around Sleeping Beauty Castle, this is one of those quiet corners of the park easily overlooked by guests. If you stand by the wishing well, you might hear Adriana Caselotti, the original voice of Snow White, singing the lovely melody "I'm Wishing," written for Walt Disney's Oscar-winning 1937 film.

Any coins tossed into the well go to charity. FYI: This is a very popular spot for guests to "pop the question."

BIRNBAUM'S BEST★ PETER PAN'S FLIGHT: "Come on everybody, here we go! Off to Never Land!" This attraction is one of the park's loveliest—and consistently one of the most popular. Based on the story by Sir James M. Barrie about a boy with an immunity to maturity and an affinity for flying—by way of Disney's 1953 animated feature—the ride's effects soar to celestial heights. Pirate ships carry travelers through the clouds and into a starry sky.

Water ripples and gleams softly in the moonlight; the lava on the sides of a volcano glows with almost the intensity of the real thing. After an ephemeral few minutes, the ships seem to drift through a waterfall and back into reality, an unloading area that is all the more jarring after the magic of the trip through Never Land.

Of the approximately 350 miles of fiber optics found throughout Fantasyland, the majority is used in this ride. The twinkling London scene is an enlarged model of an authentic map of the city.

BIRNBAUM'S BEST★ MR. TOAD'S WILD RIDE: Based on the 1949 Disney film *The Adventures of Ichabod and Mr. Toad*—which was inspired by Kenneth Grahame's classic novel *The Wind in the Willows*—this simple, zany attraction is housed in an English manor bristling with ornate chimneys that really smoke. The wild, low-tech ride is experienced from the perspective of the eccentric but lovable Mr. Toad.

Of course, he is as inept a driver as you'd expect a toad to be. During the excursion, you crash through the fireplace in his library, burst through a wall full of windows, careen through the countryside, charge headlong into a warehouse full of TNT, lurch through the streets of London, then ram into a pub and veer out again. During the two-minute journey, you'll also be berated by a judge in court, nearly collide head-on with a railroad train, and be banished to a fiery inferno. (The near-crash and train blast may be too intense for tots.)

> **Did You Know?**
> There is a shadow of Sherlock Holmes (complete with pipe and cap) in the second-story window of the manor that houses Mr. Toad's Wild Ride.

ALICE IN WONDERLAND: Traveling in oversize caterpillars, visitors fall down the rabbit hole and embark upon a bizarre adventure in that strange world known as Wonderland. They come face-to-face with Tweedledum and Tweedledee, a garden filled with singing roses, the Cheshire Cat, the Queen of Hearts and her playing-card soldiers, the White Rabbit, and other characters from Lewis Carroll's beloved story *Alice in Wonderland*.

At the end of the nearly four-minute ride, a giant un-birthday cake explodes (thanks to a dynamite "candle"), providing a suitable finish to this sweet interlude. It's understandably popular with the under-age-7 set.

MAD TEA PARTY: The sequence in Walt Disney's 1951 release *Alice in Wonderland* in which the Mad Hatter hosts a tea party for his "un-birthday" is the theme for this attraction—a group of colorful oversize tea-cups whirling wildly on a spinning tea table. Festive Japanese lanterns hang overhead. One of the park's original attractions, this ride lasts only 1½ minutes, so if the line is long, come back later.

Note: The teacups may look mild, but it's a good idea to let a reasonable interval pass after eating before you take one for a spin.

BIRNBAUM'S
★BEST **MATTERHORN BOBSLEDS:** Though it's 100 times smaller than the actual peak, Disney's version of the Matterhorn is still a credible reproduction. The use of forced perspective makes the snowy summit look much loftier than the approximately 147 feet it does reach. Even the trees and shrubs help create the illusion. Those at the timberline are far smaller than the ones at the bottom.

The ride itself, like the Space Mountain and Big Thunder Mountain Railroad attractions, has to be counted among the most thrilling at Disneyland. At the time the Matterhorn Bobsleds were dedicated, in 1959, they were considered an engineering novelty because their

dispatch system allowed more than one car to be in action at once. The ride was also the world's first tubular steel roller coaster. This classic is also considered to be Disney's first thrill ride. Refurbished in 2012, the Matterhorn has a new fleet of ride vehicles, and enhanced snowcaps, lighting, and special effects.

The adventure begins with a long climb into the frosty innards of the mountain, then makes a speeding, twisting, turning descent through a cloud of fog and past giant icicles and ice crystals. The wind howls as you hurtle toward a brief but inevitable encounter with the Abominable Snowman. The speed of the downhill flight away from the creature seems greater than it really is because much of the journey takes place inside tunnels. Splash-down is in an alpine lake.

Notes: Pregnant women, children under 3, and guests who suffer from weak backs, heart conditions, motion sickness, or other physical limitations should not take the ride. Guests must be at least 40 inches tall. At press time there were plans for a "single riders line." Check *www.disneyland.com* for updates.

PHOTO BY JILL SAFRO

STORYBOOK LAND CANAL BOATS: This 7-minute cruise through Monstro the Whale and past miniature scenes from classic Disney animated films is not one of Disneyland's major attractions, yet few who take the trip deny that the journey is one of the park's sweetest. No detail was spared, from the homes of the Three Little Pigs to the Old English village of Alice in Wonderland (where the White Rabbit boasts his very own mailbox) to the London park that Peter Pan and Tinker Bell flew over with Wendy, John, and Michael Darling on their way to Never Land.

Other storybook locales include the marketplace where Aladdin met Princess Jasmine, the Seven Dwarfs' home and jewel mine, and Cinderella's castle. At the end of the cruise, the boat drifts past Geppetto's village, Prince Eric and Ariel's castle, and King Triton's castle.

BIRNBAUM'S ★BEST★ **IT'S A SMALL WORLD:** The background music for this attraction is cheerful and singsong, sometimes maddeningly so. It does grab your attention, starting with the cheery facade, embellished with stylized representations of the Eiffel Tower, the Leaning Tower of Pisa, Big Ben, the Taj Mahal, and other landmarks. The 30-foot-tall clock with the loud ticktock and the syncopated swing is frosting on the architectural cake. The whirring of gears that marks every quarter hour alone warrants a trip to the attraction's plaza.

Boats carry guests into a land filled with more than 300 Audio-Animatronics dolls representing children (and recently added Disney characters) from 100 regions of the world. It's a pageant for the eyes, even if the ears grow weary. (If you find yourself humming "It's a Small World" for the next several hours, you can blame Richard M. and Robert B. Sherman, the Academy Award-winning composers of the music for *Mary Poppins*, among many other Disney scores.)

Topiary figures in the shapes of a giraffe, elephant, rhinoceros, lion, horse, and other friendly beasts bid guests farewell at ride's end.

Note that It's a Small World is transformed inside and out between Thanksgiving and New Year's to become as close to a winter wonderland as you're likely to find in Southern California. The dolls even sing "Jingle Bells" along with "It's a Small World."

CASEY JR. CIRCUS TRAIN: One of the key sequences in the movie *Dumbo*, in which an engine named Casey Jr. pulls a circus train up a steep hill, became the inspiration for this 3½-minute train ride that circles Storybook Land. The Storybook Land Canal Boats are better for viewing the landscaping and miniature details there, but it's worth a ride inside one of the wild-animal cage cars. Each train has two of them—plus a real caboose. Listen as the engine chugs, "I think I can" and then, "I thought I could" as it negotiates the hill.

DUMBO THE FLYING ELEPHANT: As beloved a symbol of Fantasyland as Sleeping Beauty Castle, this ride reminds all who see it of the baby elephant immortalized in the 1941 Disney film. Dumbo discovers that his inordinately large ears, which have been such a source of embarrassment, actually enable him to fly.

A mechanical marvel, Dumbo the Flying Elephant is full of filigreed metalwork, with cogs, gears, and pulleys galore. Brass pipes spew water from the base, and music is supplied by a vintage band organ housed in a small, ornate structure nearby. That figure atop the ride is Timothy Mouse, who became Dumbo's manager after the little elephant was hired to be a star by the same circus folk who once teased him. The topiary figures pay tribute to the little guy with the floppy ears.

SNOW WHITE'S SCARY ADVENTURES:
Ornamental stone ravens perch on carved stone skulls atop a stone tower, and hearts pierced through with swords lie at the base of the twisted pillars that support this brooding building. All this might lead you to expect an attraction as frightfully elaborate as the Haunted Mansion. It isn't. That said, the two-minute ride includes several fairly jarring scenes. In one, the Queen changes into a scary old hag before your eyes; in another, this wicked witch has the nerve to tempt you with a poisoned apple.

After passing a brief and joyful scene in the Seven Dwarfs' cottage, the cars travel through a creepy dungeon, visit a workshop where the Queen labors over her bubbling cauldron, and then venture into the Frightening Forest, where moss-draped trees point talon-like branches at passersby. The visit to the jewel

PHOTO BY KEITH GROSHANS

mines, where the Seven Dwarfs work, is more beautiful than scary because of the emeralds, rubies, and sapphires glowing in the darkness.

It all ends in true storybook fashion: As the evil Queen attempts to roll a stone down the side of a mountain to crush the dwarfs below, she gets struck by lightning (via a strobe effect) and tumbles over the edge of a cliff, leaving Snow White, the handsome prince, and their seven sidekicks to live happily ever after, as depicted in the mural near the exit. The music is taken from rare recordings used to create the film's original soundtrack.

Note: This attraction can be too intense for many small children. Snow White's adventures really *are* scary!

PINOCCHIO'S DARING JOURNEY:
Based on Disney's 1940 animated feature, this is a three-minute morality play of sorts, with Jiminy Cricket serving as host and guide. Pinocchio, who is the creation of the toymaker Geppetto, pays a visit to Pleasure Island and then discovers the right way to live.

As the ride vehicles move from the cheerful land of popcorn and Ferris wheels to the seamy world of Tobacco Road, Pleasure Island hues are replaced by drab shades of brown and gray. Here, little boys are turned into donkeys and sold to work in the salt mines.

Pinocchio escapes that fate, nearly becomes supper for Monstro the Whale, and winds up back home in the care of Geppetto—another happily-ever-after ending. The final scene, in which the Blue Fairy turns into a cloud of sparkles and then disappears, leaving a smattering of pixie dust on the floor, is partially accomplished via fiber optics.

Note: This attraction may be a bit frightening to some toddlers (not to mention those of us who may be spooked by the concept of turning into a donkey).

KING ARTHUR CARROUSEL:
Guests come upon this graceful park landmark as they stroll toward the Sleeping Beauty Castle passageway into Fantasyland. One of the few attractions in the park that is an original rather than a Disney adaptation, the carrousel contains 68 horses—all movable, as Walt Disney wished. Carved in Germany over a century ago, no two alike, they are as pampered as the live Belgian horses on Main Street. The ornamentation on them is gold, silver, and copper leaf. The nine hand-painted panels on top of the carrousel's main face tell the story of Sleeping Beauty.

Mickey's Toontown

Disneyland lore tells us that when Mickey Mouse burst onto the movie scene in 1928 in *Steamboat Willie*, the first synchronized-sound cartoon, his success was so great that his busy schedule demanded he practically live at the Walt Disney Studios. Thirty cartoons later, in the early 1930s, he was one tired mouse, so he moved into a quiet residence in a "toon only" community south of Hollywood. Over the years, many toon stars gravitated to Mickey's Toontown, as it quickly became known. Minnie Mouse, Pluto, Goofy, Roger Rabbit, Chip, Dale, and Gadget all live here, and Donald Duck docks his boat, the *Miss Daisy*, on Toon Lake.

HOT TIP!

There are no full-service restaurants in Toontown, just a few fast-food places with window service, and limited outdoor seating. So don't plan on having a big meal here.

One afternoon in the early 1950s, while Mickey and his close friend Walt Disney were relaxing on Mickey's front porch, Walt revealed his idea for a theme park that would appeal to "youngsters of all ages." Mickey suggested that he build it next to the secret entrance to Toontown, and the rest is history. Disneyland opened to the public in 1955, but little did anyone realize when they were drifting through It's a Small World that they were right next door to Mickey's Toontown.

In 1990, Mickey and his friends decided to open up their neighborhood and their homes to non-toons, and, in preparation, all of Toontown received a new coat of ink and paint. The grand opening took place in January 1993, marking the first new "land" to debut at Disneyland since Critter (originally Bear) Country opened in 1972.

Legend aside, the development of Toontown was a real challenge: to create a three-dimensional cartoon environment without a single straight line. Yet, as topsy-turvy as it is, Mickey's Toontown is a complete community, with a downtown area, including a commercial center and an industrial zone, plus a suburban neighborhood. The best part is that everything is meant to be touched, pushed, and jumped on. Kids do just that, while adults relish the attention to detail and the assortment of gags. Much of what's here is interactive, from the mousehole covers to the public mailboxes.

This booming toontropolis is home to ten attractions, two shops, and three fast-food eateries. The attractions are described in the neighborhood sections that follow; the shops, in the Shopping section later in this chapter; and the quick-service eateries, in the *Good Meals, Great Times* chapter of this book.

Guests enter this colorful land by walking under the Toontown train depot. The attractions are listed as they are encountered when strolling counterclockwise.

Downtown Toontown

In Toontown's "business" zone, an animated taxi teeters off the second-floor balcony of the Cab Co. A runaway safe has crashed into the sidewalk, and crates of rib-ticklers, ripsnorters, slapsticks, and wisecracks wait for passersby to lift the lids. At the Fireworks Factory, a plunger sets off quite a response when pressed; it's a good thing the Toontown Fire Department is located right next door.

Lift the receiver of the police phone outside the Power House (home to all sorts of electrifying gizmos—open the door at your own risk), and you might hear a voice over the toon police car radio, announcing, "Someone put mail in the box, and the box doesn't like it. Please respond post haste." Or step on the mouse-hole cover near the post office, and you might hear, "How's the weather up there?" or "Is it time to come out now?"

You never know what to expect once inside Toontown—but it's all bound to be "goofy."

ROGER RABBIT'S CAR TOON SPIN: FP
This chaotic, rollicking ride combines the technology of the Mad Tea Party teacups (cars here spin a full 360 degrees) and the tracks of Fantasyland attractions, such as Mr. Toad's Wild Ride. Benny the Cab and Roger Rabbit join the dizzying chase, which

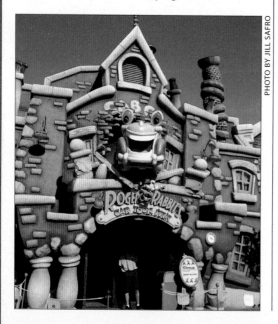

PHOTO BY JILL SAFRO

takes guests through the back alleys of the toon underworld made famous in the film *Who Framed Roger Rabbit*. The mission of each car is to save Jessica Rabbit from the evil weasels while avoiding the dreaded Dip.

ROGER'S FOUNTAIN: In this funny fountain, a statue of Roger Rabbit is suspended in midair, afloat on a column of water erupting from a broken fire hydrant that he has seemingly crashed into. He's still holding the steering wheel from the cab he was driving. Surrounding the hydrant, four floating cab tires serve as inner tubes for fish spouting arcs of water into the air.

POST OFFICE: Each kooky mailbox actually speaks in the voice of the character whose mail it receives—Mickey Mouse, Minnie Mouse, Roger Rabbit, Jessica Rabbit, Donald Duck, and Goofy. It can be quite a cacophony.

Outside, the letter box pipes in with chucklesome comments like, "Don't just stand there—mail something!"

Toon Square

Located between the downtown area and the residential section of Toontown, this district is home to local businesses and institutions, including the Toontown Skool, the Department of Ink & Paint, and the 3rd Little Piggy Bank. Toontown's three eateries—Clarabelle's Frozen Yogurt, Pluto's Dog House, and Daisy's Diner—stand side by side on the square.

TOWN HALL: Toon residents emerge from this municipal building and proceed to the bandstand out front to greet guests, entertain with their antics, and provide more relaxing photo opportunities than are often available elsewhere in Disneyland.

When a character is about to arrive, the "Clockenspiel" above City Hall comes to life: Mallets ring bells, toon hands pull whistles, and figures of Roger Rabbit and Mickey Mouse pop out of cannons, blowing horns that, in turn, produce bouquets of flowers.

GOOFY'S GAS: From the looks of it, any traveler would think twice about refueling at this station. On the other hand, it does house Toontown's public restrooms and telephones, and that's an important location to know (though we don't recommend making any important business calls here).

Pedestrians can now refuel here, too. A fruit stand, called Toontown Fruit Market (open seasonally), offers fruit and other snacks. It's also a convenient locale to purchase souvenirs. The funny water fountain beside the station dispenses refreshing H_2O.

Mickey's Neighborhood

The homes in this district sit at the base of the 40-foot-tall Toon Hills, which have their own version of the famous Hollywood sign. The attractions are described as a guest would pass them while walking counterclockwise from Mickey's Fountain.

MICKEY'S FOUNTAIN: A statue of the world's most famous mouse stands at the center of a pool surrounded by toon-style musical instruments, creating a whimsical centerpiece for the Toontown residential area.

MINNIE'S HOUSE: It's hard to miss Minnie's House. This lavender-and-pink creation has a sweetheart theme for the sweetheart inside. Here guests can peek at Minnie's living room with its chintz sofa and sophisticated magazines (*Cosmousepolitan* and *Mademouselle*) on the coffee table.

There are messages from Goofy and Mickey on the answering machine in the hallway. Guests are invited to create new fashions for Minnie on the computer in her dressing room.

In Minnie's kitchen, a cake in the oven rises when a knob is turned, pots and pans clank out a melody when the stove is switched on, and the dishwasher churns when a button is pushed. The Cheesemore refrigerator is stocked with an assortment of dairy products, including Golly Cheeze Whiz, and the shopping list left on the outside of the fridge hints at this mouse's cheeses of choice. Be sure to check out the cookies on her kitchen table (and be prepared for a little trick, courtesy of Ms. Mouse).

As you leave Minnie's House, you'll pass the wishing well in her yard. Don't think you're hearing things: It's been known to share a few parting thoughts.

MICKEY'S HOUSE: A path leads from Minnie's backyard to the front door of Mickey's House. The welcoming yellow dwelling with a tile roof, huge green door, and green shutters is home to the toon who started it all. Not only is Mickey's face on the mailbox out front, but his welcome mat is in the instantly recognizable shape of three circles—his head and ears.

HOT TIP!
Toontown closes one hour before the pyrotechnics on nights when the park is presenting a fireworks show.

In the living room stands a player piano and a curio cabinet filled with all manner of memorabilia, including Mickey's baby shoes and a picture of him with his friend Walt Disney, as well as some of Pluto's treasures—a huge bone and a half-eaten shoe. In the laundry room, the washing machine chugs merrily away, and laundry supplies, such as Comics Cleanser and Mouse 'n' Glo, are at the ready.

From here, make your way through the greenhouse and into Mickey's backyard, where you'll see Pluto's doghouse and a garden with mysteriously disappearing carrots. If you want to meet the Mouse, be sure to visit the barn out back.

FP = Fastpass attraction (see page 58)

MICKEY'S MOVIE BARN: Ever industrious, Mickey has transformed the old barn in back of his house into a workplace, and guests are welcome to visit him here. The first stop is the Prop Department, where costumes and props from some of his famous cartoons are stored.

In the Screening Room, a bumbling Goofy projects movie clips from a few "remakes" currently in progress, among them *Steamboat Willie* and *The Sorcerer's Apprentice*. Mickey is hard at work on a soundstage, but happy to take a break. Guests enter in small groups for a photo and autograph session with the "famouse" star.

Note: You can't get to Mickey's Movie Barn without going through his house. This attraction is a must for die-hard fans of the Mouse.

CHIP 'N' DALE TREEHOUSE: Just past Mickey's House stands the home of that jolly chipmunk duo, Chip and Dale. Styled to look like a redwood tree, this high-rise accommodates guests of all ages—but it's best enjoyed by small children. A spiral staircase leads to the lofty perch, whose windows provide a fine view of Toontown.

GADGET'S GO COASTER: Gadget is the brilliant inventor from the TV cartoon *Chip 'n' Dale's Rescue Rangers*. So it's only fitting that some of her handiwork is within view of their treehouse. Gadget, the ultimate recycler, has created this coaster from an assortment of gizmos that once served other purposes.

Giant toy blocks are now support beams for the tracks; hollowed-out acorns have become the cars of the train; and bridges have been created from giant combs, pencils, paper clips, and such. The thick steel tracks give the impression of a tame ride, but there are a few thrills, right up to the final turn into the station. This experience is exciting but brief (one minute), so if the line is long, save it for later.

Note: Kids must be at least 3 years old and 35 inches tall to ride Gadget's Go Coaster. Those under age 7 must be accompanied by an adult. Pregnant women should skip the trip. It may be a small coaster, but the 51-second ride is wilder than one might expect.

DONALD'S BOAT: Donald Duck's houseboat, named for his fair-feathered friend (Daisy) is docked in Toon Lake, adjacent to Gadget's Go Coaster. Parents can relax in a shaded seating area near a waterfall while their children explore the boat, which looks a whole lot like its owner.

See if you can recognize Donald's eyes in the large portholes of the pilothouse, his jaunty blue sailor's cap in the roof of the cabin, and his face in the shape of the hull. Would-be sailors can climb the small rope ladder or the spiral staircase up to the pilothouse to steer the wheel that turns the compass or to toot the boat's whistle.

GOOFY'S PLAYHOUSE: Located beside the Miss Daisy, this playground is just for kids. The garden outside Goofy's house boasts an odd assortment of delights: giant stalks bearing popcorn guarded by a Goofy-style scarecrow, spinning flowers, a leaky garden hose, and a patch with watermelons and pumpkins. Inside, young visitors can peek into Goofy's cupboards, climb on his furniture, and tickle the keys of the piano (doing so yields "goofy" sound effects rather than musical notes). Across the street is Goofy's Gas. It's not a real filling station, but is a great place to take little ones for a pit stop (it's a restroom).

TOON PARK: This tiny soft-surface enclave next to Goofy's Playhouse supplies a safe play area for toddlers. Adjacent seating gives parents and other guests an inviting place to rest and enjoy the youngsters' antics.

Tomorrowland

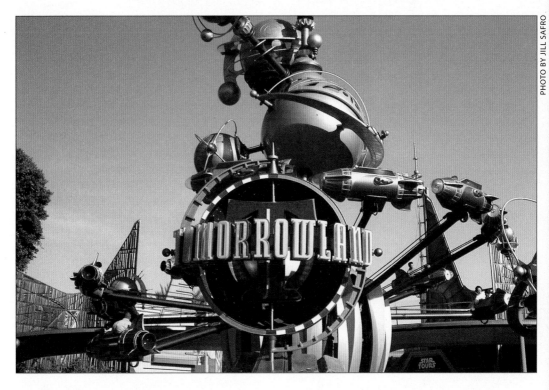

PHOTO BY JILL SAFRO

When Walt Disney was alive, the future seemed simple: We would all dress in Mylar and travel in flying saucers. The Tomorrowland he created in the fifties was set in the distant year of 1987, part Buck Rogers and part World's Fair. The latest incarnation of Tomorrowland, rededicated in May 1998, is based on a classic vision of the future, one that looks at it from the perspective of the past. The result is an innocent and hopeful place— imagine, for instance, a planet that renews itself!—more in keeping with the rest of Disneyland than with the sterile, less positive future world often depicted in contemporary films.

Visit Tomorrowland today, and you enter a visually engaging terrain, where the palette of colors is not otherworldly, but still forward-thinking. Futuristic boulders and dreamlike architecture coexist with apple, orange, lemon, and pomegranate trees that line pathways created from gray, mauve, and burgundy bricks. This landscape fires up the intellect as much as the imagination.

Galileo Galilei, Leonardo da Vinci, Jules Verne, H.G. Wells, and certainly Walt Disney would have felt at home here. Aldous Huxley probably wouldn't have.

Five of Tomorrowland's newer attractions are also at Walt Disney World in Florida: Star Tours—The Adventures Continue, *Captain EO*, Innoventions, Astro Orbitor, and Buzz Lightyear Astro Blasters (known in Florida as Buzz Lightyear's Space Ranger Spin). Other well-loved Tomorrowland attractions remain, among them Space Mountain and Autopia.

A replica of the Moonliner, a Tomorrowland icon from 1955 to 1966, sits on a pedestal near the site of its predecessor. Sleek monorail trains still glide to and from the Downtown Disney district, while traditional Disneyland Railroad trains continue to chug their way into the Tomorrowland station, a reminder that the past is indeed prologue.

The following attractions are described as you encounter them when proceeding counterclockwise from the Main Street entrance to Tomorrowland.

ASTRO ORBITOR: Towering above the entrance to Tomorrowland, this big whirligig with spinning orbs and speeding starships is a fitting symbol for Tomorrowland. Astro Orbitor, modeled on a drawing made by Leonardo da Vinci almost five centuries ago, is the successor to Rocket Jets, which gave Disneyland guests a lift for 30 years. Each ride vehicle accommodates two passengers (or two adults and one small child), who can maneuver it up and down while spinning clockwise for 1½ minutes, reveling in sweeping views of Tomorrowland, Central Plaza, and Sleeping Beauty Castle.

Note: The minimum age to ride is one year. Young children have to be in the company of an adult.

BIRNBAUM'S
★BEST★ **BUZZ LIGHTYEAR ASTRO BLASTERS:** The evil Emperor Zurg is up to no good—and it's up to that Space Ranger extraordinaire Buzz Lightyear and his Junior Space Rangers (that means you) to save the day.

So goes the story line of Tomorrowland's video game-inspired spin through toyland. The adventure is experienced from a toy's point of view. Guests begin their 4½-minute tour of duty as Space Rangers at Star Command Action Center. This is where Buzz gives his team a briefing on the mission that lies ahead. Then it's off to the Launch Bay to board the ride vehicles. The ships feature dual laser cannons, glowing lights, and a piloting joystick.

In addition to Buzz and the evil Emperor, you may recognize some other toy faces swirling about—the little green, multi-eyed alien squeaky toys, best known for their awe of "the claw." The squeakies have been enlisted to help in the fight against Zurg.

HOT TIP!
To maximize your scoring potential at the Buzz Lightyear attraction, aim for targets that are lit up, moving, or far away. They yield the most points.

Once Junior Space Rangers blast off, they find themselves surrounded by Zurg's robots, who are mercilessly ripping batteries from toys. As Rangers fire at targets, beams of light fill the air. For every target hit, you will be rewarded with sight gags, sound effects, and points. The points, which are tallied automatically, are accumulated throughout the journey. Although the vehicles follow a rigid "flight" path (they're on a track), the joystick allows riders to maneuver the ships, arcing from side to side or spinning in circles while taking aim at their surroundings.

When the star cruiser arrives at Zurg's spaceship, it's showdown time. Will good prevail over evil? Or has time run out for the toy universe? And will you score enough points to be a Galactic Hero? (Most people improve their scores with a little practice.)

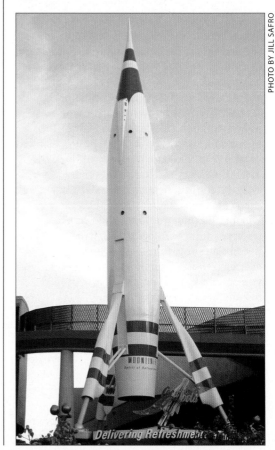

PHOTO BY JILL SAFRO

Delivering Refreshment

BIRNBAUM'S BEST **STAR TOURS—THE ADVENTURES CONTINUE:** FP
Inspired by George Lucas's blockbuster series of *Star Wars* films, this is one of the most thrilling attractions at Disneyland. It offers guests the opportunity to ride on droid-piloted StarSpeeders, the exact same type of flight simulator used by military and commercial airlines to train pilots—and explore the galaxy in a new 3-D adventure. The action here takes place in the time period between the two sets of *Star Wars* trilogies. The best part? There are dozens of different adventures to experience here—multiple visits yield multiple surprises.

This is a turbulent trip—seat belts are definitely required. Passengers must be free of back problems, heart conditions, motion sickness, and other physical limitations to ride. Guests under 40 inches tall and kids younger than 3 may not ride. Pregnant women must skip this one.

STARCADE: There are hundreds of games in this "pay as you play" arcade—incorporating motorcycles, race cars, skateboards, snowboards, bicycles, snow skis, horses, spacecraft, and tanks. Most represent whatever happens to be hottest at the moment. Costs range from 25 cents to $4 per game. There are $1, $5, and $10 change machines, as well as a cashier, on the premises.

CAPTAIN EO: This futuristic musical is actually a blast from the past—a classic spectacular known as *Captain EO*, starring Michael Jackson. Back by popular demand, this crowd-pleasing film originally ran here from 1986 through 1997.

Produced by George Lucas and directed by legendary Hollywood helmsman Francis Ford Coppola, *EO* is a thrilling, musical, space-fantasy adventure. Better yet, it's in 3-D! It's fun for all ages, but some youngsters may be frightened when EO and his crew encounter a dark planet and its villainous Supreme Leader. Of course, good prevails when the gang magically—and musically—transforms the darkness into a happy and colorful world.

In addition to the King of Pop, the 17-minute film features a cast of mythical space critters such as Hooter (a little, green, elephant-like fellow who sneezes musical notes), Fuzzball (an orange-haired monkey with butterfly wings), the golden-haired, two-headed Geex, and many more.

INNOVENTIONS: As guests scale the winding ramp that leads to this attraction's entrance, they're never quite sure what to expect—but the gadgets, gizmos, and futuristic wizardry they witness inside never cease to intrigue. Housed in the Carousel Theater (the former home of the Carousel of Progress), this is Tomorrowland's largest attraction. In it, guests see how today's emerging technologies can improve their lives. They're free to explore the world of Innoventions at their own pace, stopping to watch live demonstrations, visit the Innoventions Dream Home, and enjoy a "hands-on" experience with new products (none of them for sale) at their leisure. Exhibits may be swapped out at any time.

BIRNBAUM'S BEST **SPACE MOUNTAIN:** FP When Space Mountain first opened in 1977, it quickly rocketed to the top of just about everyone's list of favorite attractions. Well, believe it or not, the Mountain's popularity soared to new heights when the attraction was "relaunched" in the summer of 2005.

While the classic facade and essence of Space Mountain remain intact, the experience is decidedly 21st century. Brave voyagers board new vehicles in a realistic launch port. After shooting through a disorienting tunnel, riders will have a close encounter with a meteorite. After that, it's all about screeching through the darkness, past spinning stars and whirling galaxies. Add to that an edgy soundtrack (which is synchronized to each car), and you've got one out-of-this-world attraction.

If your courage fails you, just ask an attendant to direct you to the nearest escape route (aka "the chicken exit").

Note: Pregnant women and guests who have weak backs, heart conditions, motion sickness, or other physical limitations must sit this one

DISNEYLAND PARK

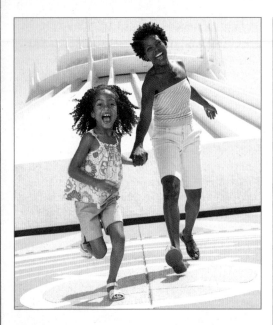

out. Children younger than 8 years old must be accompanied by an adult (kids under 3 are not permitted to ride). Guests must be at least 40 inches tall to experience Space Mountain.

AUTOPIA: FP The only attraction from the original Tomorrowland, Autopia was dubbed "The Freeway of the Future" back in 1955. Kids have always loved guiding the small sports cars around the twisting roadways (for them, a top speed of seven miles per hour is thrilling). Now pint-size motorists and their parents encounter a souped-up version of the original ride.

The Tomorrowland and Fantasyland roadways now comprise a single attraction (yes, there were two Autopias; the one in Fantasyland opened in 1959 to accommodate

spillover crowds). Guests now enter through a single boarding area in Tomorrowland and watch an entertaining pre-show on a large video screen that presents the world from a car's point of view. Drivers (and one passenger per vehicle) travel in restyled cars through 21st-century terrain, experiencing a series of happy roadside surprises along the way. At the ride's end, they may receive a commemorative driver's license as a memento. A shop proffers auto-related toys and assorted souvenirs. This attraction is quite popular with those who've not yet reached "driver's ed" age.

Note: Kids must be at least 52 inches tall and at least 7 years old to drive alone. Pregnant women and guests with back or neck problems should not ride.

DISNEYLAND MONORAIL: Who doesn't love the monorail? The first daily operating monorail in the Western Hemisphere was a novelty when it was introduced at Disneyland in 1959. Today, it's still a thrill to watch them glide through the park. The sleek, Mark VII trains were designed to evoke images of their 1959 predecessors. Straddling a concrete beamway, the monorail has rubber tires—which enable it to glide quietly—as well as braking wheels atop the beam and guiding and stabilizing wheels on either side.

The 2½-mile-long "highway in the sky" is a distinctive and integral part of Tomorrowland. The electrically-powered ride takes guests around the periphery of Tomorrowland, over to Downtown Disney and its diverting activities, and then back to Tomorrowland.

For a special experience, inform the cast member on the boarding ramp that you'd like

PHOTO BY MIKE CARROLL

BIRNBAUM'S ★BEST **FINDING NEMO SUBMARINE VOYAGE:** Uh-oh. It seems that curious little clownfish has wandered off again. And this time he's done so in Tomorrowland's submarine lagoon. The good news is the subs that used to take guests to the North Pole now provide the perfect means for monitoring the fin-challenged fish and his high-spirited underwater hijinks.

The submarine adventure begins as a quiet expedition to observe an undersea volcano. But faster than you can say, "all drains lead to the ocean," our frisky friends from *Finding Nemo* start floating and fluttering in front of a personal porthole. The whole gang's here, including Nemo's overprotective dad, Marlin, the faithful-if-forgetful royal blue tang, Dory, that totally awesome turtle dude, Crush, and more. They're on a quest to catch up with their buddy Nemo, and you're invited along for the slightly frenetic, completely kinetic undersea search. Oh, and remember that volcano you were going to observe? It erupts.

Will you survive the sub-shaking volcanic quaking and find Nemo? Yep. They don't call this "the happiest place on earth" for nothing.

This whimsical experience is appropriate for guests of all ages, provided that the guests are claustrophobia-free. Some moments may be too intense for some tots.

to sit up front in the pilot's cabin. It can usually accommodate up to five passengers. If all the seats are taken, you can always wait for the next monorail and try your luck again.

Note that by boarding the monorail in Tomorrowland, you are actually leaving Disneyland Park. If you get off at the Downtown Disney station, be sure to get your hand stamped. You'll need to show it and a valid ticket to reboard the monorail or pass through the park's turnstiles. Know that walking is also an option—as Disneyland is about a 5-minute stroll from the station.

The monorail is considered more of an attraction than a mode of transportation. It takes about the same amount of time (maybe less) to walk from the Downtown Disney station to the Disneyland Park.

HOT TIP!

A trip on the monorail yields panoramic views of the Disney California Adventure theme park and its neighbor, the Grand Californian resort. However, it does not stop at either place.

Tomorrowland Icons

MOONLINER: Beside Redd Rockett's Pizza Port, this two-thirds-scale, 53-foot-high replica of an early Tomorrowland icon stands 50 feet from the site of the original rocket. It is set on a 12-foot pedestal that doubles as a refreshment stand, called The Spirit of Refreshment. Water vapor wafts from its nozzles, but the only things "launched" here are bottled beverages (and then only by request). See page 78 for a photo of the Moonliner.

THE OBSERVATRON: This quirky icon for Tomorrowland towers above the area, constantly beaming electronic messages into space. Every 15 minutes, it comes to life in an orchestrated medley of music and motion.

Shopping

Until you get to know Disneyland, you might not expect that anyone would visit just to go shopping. But among Southern Californians, it's a top draw for the quality merchandise and appealing gift items. Mickey Mouse paraphernalia, such as key chains, mugs, T-shirts, hats, and other such souvenirs, is found here in abundance, of course, but there are some surprises, such as character-inspired costumes for kids, wireless phone accessories and items for the office, plus upscale items, such as art collectibles, jewelry, and products for the home.

Main Street, U.S.A.

CANDY PALACE: An old-fashioned pageant in pink and white, this shop is alluring at any time of day, but never more than when the candy-makers are at work in the glass-walled kitchen confecting candy canes, chocolate-covered strawberries, caramel apples, toffee, fudge, and other temptations for anyone with a sweet tooth. The products made on the premises are available for purchase, along with a bounty of chocolates, licorice, and taffy.

CHINA CLOSET: If you're in the market for figurines, picture frames, or snow globes, this is the place to go.

CRYSTAL ARTS: Glasses and pitchers, trays, and other mementos can be engraved (for free) and monogrammed while you wait, or you can purchase them unornamented. The shop also sells a selection of glass miniatures, bells, and paperweights.

DISNEY CLOTHIERS, LTD.: Disney character merchandise has always been popular, but if you want something a little more stylish, this is where to find it. The spot caters to fashion-conscious shoppers with a love for Disney gear. Almost every item in the selection of men's, women's, and children's clothing and accessories sold here incorporates Disney characters in some way.

DISNEY SHOWCASE: Featuring the latest seasonal merchandise (Disney style), this shop also offers park logo items, apparel, pins, and more. Personalization is offered (for a fee).

DISNEYANA: Collectors and the simply curious alike will discover rare and unusual Disney merchandise here, such as limited-edition art and hand-painted cels inspired by Disney animated classics. Popular pieces include crystal, bronze, and pewter figurines, and striking porcelain sculptures from the Walt Disney Classics Collection. This shop recently moved from its longtime location to a new home in The Bank of Main Street building.

   Note: Disney Imagineers and artists often drop by the shop to sign reproduction artwork, sculptures, or recently published books.

EMPORIUM: Much like an old-time variety store, this large and bustling shop offers an incredible assortment of wares, and it is home to the popular Disneyland logo merchandise. Decorative figurines, mugs, home decor, clothing, plush toys, character hats, jewelry and a variety of souvenirs make up the bulk of the stock.

PHOTO BY JILL SAFRO

FORTUOSITY SHOP: Merchandise in all shapes and sizes, including Mickey Mouse watches and alarm clocks, along with other character-laden novelty clocks, beckons from this unique emporium.

MAD HATTER: This hat shop stocks Mickey Mouse ears in black and various colors and designs. You can even get your name stitched on the back.

MAIN STREET MAGIC SHOP: Small but well stocked with gags and tricks—and books about how to pull them off—this shop has the wherewithal to inspire budding illusionists. In the market for an invisible pooch? A magic wand? An ice cube with a bug in it? This place has it all.

MAIN STREET PHOTO SUPPLY CO.: If a roving Disneyland photographer snaps your mug, this is the place to pick up the print. You can also find memory cards, batteries, film, frames, and photo albums.

MARKET HOUSE: This Disney version of an old-fashioned general store—which was recently refurbished and expanded—is actually a cleverly themed Starbucks coffee shop. Stop here for fresh-brewed coffee and specialty drinks, plus cookies, cake pops, savory snacks, and much more.

NEW CENTURY JEWELRY: Among the delicate offerings here are 14-karat-gold charms of Tinker Bell, Donald Duck, and Minnie Mouse. The marcasite character jewelry is subtle and somewhat sophisticated.

NEWSSTAND: While no actual news is offered here (No news is good news, right?), this stand stocks postcards and souvenir items. The Newsstand offers personalization and embroidery on hats, shirts, and other merchandise (for a small fee).

PENNY ARCADE: Adjacent to the Gibson Girl Ice Cream Parlor is a virtual Coney Island of food and fun. Fresh-made treats fill ornate shelves, and scrumptious saltwater taffy is available in an array of flavors. To add to the carnival atmosphere, old-fashioned arcade games that still cost a penny to play and a Welte Orchestrion line the walls.

SILHOUETTE STUDIO: Working at the rate of about 60 seconds per portrait, Disneyland's silhouette artists truly are a wonder to behold. Individual and group portraits are available.

20TH CENTURY MUSIC COMPANY: This little place carries a rather extensive selection of classic Disney music and DVDs. There is a small selection of books, too.

New Orleans Square

CRISTAL D'ORLEANS: Glasses and chandeliers, decanters and ashtrays, pitchers and paperweights are typical treasures here. All engraving, and some monogramming, is done for free.

LE BAT EN ROUGE: Do you need to cross a few Disney villain related items off your shopping list? You've come to the right place. Also lining the shelves are various tchotchkes and thingamabobs with a Tim Burton's *The Nightmare Before Christmas* theme.

LA MASCARADE D'ORLEANS: Informally known as "pin central," this little shop is filled with collector pins, lanyard starter sets, and pin-trading accessories. Cast members are happy to trade Disney pins! The shop also stocks an assortment of collectible Vinylmation figures.

MLLE. ANTOINETTE'S PARFUMERIE: This fragrant boutique carries a variety of classic and chic fragrances for men and women. The parfumerie "blends the essence of French-style elegance with American-style spontaneity." It's located in the heart of New Orleans Square.

PIECES OF EIGHT: Wares with a pirate theme are purveyed at this shop beside the Pirates of the Caribbean exit. There are pirate rings, ships' lanterns, stocking caps, and fake knives and skulls in plastic and rubber. You will also discover T-shirts, key chains, glasses, and other souvenir items imprinted with the Pirates of the Caribbean logo. In the market for a pirate sword? Look no further. And, for the right price, you may be able to fill a bag with colorful pirate booty. Arrrrrr!

PORT ROYAL CURIOS AND CURIOSITIES: Ready to give your treasured Mickey T-shirt a day off? Stop at this boutique to augment your character-oriented closet. Expect to find a large assortment of merchandise with a *Nightmare Before Christmas* theme, too (cups, coasters, bags, dolls, dresses, pajamas, shirts, and more).

PORTRAIT ARTISTS: Sit for a portrait—done in pastel or watercolor—amidst the quaint charm of a New Orleans *rue* (street). Individual and group portraits are offered.

ROYAL STREET SWEETS: Satisfy your sweet tooth (or teeth) at this stand that specializes in sugary treats.

Frontierland

PIONEER MERCANTILE: Inspired by the paraphernalia of the pioneer period in American history, this shop is home to some of *Toy Story*'s ever-popular characters and sidekicks. Expect to find plush toys, figurines, hats, shirts, books, and more. There is a "penny press" machine here, too, which allows you to convert a regular penny into a souvenir for a small fee.

WESTWARD HO TRADING COMPANY: This quaint, rustic store stocks something for the whole pin-trading frontier family, including pins, lanyards, and other pin-collecting accoutrements.

Critter Country

BRIAR PATCH: Situated near Splash Mountain, this small shop offers hats, character merchandise, and sundry souvenirs.

POOH CORNER: This *hunny* of a spot is home to a candy kitchen filled with sweet treats. Lining its many shelves are other Disneyland logo merchandise and items with a Winnie the Pooh theme. Pooh's pals from the Hundred Acre Wood are also well-represented. All kinds of Pooh products await, including plush toys, watches, infants' apparel, children's clothing, sleep shirts, and bedroom slippers. There is also a substantial selection of freshly made cookies and chocolates.

Get Your Ears Done Here

Since Disneyland first opened in 1955, there has been no more coveted souvenir of the park than a pair of Mickey Mouse ears personalized with the lucky owner's name—or that of a family member. And never have there been more styles to choose from. They can all be embroidered for a nominal fee at both locations of the Mad Hatter (in Fantasyland and on Main Street), the Gag Factory in Toontown, Tomorrowlanding in Tomorrowland, and other select locations. The shops will not embroider company names on hats.

POOH & YOU PHOTOS: Pooh and his pals from the Hundred Acre Wood can be found in Critter Country. You can take photos with your own camera or purchase any of the shots taken by one of Disneyland's photographers via Disney's PhotoPass program. For specifics regarding PhotoPass, refer to the sidebar to the right.

Adventureland

ADVENTURELAND BAZAAR: The plush jungle animals corralled here include lions, tigers, and panda bears (oh, my!).

INDIANA JONES ADVENTURE OUTPOST: This outfitter can supply the most daring expeditions with all manner of safari apparel, notably Indy's trademark headgear, as well as other rough-and-ready wear and "artifacts" related to the ever-popular archaeologist and adventurer, Indiana Jones.

SOUTH SEAS TRADERS: This is the spot to browse for surf- and safari-themed items, such as T-shirts, shorts, jackets, windbreakers, bags, belts, and a selection of hats.

Fantasyland

BIBBIDI BOBBIDI BOUTIQUE: Tucked inside Sleeping Beauty Castle, this shop offers young guests the opportunity to be transformed into "little princesses," and princely "cool knights." Makeovers are available daily. Prices vary.

ENCHANTED CHAMBER: Sparkly crowns dazzle the eyes of every young princess who enters this royal boutique, tucked inside Sleeping Beauty Castle, just to the left of the entrance to Fantasyland. From toys and jewelry and other courtly keepsakes, this little shop has made more than a few special dreams come true.

FAIRYTALE ARTS: Here guests are turned into princesses, among other things, via the magic of face painting. There is a fee.

FANTASY FAIRE GIFTS: On Disneyland's parade route, near the entrance to the Fantasyland Theatre, this open-air stand stocks special souvenirs and yummy treats spun from the colorful tales and sights in Fantasyland.

IT'S A SMALL WORLD TOY SHOP: The whimsical structure near the entrance to It's a Small World stocks an assortment of Disney-themed toys, dolls, pins, and plush toys featuring the Disney characters.

LE PETIT CHALET GIFTS: As cozy as a warm cup of cocoa on a winter evening, this small Swiss shop, nestled at the base of the Matterhorn, is the repository of traditional Disneyland gifts and souvenirs.

MAD HATTER: Always a great place for hats and plush character caps—and Mouse ears, of course (they'll embroider them for you for a small fee). The selection of novelty headgear includes items such as Donald's sailor cap, a hat sporting Goofy's ears, and more.

STROMBOLI'S WAGON: Located near the Village Haus restaurant, this stand offers a wagonful of wares—everything from Disney plush toys to Mickey Mouse sunglasses. Some of the smaller items available here include character key chains, pens, buttons, and candy. The shop is named after one of the villains from *Pinocchio*.

Mickey's Toontown

GAG FACTORY: A Laugh-O-Meter outside this shop gives some indication of the fun to be found inside, along with an assortment of character merchandise—plush toys, stationery,

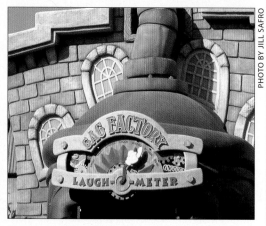

PHOTO BY JILL SAFRO

souvenirs, T-shirts, novelty headwear, and candy—all featuring the Fab Five (Mickey, Minnie, Pluto, Donald, and Goofy) and their friends. Take a moment to admire the toon architecture, especially the pillars at the back of the store. The Gag Factory will stitch your name on mouse ears for a small fee.

MICKEY & ME PHOTOS: Trying to get your photo taken with Mickey on busy days can be challenging, but if you follow this tip, it's a piece of cake: Mickey can often be found working in the Movie Barn behind his house in Toontown, and he's always happy to stop what he's doing to greet his guests and pose for pictures. You can take as many photos as you like with your own camera (at no charge) or purchase any of the shots taken by a Disneyland photographer via Disney's PhotoPass program. For details on PhotoPass, see page 85. Note that the line to meet the Mouse is often a long one. But to his legions of loyal fans, it's well worth the wait.

Tomorrowland

AUTOPIA WINNER'S CIRCLE: Racing enthusiasts will enjoy the Autopia-inspired souvenirs and toys offered at this small shop.

LITTLE GREEN MEN STORE COMMAND: "Sharp" traders know they can find an excellent selection of pins and Vinylmation collectibles at this spot. The ultimate pin destination at Disneyland offers open and limited-edition pins, lanyards, and pin-trading accessories, as well as souvenirs and toys featuring Pixar characters.

THE STAR TRADER: The Star Trader is the repository of everything from T-shirts and jewelry to novelty headwear, mugs, key chains, candy, and much more—all emblazoned with the likenesses of Disney characters.

Toys featuring Buzz Lightyear, Woody, and the gang from *Toy Story* can also be found here, along with hundreds of stuffed animals. In the section over by the Star Tours attraction exit, the *Star Wars* legends have come to collectible life. It's even possible to build your own lightsaber.

TOMORROWLANDING: Whether it's the Jedi Force that draws you to Tomorrowland or a desire to help find Nemo, what you'll actually find here is a super-sized assortment of headwear.

Pin Trading, Disney Style

It's one of the biggest collectible crazes to sweep through Disney's land—pin trading. These small enamel pins (there are hundreds of different styles) can be purchased all over the property, but buying them is only half the fun. The real joy comes when you encounter another pin trader with a worthy swap. To get a head start, bring pins from home (Disney Stores carry pins, too). Once on-property, keep an eye out for cast members sporting a good selection of pins— they tend to be agreeable to almost any trade. And when negotiating a trade with a Disneyland cast member, always remember these rules: (1) only Disney pins may be traded, and (2) every trade must be an even pin-for-pin exchange.

Entertainment

Together with Walt Disney World, Disneyland presents more live entertainment than any other organization in the world. What follows is typical of the variety you can expect. Check a park Times Guide for daily offerings.

Performers & Live Shows

Performers stroll, march, croon, and pluck their way through Disneyland every day—so frequently that all you usually have to do to find them is follow your ears.

Fantasyland

MICKEY AND THE MAGICAL MAP: Mickey Mouse reprises his classic role of sorcerer's apprentice in this brand-new, toe-tappin' and eye-poppin' performance. What's magic about the map? It transports dreamers to all the places they can imagine. Pretty cool! But the massive map has an empty spot—and Mickey takes it upon himself to fill it. As he swings his paintbrush, the audience is transported into the worlds of *The Jungle Book*, *Tangled*, *Lilo and Stitch*, *Pocahontas*, *Mulan*, and *The Princess and the Frog*. Dozens of singers and dancers join the Mouse, making this musical magical for all ages. For the best views, don't sit up front. The 22-minute show is usually presented several times a day. Check a park Times Guide for specifics.

Main Street, U.S.A.

ATMOSPHERE BANDS: Look and listen for a variety of musical groups who perform near the Fire House and Sleeping Beauty Castle on select days.

DAPPER DANS OF DISNEYLAND: The official greeters of Main Street, U.S.A., this classic singing quartet performs standards in perfect four-part harmony. The colorfully clad performers may be found strolling on the sidewalk, planted by a storefront, or whizzing by on a bicycle built for four.

DISNEYLAND BAND: A presence in the park since opening day in 1955, Disneyland's signature musical group specializes in turn-of-the-century band music and Disney tunes, but it can play just about anything. The band performs inside the main entrance when the park opens, in Town Square (at the South end of Main Street), and at other locations.

FLAG RETREAT: The flag at Town Square is lowered just before sunset each day (times vary). The ceremony is often highlighted by a performance by the Disneyland Band or the Dapper Dans. The band has been known to perform several rousing marches per show. On the band's day off, the Dapper Dans perform a capella renditions of American classics. "The Star-Spangled Banner" makes for a stirring finale. (We get choked up during this touching ceremony.) It is a rewarding experience that captures the essence of what Walt Disney hoped guests would feel as they experienced Main Street, U.S.A. Usually presented daily.

MAIN STREET PIANO PLAYER: Piano players are often on hand to tickle the ivories on the snow-white upright piano at the Corner Café. Presented daily.

New Orleans Square

JAMBALAYA JAZZ: This group plays down-home New Orleans jazz with plenty of soul. Fetch yourself a mint julep (sans alcohol) or a bowl of gumbo, and let the music wash over you like the mighty Mississippi.

ROYAL STREET BACHELORS: Their style is early traditional jazz and blues, with a mellow four-beat sound similar to that once commonly heard in the Story-ville section of the Crescent City. The Bachelors can be found performing throughout the Square.

Frontierland

BILLY HILL AND THE HILLBILLIES: Dishing up a lively mix of bluegrass and comedy on the Golden Horseshoe Stage, these four brothers, all named Billy and all first-rate musicians, never take themselves—or their guests—too seriously. This group also performs at Big Thunder Ranch during select times of year.

BIG THUNDER RANCH JAMBOREE: There's a rootin', tootin' Western-style celebration going on . . . yee-ha! Cowgirls and cowboys of all ages flock here to enjoy live music, family activities, and seasonal entertainment.

LAUGHING STOCK CO.: Sheriff Clem Clodhopper has no desire to marry Mayor McGillicuddy's daughter, Sally Mae, but neither of them will take no for an answer. An old-time serial in three parts is played out as the dysfunctional trio finagles to get Sally Mae hitched to someone (anyone), even an unsuspecting park guest. Check a park Times Guide for the performance schedule.

Tomorrowland

JEDI TRAINING ACADEMY: *Star Wars* fans and Jedi-wannabes can learn the ways of "the Force" right here in Disneyland. A Jedi Master is on hand to teach guests dos and don'ts of using a lightsaber, as well as help them fend off an unexpected march of Stormtroopers. Expect a special appearance by one notable Dark Lord who'll attempt to lure you to the dark side. Check a park Times Guide for exact times and dates.

Parades

No Main Street is complete without a parade, and Disneyland has plenty. The usual route runs between Town Square and the promenade in front of It's a Small World—or vice versa. The direction and route can vary, so it's wise to ask at the Information Center at City Hall or Central Plaza.

MICKEY'S SOUNDSATIONAL PARADE: Meant to evoke happy, musical Disney memories, this parade showcases dozens of beloved Disney characters, including the Mouse himself. It is usually presented each afternoon. Check a park Times Guide or Tip Board for current details and showtimes.

Where to Watch the Parade: The best vantage points from which to see the parades are the platform of the Disneyland Railroad's Main Street depot, Town Square near the flagpole, and the curb on either side of Main Street. If you'd like to avoid crowds, any viewing location other than Main Street would be better.

Two other options are the terrace outside the Plaza Inn (but be aware that the seating is limited here) and the tables in the courtyard of the Carnation Cafe, where the view may be partially obstructed. Better still, plan to catch a later parade on nights when more than one is scheduled—it's usually less crowded.

HOT TIP!

The park Times Guide provides a current listing of entertainment offerings and schedules. Pick up a copy at the main entrance, City Hall, or at one of the Tip Boards on Main Street. It's free! Note that custodial cast members tend to carry extra copies of park guidemaps and Times Guides, too. Just ask.

You can also stand on either side of the promenade area in front of It's a Small World, whose multicolored facade provides a whimsical, only-at-Disneyland backdrop. Wherever you decide to station yourself for the parade, plan to arrive about 20 to 45 minutes beforehand to claim your piece of turf.

Fireworks

FIREWORKS SPECTACULAR: An impressive fireworks show called "Remember . . . Dreams Come True" is presented seasonally, and "Magical . . . Disney's Nighttime Fireworks Spectacular" is presented during the summer. Both shows ignite the sky with a kaleidoscope of colors over Sleeping Beauty Castle. After dark (on Friday, Saturday, and summer nights), Tinker Bell and Dumbo fly in to start the spectacular light show in fantastic fashion. That's followed by the stories of the wishes of classic Disney characters, from Cinderella to Aladdin—all to the accompaniment of a medley of Disney tunes and other musical favorites. More than 200 pyrotechnic shells are fired in all, one every couple of seconds, in time to the music. Specially themed fireworks shows are presented during all major holiday seasons. Check a Times Guide for the schedule.

Where to Watch: One of the best areas is about midway down Main Street, U.S.A., near the Main Street Photo Supply Company. (Be sure to face Sleeping Beauty Castle!) Another great spot is near It's a Small World—keep your eye out for a special projection effect that's unique to this area.

Dancing

Bands play several sets in Tomorrowland on Saturdays year-round and nightly during peak seasons. Feel free to sway to the songs. If you'd like a higher-octane dance party, consider "hopping" to Disney California Adventure for the nightly Mad T Party— an interactive dance party based on Tim Burton's *Alice In Wonderland*.

Special Occasions

Along with plenty of special events in the parks and hotels year-round (some require special admission tickets), Disneyland celebrates three major seasons each year: Summer (including the Fourth of July), Halloween (September through October), and the winter holidays (mid-November through early January).

SUMMER: While plenty of folks are on vacation, Disney offers a full slate of atmosphere entertainment and spectaculars from Memorial Day to Labor Day. Expect longer wait times at attractions and plan to use Fastpass (see page 58) as often as possible. Along with daytime diversions, the nighttime spectacular **Fantasmic!** (see page 91) is a lovely capper to a day in the park. Past years have seen a patriotic, pyrotechnic tribute to the U.S.A. on July 4th in a celebration known as Disney's Celebrate America! A Fourth of July Concert in the Sky.

HALLOWEEN: Halloween Time at the Disneyland Resort brings a palette of fall colors, pumpkins, and trick-or-treat touches, along with the extra-spooky *Nightmare Before Christmas*-themed Haunted Mansion (see page 10). Spirited family fun can also be found at Disney's Halloween Time Carnival at Big Thunder Ranch in Frontierland.

WINTER HOLIDAYS: This jolly period stretches from November through New Year's, when the entire park glows with holiday themes. (We have witnessed the yuletide holiday decorations in place as early as October.)

The Disneyland Resort officially begins to celebrate the holidays in November when Jingle Jangle Jamboree, Sleeping Beauty Castle's Wintertime Enchantment, and the merriest attraction on Earth—It's a Small World Holiday—return for the season.

It's a Small World Holiday celebrates yuletide customs around the world. The singing dolls add "Jingle Bells" to their repertoire in numerous languages, and the clock on the whimsical facade dons a Santa hat.

Main Street, U.S.A., is decked out in traditional red and green, including hundreds

PHOTO BY JILL SAFRO

of poinsettias and a huge Christmas tree that's surrounded by oversize holiday packages. But the true star of the Main Street festoonery has to be Sleeping Beauty's Castle. It's draped in a blanket of thousands of twinkling lights. Other highlights include the chance to meet the man in the red suit, Santa himself. To do so, check a Times Guide for **Jingle Jangle Jamboree**. And don't miss **Believe . . . In Holiday Magic**—in addition to festive fireworks, it brings with it a dusting of snow.

On select nights at the beginning of the season, a candlelight procession ending at Town Square takes place. Special music is provided by a large choir, and a holiday story is read by a well-known entertainer. (**A Christmas Fantasy Parade**, a Disney holiday favorite, takes place throughout the holiday season.)

Live entertainment and a spectacular fireworks show on **New Year's Eve** (no special ticket required) provide the grand finale for this happy holiday season.

For more information about seasonal happenings in the park, call 714-781-7290 or visit *www.disneyland.com*.

Where to Find the Characters

Look for the Disney characters in Town Square on Main Street, U.S.A., as well as in Mickey's Toontown, where they live. Tinker Bell and her fairy friends appear at Pixie Hollow. Princesses hold court at Fantasy Faire on Main Street. Pooh and his pals congregate in Critter Country. In Adventureland, Aladdin and Jasmine often stop to interact outside Aladdin's Oasis.

Cast members at the Information Board can help locate characters. Also refer to the *Good Meals, Great Times* chapter of this book, and your Disneyland Times Guide.

Imagination Runs Wild in Fantasmic!

These 22 minutes of magic, music, live performances, and special effects light up the Rivers of America nightly on weekends, holidays, and throughout the summer season. More than 50 performers put on an unforgettable show in a dazzling display of pyrotechnics, giant props, and impressive new hi-def video and lighting. In this tale of good versus evil, it's up to Mickey to overcome an array of villains. He first appears in cartoon form at the tip of Tom Sawyer Island and uses his imagination to make comets shoot across the sky while the river waters dance. Mickey materializes in a cone of light, and a shower of sparks seems to shoot from his fingers.

Spectacular technology makes Fantasmic! all the more fantastic. Mickey works his magic and a special film sequence appears,

Disney villains attempt to disrupt Mickey's fantasy. Fearsome creatures all have an opportunity, including an animated Maleficent, who morphs into the 45-foot-tall, fire-breathing dragon from *Sleeping Beauty*.

The villains turn Mickey's dreams into nightmares, and he must overcome them with his own powers of goodness, plus a little help from his friends. The sailing ship *Columbia* glides through the show with the swashbuckling cast of *Peter Pan* on board, and the *Mark Twain* riverboat brings along a host of favorite Disney characters.

Where to Watch: The best spots are in front of Pirates of the Caribbean (be sure you can see the water and a clear view of Tom Sawyer Island, and get there at least one hour early). If you decide to splurge, book Premium Viewing seats. They are set at the water's edge

seemingly in midair above the river. This effect is achieved by projecting digital images onto three giant mist screens, each one 30 feet tall by 50 feet wide. The screens are transparent, so that the live performers behind and in front of them appear to be interacting with the filmed images.

In one scene, Monstro the Whale from *Pinocchio* makes waves in the real water of the Rivers of America. In the "Pink Elephants on Parade" scene, the animated pachyderms from *Dumbo* interact with live performers in flexible, glow-in-the-dark elephant costumes. The illusions build toward a confrontation of good and evil, in which

and come with tasty treats and beverages. The cost is about $59 per adult, $49 per child. Call 714-781-4400 to reserve. The ticket office opens at 8 A.M. We recommend calling as soon as it opens, exactly one month before your desired reservation date. Late arrivals can usually find a decent place to watch near Haunted Mansion.

Note: Fantasmic! is shown twice nightly during the summer, and there can be a crush of people trying to leave after the show. The later show is always less crowded. Some of the effects are quite realistic and may be too intense for very young viewers.

Hot Tips

❋ Tuesday, Wednesday, and Thursday are the least crowded days to visit year-round. If you must come on a weekend, choose Sunday over Saturday.

❋ Measure your child's height before your visit so you'll know ahead of time which attractions he or she may be too short to ride. This can prevent intense disappointment later.

❋ Wear comfortable walking shoes. Blisters are the most common malady reported to First Aid.

❋ Main Street, U.S.A., often opens half an hour before the rest of the park. Take advantage of this to grab a quick snack, shop, or mingle with Disney characters.

❋ Check the daily entertainment schedule in a current Times Guide and plan your day accordingly.

❋ Wait times posted at the attractions and on the Information Board at the north end of Main Street, U.S.A. (on the Adventureland side), are updated every hour.

❋ Break up your time in the park (unless you have only one day). Arrive early, see the major attractions until things get busy, return to your hotel for a swim or a nap, then go back to the park. Remember, you must have your hand stamped and your ticket to re-enter Disneyland.

❋ An attraction may reach its Fastpass limit before the end of the day, especially if the park is packed. Be sure to get yours early if you don't want to wait in the standby line.

❋ Try to stop for lunch before 11:30 A.M. or after 2 P.M., and dinner before 5 P.M. or after 8 P.M. to avoid long lines (which tend to be a bit shorter toward the left side of the fast-food counters).

❋ On crowded days, you can make your way between the east and west sides of the park most quickly via the Big Thunder Trail.

❋ For a change of pace foodwise, head to Downtown Disney or one of the three hotels on property. They have something for every budget and taste—from simple to sublime, ravioli to rack of lamb—as well as buffet meals with popular Disney characters (at the Disneyland resorts only).

❋ Avoid rides such as Star Tours, Splash Mountain, the Matterhorn Bobsleds, and the Mad Tea Party immediately after meals (for obvious reasons).

❋ The lines are longest for the Disneyland Railroad at the Main Street station, but they tend to move quickly (lots of passengers disembark at this stop).

❋ Try to visit the major attractions—Space Mountain, Star Tours, the Indiana Jones Adventure, Big Thunder Mountain Railroad, Finding Nemo Submarine Voyage, Haunted Mansion, the Matterhorn Bobsleds, and Splash Mountain—early or during parades. The lines move faster then.

❋ During the busy afternoon hours, go to the smaller attractions, where the wait times are comparatively shorter; the *Mark Twain* riverboat is always a good choice. The afternoon is also prime time for shopping, enjoying outdoor musical performances, taking in a show at the Golden Horseshoe Stage, or watching the Flag Retreat on Main Street, U.S.A.

❋ Shops are a good place to escape the midday heat, but steer clear of them in late afternoon and at the end of the park's operating hours, when they tend to be the most crowded.

❋ For most attractions, if you're in line even one minute before the park closes, you'll be allowed on. This is a great tactic for Splash Mountain and the Indiana Jones Adventure.

❋ Avoid the crowds by returning your stroller before the evening's fireworks presentation comes to an end.

Disney California Adventure

F ame, fortune, and fun in the sun have lured adventurous spirits to California for centuries. But now visitors have an alternative way to enjoy the glories of the Golden State: through Disney's eyes. In February 2001, the company officially unveiled its California Adventure theme park—and it's been a work-in-progress ever since. To that end, an amazing, billion-dollar expansion is finally complete. New themes and attractions have joined the landscape, while some veteran rides have been "re-imagined." The result? An adventure to excite even the most devoted Disneyland Park devotees.

Disney California Adventure sits snugly in the heart of the Disneyland Resort, sharing an entrance esplanade with Disneyland, neighboring Downtown Disney District, and the Disney hotels. But once you set foot inside the park, you're in a world all its own. Districts blend into each other, and no matter where you stand, you're sure to see (or hear whoops and hollers coming from) one of the park's icons—the spooky-but-spectacular Twilight Zone™ Tower of Terror, the sierra-inspired Grizzly Peak mountain, Paradise Pier's coaster, California Screamin,' and the recent addition and instant classic, Radiator Springs Racers.

With a small vineyard, upscale restaurants, scream-inducing thrill rides, and attractions tailored for tots, the 66-acre theme park has something for everyone to enjoy. California, here we come!

DISNEY CALIFORNIA ADVENTURE

PARADISE PIER

PACIFIC WHARF

GRIZZLY PEAK

CONDOR FLATS

CARS LAND

A BUG'S LAND

HOLLYWOOD LAND

BUENA VISTA STREET

HOLLYWOOD LAND
1. Disney Animation
2. The Twilight Zone™ Tower of Terror
3. Hyperion Theater
4. Muppet*Vision 3-D
5. Monsters, Inc.—Mike and Sulley to the Rescue!
6. Disney Junior—Live on Stage!

A BUG'S LAND
7. It's Tough to Be a Bug!
8. Flik's Fun Fair

CONDOR FLATS
9. Soarin' Over California

GRIZZLY PEAK
10. Grizzly River Run
11. Redwood Creek Challenge Trail

PARADISE PIER
12. The Little Mermaid—Ariel's Undersea Adventure
13. California Screamin'
14. Golden Zephyr
15. Jumpin' Jellyfish
16. Goofy's Sky School
17. Silly Symphony Swings
18. Mickey's Fun Wheel
19. Toy Story Mania!
20. King Triton's Carousel
21. World of Color

CARS LAND
22. Luigi's Flying Tires
23. Mater's Junkyard Jamboree
24. Radiator Springs Racers

94

Getting Oriented

Disney California Adventure (formerly known as Disney's California Adventure) is smaller than Disneyland Park, so guests should have no trouble covering all of it on foot—as long as they wear comfortable walking shoes.

The entrance area is known as Buena Vista Street. Several distinct districts compose the rest of Disney California Adventure. East of Buena Vista Street lies Hollywood Land. It's a mock studio backlot where guests can, among other things, learn about animation, take in a stage show based on the animated feature *Aladdin*, and enjoy a lighthearted attraction known as Monsters, Inc.—Mike and Sulley to the Rescue!

West of Buena Vista Street is Condor Flats, home of the beloved Soarin' Over California attraction. Pacific Wharf is a district dedicated to the cultures, industries, and natural beauty that have shaped California, complete with a winery. The adjacent Grizzly Peak features a thrilling white-water rapids attraction known as Grizzly River Run.

The Paradise Pier neighborhood has nostalgic thrill rides with a modern twist, located around a lagoon. (This is the place to race to first thing in the morning if you want to experience Toy Story Mania.)

A Bug's Land is something of a mini-park within a park—designed for mini theme park guests. Finally, the all-new Cars Land offers guests the opportunity to experience all the thrills of Radiator Springs. Don't miss Luigi's Flying Tires, Mater's Junkyard Jamboree, and the park's newest "E-Ticket" attraction, Radiator Springs Racers.

Guests park in either the six-level Mickey & Friends parking structure or the *Toy Story* lot on Harbor Boulevard, which can be accessed from the I-5 freeway.

Parking Fees: Guests arriving in passenger vehicles pay about $16 to park. (The fee for vans and buses is $21; for trucks and buses with extended trailers, $26.) You may leave the lot during the day and return later the

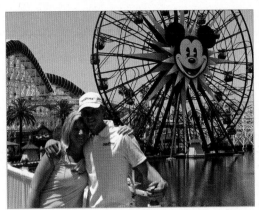

same day at no extra fee. Just hold on to your parking stub as proof of earlier payment.

Lost Cars: Even if you take careful note of where you parked your car, you might have trouble remembering or recognizing the exact spot when you return hours later. Hundreds more vehicles will likely be parked around yours. If this happens, tell a cast member approximately when you arrived. With that little bit of information, parking lot personnel can usually figure out the car's general location, and someone will then comb the lanes for it on a scooter.

GETTING AROUND

You'll have to depend a lot on your feet— other than the Red Car Trolley ride, there's no transportation in this park. Wheelchairs and Electric Conveyance Vehicles are available.

Guests staying at Disney's Grand Californian hotel have their own private entry into Disney California Adventure park. (Guests enter and exit through turnstiles located near Grizzly River Run. It may be used by guests staying at the Disneyland Hotel and Disney's Paradise Pier Hotel, too.) All other visitors enter and exit the park through the main entrance, just across the esplanade from Disneyland's front gate. From here, trams and shuttles transport guests to the two resort parking areas. Since the area is pedestrian-friendly, guests may also opt to walk from the park along the esplanade to the hotels and the Downtown Disney part of the property.

HOT TIP!

When you enter Disney California Adventure through the Entry Plaza, east is to your left and west is to your right.

Park Primer

BABY FACILITIES

Changing tables, baby-care products, and facilities for nursing can be found at the Baby Care Center.

DISABILITY INFORMATION

Many park attractions and nearly all shops and restaurants are accessible to guests using wheelchairs. Services are also available for those with visual or hearing disabilities. Ask about these services at Guest Relations.

FIRST AID

Minor medical problems are handled at the First Aid Center, by the park's main entrance.

GUIDED TOUR

The *Welcome to Disneyland* tour is available daily. The 2½–hour journey takes guests through Disneyland Park and Disney California Adventure, with stops at several attractions, shows, and interactive experiences. Park admission is required, but not included. For current pricing, schedule, or to book a tour, call 714-781-4400, or stop by the park's Guest Relations center.

HOURS

Disney California Adventure is generally open from 10 A.M. to 8 P.M. Monday through Thursday, and 10 A.M. to 9 P.M. Friday, Saturday, and Sunday. For the exact times, visit *www.disneyland.com* or call 714-781-4636.

INFORMATION

Guest Relations/Visitor's Center, located near the park's main entrance, is equipped with guidemaps, Times Guides, and a helpful staff. Maps and Times Guides are also available at most park shops. The Information Kiosk, in Carthay Circle Plaza, is an excellent resource for attraction wait times and show schedules. Information is updated every hour.

LOST & FOUND

The theme park's Lost & Found department is on the left (east) side of the park's main entrance. If you find a lost item, you'll be asked to fill out a card with your name and address; if the object isn't claimed within 60 days, you have the option of keeping it.

LOCKERS

Lockers are located near the park's main entrance. Rental fees range from $7 to $15 per day, depending on size. They are available for unlimited use throughout the day.

LOST CHILDREN

Report lost children at the Baby Care Center, or alert the closest employee to the problem.

MONEY MATTERS

There are several ATMs in the park. Currency may be exchanged at Guest Relations, and Disney Dollars may be purchased at ticket sale windows. Cash, credit cards, traveler's checks, Disney gift cards, Disney Dollars, and Disneyland Resort Hotel IDs are accepted for most purchases.

SAME-DAY RE-ENTRY

Be sure to have your hand stamped as you exit the park, and hold on to your ticket if you plan to return later the same day.

STROLLERS & WHEELCHAIRS

Strollers, wheelchairs, and Electric Conveyance Vehicles (ECVs) can be rented outside the main entrance to Disneyland Park. If you need a replacement, just present a receipt.

Ticket Prices

Although prices are likely to change (they always do), the following will give you an idea of what you can expect to pay in 2014. For current prices, visit *www.disneyland.com* or call 714-781-4636.*

One-Day Ticket	ADULTS	CHILDREN**
(one park)	$92	$86
One-Day Ticket (hopper)	$137	$131
Two-Day Ticket (hopper)	$210	$197
Three-Day Ticket (hopper)	$260	$244
Four-Day Ticket (hopper)	$285	$265
Five-Day Ticket (hopper)	$300	$279
Two-Park Deluxe Annual Passport		$499
Two-Park Premium Annual Passport		$669
Premier Annual Passport		$979

*Discounts may be available through the Website.
**3 through 9 years of age; children under 3 free

Buena Vista Street

When a young Walt Disney took the train from Kansas City to Los Angeles in 1923, he discovered a bustling metropolis teeming with pedestrian boulevards, shops, restaurants, and shiny red trolley cars. Buena Vista Street, the new entrance to the park, sends guests back to this era—to an idealized version of a city beaming with optimism and opportunity.

Follow festive Buena Vista Street, which begins inside the turnstiles, to the Carthay Circle Theatre—a replica of the theatre where *Snow White and the Seven Dwarfs* premiered in 1937. Or enjoy a trip back in time by hopping aboard a trolley.

RED CAR TROLLEY: The Red Car Trolley system revives the gone-but-not-forgotten Pacific Electric Railway right here in Disney California Adventure. This jolly trolley transports guests between Buena Vista Street and The Twilight Zone™ Tower of Terror by way of Hollywood Land.

Hollywood Land

Lights! Camera! Action! The spotlight is on you in the glitzy Hollywood district of Disney California Adventure, where the action unfolds all around you. Motion picture soundstages and backlot scenery provide the setting for the movie-making antics and entertaining demonstrations that reveal a few tricks of the trade. No movies are actually filmed here, so you'll have to keep waiting for your big break. But you can think of this area as the "Hollywood that never was and always will be."

Turn onto Hollywood Boulevard and enter into Disney's version of the legendary street. And it all fits neatly into a two-block strip. Some of Disney California Adventure's most popular attractions lie within this zone, including The Twilight Zone™ Tower of Terror, Turtle Talk with Crush, Muppet*Vision 3-D, and much more.

In contrast to starstruck Hollywood Boulevard, the backlot area peels away the facade and takes a backstage look at Hollywood without its makeup. Alongside soundstage buildings, behind-the-scenes support departments do their unseen, essential work: props are put into position, klieg lights are set to shine on the scene, and the crew is busy making sure every performer is on his or her mark before the director yells "Action!"

BIRNBAUM'S BEST **MUPPET*VISION 3-D:** One of the best shows in the park, much of the appeal of this movie is in the details. In fact, a digital projection system makes the detail crystal clear—so if you haven't seen it lately, you haven't seen it!

A funny song-and-dance pre-show, hosted by Gonzo and viewed on TVs, gives clues about what's to come. The theater (set inside a soundstage) looks just like the one from Jim Henson's classic television series *The Muppet Show* and comes complete with an orchestra of penguins. Even the two curmudgeonly fellows, Statler and Waldorf, are sitting in the balcony, bantering with each other and flinging barbs at the performers and the audience.

The production comes directly from Muppet Labs, presided over by Dr. Bunsen Honeydew and his long-suffering assistant, Beaker, and introduces Waldo, the "spirit of 3-D." Among the highlights is Miss Piggy's solo, which Bean Bunny turns into quite a fiasco. Sam Eagle's patriotic finale leads to trouble as a veritable war breaks out, culminating with a cannon blast from the rear of the balcony, courtesy of everybody's favorite Swedish Chef.

The 3-D effects, impressive as they may be, are only part of the show: There are appearances by live Muppet characters and lots of details built into the walls of the huge theater. Including the pre-show, expect to spend about 25 minutes with Kermit and company. Shows run continuously.

BIRNBAUM'S BEST **MONSTERS, INC.—MIKE AND SULLEY TO THE RESCUE!:** A monster's-eye spin through Monstropolis, this colorful, slow-moving attraction was inspired by the hit film *Monsters, Inc.* It invites guests to follow affable monsters Mike and Sulley as they valiantly attempt to deliver Boo safely back to her room—all the while dodging trucks, helicopters, and the occasional yellow-suited member of the Child Detection Agency.

DISNEY JUNIOR—LIVE ON STAGE!: Fans of Playhouse Disney—Live on Stage (the show that used to play here) should enjoy this new production. It brings back three audience favorites—*Mickey Mouse Clubhouse*, *Handy Manny*, and *Jake and the Never Land Pirates*—and introduces elements of Disney Junior's new series, *Sofia the First*. (Sofia, Disney's youngest princess, shows guests that a true princess is much more than pretty dresses and sparkling jewels.) Very young guests tend to be the most enthusiastic members of the audience for this show.

The performance space holds large crowds (of mostly tiny people) at a time. There are just a handful of seats, but there's plenty of room to sprawl out on the carpeted floor.

This show is presented daily. The park Times Guide lists the performance schedule.

BIRNBAUM'S ★BEST **DISNEY ANIMATION:** When you look around at all the attractions, themed hotels, and dozens of familiar animated faces that Disney has become famous for, it's almost impossible to remember it all started with a simple sketch of a mouse. This behind-the-scenes exploration invites guests to step into Disney's wonderful world of animation. Here visitors are given an insider's look at the process, the heritage, and, above all, the artistry of this world-renowned art form, along with a possible preview of an animated feature that is currently in progress.

Animation Courtyard: This central area makes visitors feel as if they are stepping into an animated film. Sketches and artwork from Disney and Pixar film classics are projected onto giant screens that circle the colorful atrium as familiar tunes fill the air. From this hub, guests may progress to several interactive animation attractions.

Animation Academy: Inspired by the animation art in the courtyard, this attraction lets guests take a crack at drawing their favorite Disney characters. With step-by-step guidance provided by a Disney animator, you will use basic shapes and simple techniques to create your own souvenir sketch, suitable for framing. (Well, that's the goal, anyway!) Be sure to check out the *Toy Story* zoetrope as you exit—it's pretty cool!

Sorcerer's Workshop: Budding animators and artists particularly get a kick out of these three rooms. They are built around interactive exhibits featuring animation special effects. At Ursula's Grotto, for example, you can supply the voice of a favorite character from *The Little Mermaid*, and then see and hear the completed scene containing your own vocals. At Enchanted Books, you can take a personality survey (hosted by *Beauty and the Beast*'s Lumiere and Cogsworth) to determine to which Disney character or villain you are most similar.

Turtle Talk with Crush: If ever there were an attraction that left guests smiling and asking, "How do they do that?!"—this is it. The concept is simple enough: a ten-minute, animated show featuring the surfer-dude sea turtle from *Finding Nemo*. The amazing part? The cartoon critter actually interacts with the audience. In doing so, he imparts turtle-y wisdom, answers questions, and cracks more than a few jokes. You have to see it to believe it. To do that, you'll have to wait—the show is extremely popular with guests of all ages. It so totally rocks, dude.

DISNEY'S ALADDIN—A MUSICAL SPECTACULAR: Disney brings Broadway to its backyard with this 40-minute show, presented on the grand stage of the 2,000-seat Hyperion Theater. Inspired by the animated feature of the same name, this production tells the story of Aladdin, the magic lamp, and his trusty blue sidekick, Genie. The engaging staging even includes a magic carpet ride or two. Don't forget to look up!

You'll recognize all your favorite songs from the classic Disney film, and be introduced to a new one, penned by renowned composer Alan Menken.

Note: The show is quite popular, and the schedule varies. Check a park map for the performance schedule, and plan to arrive early.

BIRNBAUM'S ★BEST **THE TWILIGHT ZONE™ TOWER OF TERROR:** FP The Hollywood Tower Hotel houses a creepy-yet-thrilling ride. On the facade of the 199-foot-tall building hangs a sparking electric sign. As the legend goes, lightning struck the building on Halloween night in 1939. An entire guest wing disappeared, along with an elevator carrying five people.

The line for the popular ride runs through the hotel lobby, where dusty furniture, cobwebs, and old newspapers add to the eerie atmosphere. As guests enter the library, they see a dark TV set suddenly brought to life by a bolt of lightning. Rod Serling invites them to enter The Twilight Zone.

Guests are led toward the boiler room to enter the ride elevator. (This is your chance to change your mind about riding. Simply ask the attendant to direct you toward the "chicken exit.") Once you take a seat in the elevator, the doors close and the room begins its ascent. At the first stop, the doors open and guests have a view down a corridor. Among the many effects is a ghostly visit by the hotel guests who vanished. The doors close again and you continue your trip skyward.

At the next stop, you enter another dimension, a combination of sights and sounds reminiscent of *The Twilight Zone*™ TV series. In fact, Disney Imagineers watched each of the 156 original *Twilight Zone* episodes at least twice for inspiration. This part of the ride is rather suspenseful, as you can't quite tell when you're going to take the plunge. What happens next depends entirely upon the whim of Disney Imagineers, who have programmed the ride so that the drop sequence can change.

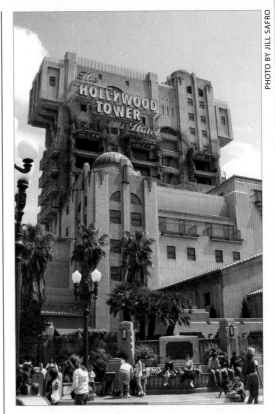

At press time, the elevator was taking an immediate plunge (of about eight stories) before shooting up to the 13th floor. At the top (about 157 feet up), passengers can look out at the park below. Once the doors shut, you plummet 13 stories. The drop lasts about two seconds, but it seems a whole lot longer.

Just when you think it's over, the elevator launches skyward, barely stopping before it plunges again. And again. From the time you are seated, the trip takes about five minutes.

Note: You must be at least 40 inches tall to ride. It is not recommended for pregnant women, or people with heart conditions or back and neck problems. Though thrilling (and rather scary), the drops are surprisingly smooth. Still, if you are susceptible to motion sickness, skip this one.

Did You Know?

The "Hyperion" name has a special Disney heritage. The Walt Disney Studios moved to 2719 Hyperion Street, Los Angeles, in 1926. It was there that Mickey Mouse was born. In 1940, Walt moved his studios to a bigger lot in Burbank, but he took some of the original Hyperion buildings with him.

Condor Flats

Inspired by California's aviation history, this airfield and its display area pay tribute to famous flyers and their precious planes. A huge aircraft hangar, the focus of this site, houses the Soarin' Over California attraction.

SOARIN' OVER CALIFORNIA: FP It's no wonder California has an ongoing romance with aviation—how better to experience its breathtaking landscapes than by soaring through the skies above them? On this smooth, high-flying attraction, you're suspended up to 45 feet in the air above a giant Omnimax projection dome that showcases some of the state's most glorious sights. With the wind in your hair and your legs dangling in the breeze, the hang glider feels so convincingly real that you may even be tempted to pull up your feet for fear of tripping over a treetop as you dip down toward the ground. During the journey, flyers glide toward the Upper Yosemite Falls of Yosemite Valley, past an active naval aircraft carrier in San Diego Bay, by San Francisco's Golden Gate Bridge, then down over the vast desert of Death Valley and the lush wine country of Napa Valley, and up past skiers swooshing down the slopes in Lake Tahoe.

In all, the airborne trip takes about 5 minutes and employs synchronized wind currents, scent machines, and a moving musical score set to a film that wraps 180 degrees around you, making this a thoroughly enveloping experience. It's a hit with guests of all ages.

HOT TIP!
For a really soaring experience, try to sit in the first row—it flies the highest, while the third row stays closest to the ground.

Note: You must be 42 inches tall and free of back problems, heart conditions, motion sickness, and any other physical limitations to ride. If you're afraid of heights, you should definitely skip this one.

Grizzly Peak

Just south of Condor Flats lies Grizzly Peak recreation area. Its centerpiece is the unmistakable grizzly bear-shaped mountain peak that juts 110 feet into the California Adventure skyline. The eight-acre mini wilderness surrounding Grizzly Peak pays tribute to California's spectacular natural beauty.

GRIZZLY RIVER RUN: FP Disney legend says that Grizzly Peak was once chock-full of gold—which made it a magnet for miners in search of riches, as is evidenced by the mining relics scattered about the mountain. But the gold rush has come and gone, and the peak has since been taken over by another enterprising group—the Grizzly Peak Rafting Company. They converted the area into a rafting expedition known as Grizzly River Run.

Each circular raft whisks eight passengers on a drenching tour of Grizzly Peak. The trip begins with a 45-foot climb, and it's all gloriously downhill from there. Fast-moving currents send adventurers spinning and splashing along the river, bumping off boulders and rushing through an erupting geyser field. Because the raft is constantly spinning as it moves through the water, each rider's experience is slightly different, but one thing's for sure—everyone gets wet. During the expedition, rafters encounter two major drops. It's the 21-foot drop that earns Grizzly River the distinction of being the world's tallest, fastest raft ride.

HOT TIP!

Don't bring cameras or other valuables that must stay dry on Grizzly River Run. They will get drenched! Leave them with a non-riding member of your party or in a nearby (free) short-term locker.

Note: Passengers must be free of back and neck problems, heart conditions, motion sickness, and other physical limitations to ride. Pregnant women, guests not meeting the 42-inch height requirement, and children under age 3 will not be permitted to board.

REDWOOD CREEK CHALLENGE TRAIL: Russell and Dug, from the animated feature *Up*, want to help you earn Wilderness Explorer badges while navigating forested paths, climbing rocks, swinging on rope bridges, and zipping down slides. Russell has left hints throughout the trail to help guests get those badges. Think you're up to the challenge? Lace up your sneakers and give it a try!

Of course, even the most intrepid explorers need directions. Fortunately, there are maps available at the trail's entrance—just ask a park ranger. After consulting the detailed map, you can start the quest to earn badges in tracking, bravery, rock climbing, wolf howling, animal spirit, and puzzle solving.

Afterward, head to the Ahwahnee Camp Circle for a special ceremony with Russell. Wilderness Explorer ceremonies take place throughout the day. For showtimes, check a park Times Guide. Need a hand to assist you through the course? Just whistle for one of the workers outfitted in ranger gear. He or she will be happy to help.

Pacific Wharf

Inspired by Monterey, California's Cannery Row, this industrial waterfront salutes the diverse cultures, products, and industries that make California so international in nature. Guests can tour a working bakery and watch local products, such as fresh-baked San Francisco sourdough bread, being prepared. There are also many tables scattered about, making this a good place to stop to enjoy a rest or a snack.

THE BAKERY TOUR: Soft sourdough bread is featured at this working bakery. While baking tips are shared in the walk-through corridor tour (courtesy of a video), the famous Boudin-family recipe remains a well-kept secret.

HOT TIP!

Little ones love to romp in the splash zone near Flik's Flyers and under the giant, leaky hose across from Francis' Ladybug Boogie. Swim diapers are an absolute must for the area known as Princess Dot Puddle Park.

A Bug's Land

FLIK'S FUN FAIR: Guests of all ages are invited, but this area caters to the little ones. Who better to enjoy the experience of seeing the world from the vantage point of a bug? Somewhat of a park within a park, Flik's Fun Fair boasts a total of four honest-to-goodness, kid-pleasing attractions, plus a splash zone for tots—all of them ostensibly built by a bug:

Flik's Flyers is a hot air "balloon" ride that Flik cleverly crafted with (giant) leaves,

PHOTO BY JILL SAFRO

twigs, and old food containers. This ride is big with fans of Disneyland's Dumbo the Flying Elephant (the line here is usually shorter). The ride lasts about a minute and a half.

Francis' Ladybug Boogie: Stop here to spin yourself silly. The Francis vehicles "boogie" for about 90 seconds per ride. It's good for guests of all ages—provided they didn't just enjoy a big snack. Spinning on a full stomach is a no-no!

Heimlich's Chew Chew Train: A simple railroad ride, here Heimlich treats guests to a 2-minute gustatory sojourn—all the while clutching his precious piece of candy corn.

Princess Dot Puddle Park is a micro-water park themed around a giant lawn sprinkler. Tots must wear swim diapers here.

Tuck and Roll's Drive 'Em Buggies is an old-fashioned bumper car experience, courtesy of everyone's favorite Hungarian pill bugs. Guests must be at least 48 inches tall to drive and 42 inches tall to ride shotgun.

BIRNBAUM'S ★BEST★ IT'S TOUGH TO BE A BUG!: The underground Bug's Life Theater, just inside the entrance to A Bug's Land, features an eight-minute, animated 3-D movie augmented by some surprising "4-D" effects. The stars of the show are the world's most abundant inhabitants—insects. They creep, crawl, and demonstrate why, someday, they just might inherit the earth. It's a bug's-eye view of the trials and tribulations of their multi-legged world.

As guests enter the dark auditorium, the orchestra can be heard warming up amid the chirps of crickets. When Flik, the emcee (and star of *A Bug's Life*), makes his first appearance, he dubs audience members honorary bugs and instructs them to don their "bug eyes" (or 3-D glasses). Then our oh-so-mild-mannered hero introduces some of his not-so-mild-mannered pals, including a Chilean tarantula, a duo of dung beetles, and "the silent but deadly member of the bug world"—the stinkbug. Hopper, Flik's nemesis and the leader of the evil grasshopper pack, crashes the show and adds to the antics. What follows is a manic, often hilarious, not-to-be-missed revue.

Note: The combination of intense special effects and frequent darkness tends to frighten toddlers and young children. In addition, anyone leery of spiders, roaches, and their ilk is advised to skip the performance, or risk being seriously bugged.

Cars Land

Ladies and gentlemen, start your engines—a real-life Radiator Springs has sprung up in the area between A Bug's Land and Paradise Pier. This 12-acre *Cars*-themed town invites guests to enjoy the following attractions:

LUIGI'S FLYING TIRES: Hop aboard a stack of giant tires and enjoy a giggle-inducing "flight." Part bumper car, part flying saucer, these wacky wheels are fun for everyone. The attraction, which sits behind Luigi's Casa Della Tires, bears some resemblance to the Flying Saucers ride that once operated in Disneyland's Tomorrowland. It's a "wheel" hoot! Guests must be at least 32 inches tall to experience this ride. Expectant mothers and guests with health problems are advised to skip flying with Luigi.

MATER'S JUNKYARD JAMBOREE: This attraction is a tractor-pulling dance party hosted by everyone's favorite tow truck. As baby tractors pull the junkyard cart (with you in it), the cart gets whirled and twirled in time to tunes pumped through Mater's junkyard jukebox. To ride, guests must be at least 32 inches tall. Don't ride on a full stomach!

BIRNBAUM'S BEST **RADIATOR SPRINGS RACERS:** Fasten your seatbelts—this bona fide "E-Ticket" attraction will set your heart racing as you compete with other speed seekers. Using technology similar to that of Epcot's beloved Test Track attraction, Imagineers have devised a thrilling experience for guests: a high-speed tour of Ornament Valley, featuring hairpin turns, steep banks, and a head-to-head race to the finish. Sally, Luigi, Guido, Ramone, and other *Cars* friends zoom around this revved-up racetrack.

Note: Guests must be at least 40 inches tall and without health conditions. Expectant mothers must skip this race.

Paradise Pier

It's all about fun in the sun at Paradise Pier, a throwback to California seaside boardwalks of yesteryear. Like most classic amusement zones, the rides here offer simple thrills of speed and weightlessness—but don't let the nostalgic look fool you: The technology is quite current.

At night, the district undergoes a dazzling transformation. Thousands of tiny lights illuminate the rides and building facades, creating a magical display—especially as you soar past them on one of Paradise Pier's most thrilling attractions.

BIRNBAUM'S BEST **CALIFORNIA SCREAMIN':** FP Like many classic boardwalks, the centerpiece of Paradise Pier is a gleaming roller coaster. A steel coaster, California Screamin' is designed to look (and sound) like an old-fashioned wooden coaster, but the thrills are as modern as they get. The ride starts at lagoon level, where the long car bursts up the track as if catapulted up by a crashing wave. The car goes from zero to 55 miles per hour in 4.7 seconds—before reaching the first hill. Several long drops are combined with an upside-down loop, plus a blasting soundtrack. The result is the longest and fastest coaster in the Disneyland Resort.

Along the way, vehicles travel through blue "scream" tubes that trap guests' yells as they test their vocal cords on the big drops, magnifying the hoots and hollers and adding to the excitement. Every time you approach a tube, you know you're in for a big thrill, so brace yourself and prepare to scream!

Daredevils should be sure to enjoy this ride after the sun goes down, when the night sky is speckled with the pier's glowing lights, and the topsy-turvy twists and turns on the roller coaster will prove even more disorientingly exciting—and scary!

FP = Fastpass attraction (see page 58)

Note: Passengers must be at least 48 inches tall and free of back problems, neck problems, heart conditions, motion sickness, pregnancy, and other physical limitations to ride.

MICKEY'S FUN WHEEL: A modern loop-de-loop, this gleaming Ferris wheel, centered by a huge Mickey face, takes guests on a head-spinning trip. If you think this is a run-of-the-mill Ferris wheel, you're in for quite a surprise: While the wheel turns, most of its cabins rotate in and out along the interior edges of the wheel's giant frame—which creates a dizzying effect. At 150 feet, this is one of the park's tallest attractions, and while it may wreak havoc on sensitive stomachs, thrill seekers rave over its ride within a ride. FYI: This attraction used to be called the Sun Wheel.

Note: Passengers must be free of back problems, heart conditions, motion sickness, and other physical limitations to ride. Afraid of heights? Better skip this one!

HOT TIP!

A few Mickey's Fun Wheel cars remain fixed on the edge as the wheel spins. Request to sit in one of these if you'd prefer to take a more tranquil trip. They are easy to identify—just look for the cars that are marked with an image of Mickey Mouse. (Swinging gondolas are emblazoned with Minnie, Goofy, Pluto, and Donald Duck.)

SILLY SYMPHONY SWINGS: This re-themed ride, which opened in 2010, pays tribute to some of Walt Disney's earliest animated triumphs—the *Silly Symphonies*. The specific symphony highlighted here is the 1935 cartoon called *The Band Concert*. Riders take flight in swings, while band leader Mickey and his barnyard band serenade them with a rousing rendition of the *William Tell Overture*.

As the attraction's momentum picks up, a cyclone reveals itself as guests swirl higher and higher. Skip it if you fear heights.

Note: Riders must meet the Silly Symphony Swings height requirement of 48 inches to ride solo. (Guests between 40 and 48 inches may ride in a double swing. Those under 40 inches are not permitted to take this flight.) All guests must be free of back problems, heart conditions, motion sickness, and other physical limitations to swing here.

GOOFY'S SKY SCHOOL: [FP] At this mini roller coaster attraction, guests of most sizes climb into crop dusters and follow the same fluky flight path taken by the Goof himself. The planes zip through the farm and crash through a barn, causing quite a ruckus among the chickens. Don't let the size fool you. This roller coaster proves that big thrills come in small packages. Although guests as young as three are allowed to ride, it may be too turbulent for some.

Note: Although it's small as roller coasters go, the ride's sudden stops and herky-jerky motion during turns may prove too scary for riders not used to more strenuous coasters. Riders must be at least 42 inches tall and free of back problems, neck problems, heart conditions, motion sickness, and any other physical limitations to take this jolting ride.

JUMPIN' JELLYFISH: A dense kelp bed tops this sea-themed attraction, from which riders sitting in brightly colored jellyfish seats are lifted straight up in the air. When you reach the top, hang on to your tentacles! A parachute unfolds, and fish and friends float safely back down to the ground. While the trip

PHOTO BY JILL SAFRO

is a gentle one with special appeal for younger riders, it might take a few minutes for guests with the most sensitive of stomachs to get their land legs back.

Note: All guests must be at least 40 inches tall and free of back problems, heart conditions, motion sickness, and any other physical limitations to ride.

THE LITTLE MERMAID—ARIEL'S UNDERSEA ADVENTURE: In the first attraction ever to feature everyone's favorite Disney mermaid, guests are invited to board (continuously moving) clam-mobiles and embark on a jolly journey above and below sea level. Along the way, they join Ariel, Flounder, and all of their aquatic acquaintances, and enjoy major musical moments and pivotal plot points from the classic animated feature. It's fun for the whole family.

GOLDEN ZEPHYR: Disney Imagineers took the rocket ride to new heights with the launch of Astro Orbitor in Disneyland. But long before those space-age ships took off, riders were taking flights in rocket-shaped swings on boardwalks and amusement piers across America. Disney pays homage to those old-fashioned attractions with rocket ships that take guests for a spin beneath the Golden Zephyr tower. As speed picks up, the rockets lift into the air and fly over the lagoon several times before touching down for a landing. The ride lasts about a minute and a half.

Note: Passengers must be free of back, neck, and heart problems, motion sickness, and other physical limitations to ride. This attraction does not run when it's windy. There is no height requirement, but youngsters must be able to sit unassisted. Afraid of heights? Sit this one out.

GAMES OF THE BOARDWALK: The games of skill and chance that make up Paradise Pier's Midway are themed with Disney and Pixar characters. Guests can try their hand at amusements like Goofy About Fishin' (magnetic fishing game), Dumbo's Bucket Brigade (water squirting contest), Casey at the Bat (baseball toss), and Bullseye Stallion Stampede (wooden ball-propelled horse race).

Note: To play the games, you must buy a special Playcard with prepaid credits (the games do not accept cash). Playcard machines are located nearby, and the cards can be recharged with additional credits.

HOT TIP!

If you want to sip wine or any other potent potable anywhere at the Disneyland Resort, you'll have to prove you are at least 21 years old. (That's the legal drinking age in California). To do so, you must present an official, government-issued photo ID. (A driver's license or passport will do the trick.) If you can't produce proper ID, you won't be allowed to imbibe. No exceptions.

KING TRITON'S CAROUSEL: Take a spin on one of California's native aquatic creatures on this colorful merry-go-round, located on the boardwalk. The deep-sea theme is carried out in aquatic detail right down to the ride

vehicles themselves. The only horses you'll find here are golden sea horses. They're joined by dolphins, sea otters, seals, and fish, which move to classic organ tunes as the elegant carousel revolves. Be sure to notice all of the fish and marine mammals as they float by—each one was hand-carved, and no two of the creatures are exactly alike.

BIRNBAUM'S BEST

TOY STORY MANIA!: This beloved attraction is an energetic, interactive toybox tour with a twist: Guests wear 3-D glasses as they take aim at animated targets with spring-action shooters. The adventure is about as high-tech as they come, yet rooted in classic Midway games of skill. As points are scored, expect effusive encouragement from a colorful cast of cheerleaders—*Toy Story*'s Woody, Buzz, Hamm, Rex the Dinosaur, and, of course, the Little Green Men.

Fans of Disneyland's Buzz Lightyear Astro Blasters will no doubt delight in this adventure, which takes the experience of the interactive attraction into a whole new dimension. As far as skill level goes, there's something for everyone—from beginners to seasoned gamers alike. (Most folks up their score with a little practice.)

This is an insanely popular destination with guests of all ages. If you want to up your chances of riding without surrendering a significant chunk of the day to waiting in line, make a beeline for Toy Story Mania when the park opens first thing in the morning. You'll be glad you did!

FP = Fastpass attraction (see page 58)

Shopping

Buena Vista Street

ATWATER INK AND PAINT: Shoppers enjoy the quaint ambiance of a 1930s Hollywood-style market house as they peruse decorative items for the home, seasonal merchandise, kitchen gadgets, towels, dinnerware, and more.

BIG TOP TOYS: Teeming with toys, Big Top sells innovative and interactive toys and games, plus plush character merchandise. You'll also find items inspired by theme park attractions. such as the Red Car Trolley, plus a selection of souvenirs featuring Oswald the Lucky Rabbit.

ELIAS & CO.: Paying tribute to the opulent art deco-style buildings of yesteryear, this sprawling emporium features an array of fashion finery for the whole family—it rivals Disneyland Park's Emporium shop in size. They stock clothing, snacks, accessories, watches, and hats. Familiar with the fedoras that Walt Disney sported? Swing by this shop to pick up your very own. FYI: Elias was Walt's middle name and his dad's first name.

JULIUS KATZ & SONS: With its vast array of pins, this trading destination is a hot spot for collectors. The shop's name was inspired by Julius the Cat, a featured character in Walt Disney's classic *Alice in Cartoonland* shorts.

KINGSWELL CAMERA: Stop here to view and purchase photos taken by Disney's PhotoPass team of roving photographers. You'll also find memory cards, cameras, batteries, film, photo albums, and other camera-related souvenirs. The shop's name comes from Walt Disney's first California address. When he arrived in Los Angeles in 1923, he rented a room from his Uncle Robert on Kingswell Avenue. It's where the Walt Disney Company was born.

LOS FELIZ FIVE & DIME: In addition to the park attraction- and California-themed clothing and souvenirs, there is a selection of Disney character items. It's possible to have some items personalized (for a fee).

OSWALD'S: Stop here for autograph books, hats, bags, and souvenirs themed to the park and to Cars Land.

TROLLEY TREATS: If the thoughts of "mountains of candy" and "rivers of fudge" make you smile, this is the shop for you. Temptations include caramel apples, toffee, chocolate-dipped strawberries, fudge, and seasonal selections such as house-made marshmallows. Choose from packaged candy or items made fresh in the display kitchen. It's fun to watch the candy makers at work—and it's even more satisfying to gobble up their creations.

Hollywood Land

GONE HOLLYWOOD: A glamorous, larger-than-life boutique, Gone Hollywood celebrates the shopping styles of Hollywood's rich and famous. Here you will find apparel and accessories—most with a Disney twist.

OFF THE PAGE: The magic of Disney animation leaps off the page at this shop that showcases collectible Disneyana pieces. Cels, limited-edition prints, books, and figurines are sold here, as are attraction-inspired items. Guests may interact with artists as they sketch classic Disney characters.

PHOTO BY MIKE CARROLL

STUDIO STORE: This stand reflects the Muppets' irreverent sense of humor. The wares include clothing, toys, and souvenirs featuring Kermit, Miss Piggy, Animal, and other Muppet friends, plus items featuring Mike, Sulley, and Boo (stars of the nearby attraction, Monsters, Inc.—Mike and Sulley to the Rescue!). The store is near the Muppet*Vision 3-D attraction.

DISNEY CALIFORNIA ADVENTURE

TOWER HOTEL GIFTS: The exit lobby of the Twilight Zone Tower of Terror does double duty as a gift shop. The store sells souvenirs themed to the attraction (pins, shirts, hats, etc.), plus Tower Hotel items such as robes and bellhop bells. This is also the place to buy the photo taken on the attraction. The shot is snapped just before the big drop, so that look of horror is captured forever!

Condor Flats

FLY 'N' BUY: When you see the large selection here, you know this is no fly-by-night operation. The aviation-inspired merchandise includes authentic aviator jackets for kids, T-shirts, hats, souvenirs, toys, pins, and glow merchandise.

Grizzly Peak

EMBARCADERO GIFTS: The mementos here are themed to nearby Ariel's Undersea Adventure attraction. Look for shirts, pins, mugs, books, and assorted playthings.

RUSHIN' RIVER OUTFITTERS: This outpost is the perfect place to gear up for an outdoor adventure. Expect to find a variety of Rushin' River apparel, headwear, towels, ponchos, plus plush toys and more.

Cars Land

RADIATOR SPRINGS CURIOS: Hit the brakes to make a quick stop at this country-style mercantile. You may be tempted to fill the trunk with the latest Disney California Adventure logo merchandise, *Cars*-themed paraphernalia, and accessories. There is also a substantial supply of collector pins.

RAMONE'S HOUSE OF BODY ART: Ramone stocks all manner of items with a *Cars* theme (hey, this *is* Cars Land). There are T-shirts, hats, and Radiator Springs merchandise.

SARGE'S SURPLUS HUT: Young (and young-at-heart) racers rejoice: Sarge has a super supply of clothes and toys that were designed with you in mind. Among the wares are costumes, hats, toys, and snacks. For many *Cars* fans, it's well worth making the pit stop—even if it's just to browse.

Paradise Pier

MIDWAY MERCANTILE: This small spot features toys, games, and other merchandise inspired by characters from *Toy Story* films.

POINT MUGU TATTOO: Merchandise with a World of Color theme (see page 108) are the stock-in-trade at this shop. Point Mugu has apparel and accessories with a California theme. Oddly enough, there are no tattoos for sale here. Though you can get your face painted on the boardwalk (for a fee).

SEASIDE SOUVENIRS: An open-air souvenir stand, Seaside offers character merchandise, hats, glow items, and more.

SIDESHOW SHIRTS: The spotlight here is on shirts of all sorts—tanks, tees, and sweatshirts representing Disney attractions, characters, and films. To complete the look, hats with similar logos are also available for purchase.

PHOTO BY JILL SAFRO

TREASURES IN PARADISE: Treasure awaits little princesses at this seaside location. The shop stocks princess-inspired costumes, apparel, and accessories. Other treasures include *Phineas & Ferb* T-shirts and hats, Mouse ears, watches, jewelry, and candy. This is also the place to pick up Duffy the Disney Bear and Duffy-themed souvenirs. There is a Duffy meet-and-greet location near the entrance.

HOT TIP!

Still haven't quenched your thirst for shopping? Head to the World of Disney in nearby Downtown Disney. It's teeming with Disney character merchandise and souvenirs. (And it's one of many spots to offer a discount to Annual Passholders.)

Entertainment

As Disney California Adventure evolves, new entertainment offerings emerge. For updates, go to *www.disneyland.com*. Check a park Times Guide for schedules.

FIVE & DIME: This singing group travels Buena Vista Street in their jalopy, hoping to get their big break in the music world.

MAD T PARTY: Journey down a glowing rabbit hole and enter a wonderland filled with pulsating lights, color, and music. Mad T Party is a vibrant nighttime dance party.

MINNIE'S FLY GIRLS CHARTER AIRLINE: Minnie is joined by three far-out flight attendants in this "travelogue" of song and dance in Condor Flats.

OPERATION PLAYTIME: A rhythmic squad of *Toy Story*'s Green Army Men are on a mission to serve, protect, and entertain! The plastic platoon engages guests with games and percussive shenanigans.

PHINEAS AND FERB'S ROCKIN' ROLLIN' DANCE PARTY: This lively show features music (courtesy of a deejay), games, and appearances by Phineas and Ferb. Feel free to dance and sing along!

PIXAR PLAY PARADE: This peppy, interactive processional features the colorful worlds of Disney-Pixar pals.

RED CAR NEWS BOYS: Mickey Mouse joins the fun as the boys hawk newspapers in this peppy musical show at Buena Vista Street's Red Car Trolley.

RED TO THE RESCUE: Red the Fire Truck needs help watering the flowers and cleaning up Cars Land. Visit him near Luigi's Flying Tires.

BIRNBAUM'S BEST **WORLD OF COLOR:** FP Arrive early and be prepared to be dazzled. This 25-minute nighttime spectacular, presented on select evenings on Paradise Bay, is a kaleidoscopic journey of music, animation, effects, and, of course, brilliant color. Get a Fastpass if you can.

FP = Fastpass attraction (see page 58)

Hot Tips

✳ Disney characters (including Mickey Mouse) make scheduled appearances throughout the day. Check a park Times Guide for specifics.

✳ Take advantage of Disney's free, time-saving Fastpass system whenever possible.

✳ Check the Information Board often to get an idea of showtimes and crowds.

✳ Many attractions have height restrictions— measure the kids before you leave home.

✳ Golden Vine Winery offers wine tastings (for a fee).

✳ The line for Soarin' Over California tends to dwindle a bit by midday. Ride it then if you choose to forgo the Fastpass option (the experience is enjoyable any time of day).

✳ Shops on Buena Vista Street usually stay open a half hour after the park closes.

✳ On hot days, head to Grizzly River Run or Princess Dot Puddle Park. These splashy spots provide much-needed heat relief.

✳ The jarring motion of California Screamin' can wreak havoc on a digital camera. Store yours in a locker or leave it in the care of a non-riding member of your party.

✳ Ready for a break from the park? Head to neighboring Downtown Disney District for a shopping spree or to grab a bite to eat. There are several (relatively) cost-efficient snacking spots (i.e., Wetzel's Pretzels, Häagen-Dazs, Napolini, Tortilla Jo's, Jamba Juice, Earl of Sandwich, and La Brea Bakery).

✳ Toy Story Mania! has maniacally devoted fans. To minimize the amount of time spent on line, set the alarm, get to the park before it opens, and head straight to this attraction after passing through the turnstile.

✳ Don't risk water-logging your valuables while riding Grizzly River Run. Take advantage of the complimentary lockers (located near the ride's exit). Each locker may be used for free for up to one hour.

Good Meals, Great Times

D ining at the Disneyland Resort is definitely an adventure—and not just in Adventureland. There's more to any meal in a theme park, Downtown Disney, or a Disneyland Resort hotel than just food. Disney friends such as Mickey, Minnie, Goofy, Tigger, Pooh, Chip and Dale, or Donald Duck might drop by your table to say hello. A colorful parade or a romantic paddle wheeler could drift by. Or you might find yourself surrounded by twinkling stars (in the middle of the day!) as you savor Cajun cooking in a bayou setting.

In this chapter, the Disneyland Resort restaurant section is divided by location (Disneyland Park, Disney California Adventure, the three Disney hotels, and Downtown Disney). Within the theme parks, eateries are arranged by area, and then by category—table service or fast-food and snack facilities, including food courts; individual eateries are alphabetized within each category.

If you're hankering for something to do after dinner, or you just need to take a break from the theme parks, you'll find plenty of suggestions at the end of the chapter. Downtown Disney, the property's dining and entertainment district, is party central. Or for a more relaxed atmosphere, chill out in a lounge at one of the three Disneyland Resort hotels.

Dining
In Disneyland Park

Restaurant Primer

Eateries in this chapter have been designated inexpensive (lunch or dinner under $15), moderate ($15 to $29), expensive ($30 to $50), and very expensive ($51 and up). Prices are for an entrée, a soft drink, and either soup, salad, or dessert for one person, excluding tax and tip.

The letters at the end of each entry refer to the meals offered: breakfast (B), lunch (L), dinner (D), and snacks (S). An asterisk (*) after a letter means that the meal is served only during the park's busy seasons.

Cash, credit cards, traveler's checks, Disney Dollars, and Disney gift cards can be used as payment at all of the following full-service restaurants and fast-food spots. Disneyland Resort hotel guests can charge meals from most theme park eateries to their rooms. Only cash is accepted at snack carts.

While only a few park restaurants (Blue Bayou, Big Thunder Ranch Barbecue, Cafe Orleans, Carnation Cafe, and Plaza Inn [breakfast only] in Disneyland, and Ariel's Grotto in California Adventure) take reservations, you can book a table at most Downtown Disney spots and at the Disney hotels. Unless otherwise noted, make reservations by calling 714-781-3463.

One of the most popular foods in Disneyland is the hamburger, followed closely by ice cream and *churros* (sticks of deep-fried dough rolled in cinnamon and sugar). But fitness-minded eaters will be happy to find fish, salads, grilled chicken, and vegetable stew, plus fresh

fruit and juices. Disneyland's table-service restaurants, the Blue Bayou, Cafe Orleans, Big Thunder Ranch Barbecue, and the Carnation Cafe, provide full-course meals and lighter fare, plus a welcome break from long lines and the California sun.

Main Street, U.S.A.

TABLE SERVICE

CARNATION CAFE: On the west side of Main Street, near Town Square, this outdoor cafe is exceptionally pleasant, especially in springtime, when its planters are bursting with seasonal flowers. Stroll through a gazebo to enter the courtyard dining area filled with umbrella-shaded tables and surrounded by a cast-iron fence; from your table you'll get glimpses of any passing parade. Breakfast choices include Mickey Mouse waffles, cinnamon-roll French toast, sticky buns, "croissantwiches" (egg, cheese, and ham grilled in a croissant), apple pancakes, and fruit, yogurt, and granola parfait, along with coffee or tea and orange juice.

For lunch and dinner, sandwich plates are the big draw, along with potato soup and chef salad. Sandwiches include a steak melt and croissant chicken club. A meatloaf stack, pot pies, soup, and kids' specials are also on the menu, along with desserts such as banana splits, fruit pies, and specialty coffees. This cafe is one of four restaurants at Disneyland that offer table service for lunch and dinner (Big Thunder Ranch Barbecue, Blue Bayou, and Cafe Orleans are the others). **B L D** $–$$

FAST FOOD & SNACKS

JOLLY HOLIDAY BAKERY CAFE: A festive tribute to Disney's beloved film *Mary Poppins*, the Jolly Holiday is located at the far end of Main Street, in the space once occupied by the Plaza Pavilion restaurant. There is always a steady supply of fresh-baked pastries here, including cookies and cupcakes. Coffee drinks are available all day (hot and iced). Also on the menu (after 10:30 A.M.): soups, salads, quiches, and sandwiches (including tomato

HOT TIP!

For a jolt of java, head to the Blue Ribbon Bakery on Main Street, Bengal Barbecue in Adventureland, or Royal Street Veranda in New Orleans Square. Their iced and hot specialty coffees are sure to please.

and mozzarella, chicken Waldorf on brioche, turkey, and roast beef on a toasted onion roll). Wash it down with a soft drink—"merry cherry lemonade," anyone? Kids' meals are available as well. **B L D S** $

GIBSON GIRL ICE CREAM PARLOR: A perennially popular place, with a polished-wood soda fountain, marble countertop, and black-and-white-checkered floor, the parlor serves up a delightful array of scoops and toppings in paper cups, handmade waffle cups, and plain or chocolate-dipped cones. We are big fans of the "firehouse dalmatian mint sundae" (hold the cherry). Don't be daunted by the long line; it moves quickly. **S** $

LITTLE RED WAGON: Between the Main Street Photo Supply Co. and the Plaza Inn, it's a throwback to the delivery trucks of the early 1900s, with ornate beveled and gilded glass panels. Step right up and get your hand-dipped corn dogs, the specialty of the wagon. A selection of soft drinks and chips is also served. **L D S** $

MAIN STREET CONE SHOP: Located between Disney Clothiers Ltd. and Market House, this busy window dispenses single or double cones. Two-scoop sundaes are smothered in hot fudge or caramel and topped with whipped cream and a cherry. Ice cream bars, apple slices with caramel, and soft drinks are also served. Tables with umbrellas provide a pleasant resting spot. **S** $

MAIN STREET FRUIT CART: Parked between Disney Clothiers Ltd. and Market House, this old-fashioned cart is stocked with fresh fruit and chilled juices, bottled water, and soft drinks. It's the perfect pit stop for a healthy snack. **S** $

MARKET HOUSE: Wait—this place has been around forever . . . how can it be new? Well, this quaint Victorian-style market recently underwent a major metamorphosis. It still offers a generous selection of snack items, but now it also serves all kinds of coffee and tea concoctions, courtesy of Starbucks. It's possible to get light breakfast selections here, too. **B S** $

PLAZA INN: On the east side of Central Plaza, this eatery is the one Walt Disney was most proud of, and with good reason. Tufted velvet upholstery, gleaming mirrors, and a fine, ornate floral carpet elevate this cafeteria well above similar eateries. Two ceilings are stained glass framed by elaborate painted moldings. Sconces of Parisian bronze and Baccarat crystal are mounted on the walls, and two dozen basket chandeliers hang from the ceiling.

Where to Dine with the Characters

Character meals take place at Disneyland Park's Plaza Inn (breakfast with Minnie and friends) on Main Street; Ariel's Grotto in Disney California Adventure (princesses); Paradise Pier Hotel (breakfast with Mickey and friends); Storytellers Cafe (breakfast with Chip and Dale) in the Grand Californian Hotel; and Goofy's Kitchen in the Disneyland Hotel (brunch and dinner with Goofy and his pals).

The setting, including front-porch and terrace dining (with heat lamps to keep guests toasty at night), creates a lovely backdrop for the food—penne pasta with marinara, Bolognese, or Alfredo sauce; chicken with a spiced sauce, served with mashed potatoes and mixed vegetables; pot roast served with veggies and potatoes; Cobb salad; and desserts.

An extremely popular character breakfast is held here daily, from park opening until 11 A.M. Minnie Mouse and her pals make the rounds, signing autographs and posing for pictures with guests. A fixed-price buffet features omelets, scrambled eggs, French toast, Mickey waffles, sausage, bacon, bagels, yogurt, fresh fruit, pastries, cereal, and more. **B L D S** $–$$

REFRESHMENT CORNER: Better known as Coke Corner, this lively eatery at the northern end of Main Street, opposite Main Street Photo Supply Co., is presided over by a talented ragtime pianist who tickles the ivories periodically throughout the day while visitors nibble hot dogs, chili cheese dogs, turkey dogs, or chili in a bread bowl. Mickey Mouse pretzels with cheese, potato chips, soft drinks, lemonade, and coffee are sold, too. **L D S** $

Adventureland

FAST FOOD & SNACKS

BENGAL BARBECUE: Opposite the entrance to Tarzan's Treehouse, this is a great place to munch on a skewered snack of bacon-wrapped asparagus (a local favorite), or chicken, beef, or veggies. Other menu items include fresh fruit with yogurt topping, Mickey Mouse pretzels, and tiger tails (bread sticks). Cookies, chips, and soft drinks are also available. There is limited seating. **L D S** $

TIKI JUICE BAR: Located at the entrance to Walt Disney's Enchanted Tiki Room, this thatched-roof kiosk sells fresh Hawaiian pineapple spears and pineapple juice, but the biggest draw here is the Dole Whip soft-serve—an extremely refreshing pineapple sorbet (it's nondairy). It's presented by Dole Pineapple. **S** $

TROPICAL IMPORTS FRUIT CART: A close neighbor of the Jungle Cruise, this stand offers fresh fruit, dill pickles, trail mix, chilled bottled water, and soft drinks. There is a selection of plush animals, too. **S** $

Critter Country

FAST FOOD & SNACKS

CRITTER COUNTRY FRUIT CART: This peddler's cart is filled with refreshing selections, including fresh fruit, trail mix, dill pickles, chilled bottled water, and soft drinks. It's perfect if you need some fortification after taking the big Splash Mountain plunge. **S** $

HARBOUR GALLEY: This tiny place, tucked into the shanties that line the docking area for the *Columbia*, offers bread bowls overflowing with New England clam chowder, vegetarian chili, and broccoli and cheddar cheese soup; steak or grilled salmon salads; fresh fruit plates; kids' "power packs" (hearty snack packs with string cheese, yogurt, sliced apples, and crackers); soft drinks; and desserts. **L D S** $

HUNGRY BEAR RESTAURANT: A rustic, waterside classic, this eatery serves veggie burgers, chili cheeseburgers, fried green tomato sandwiches (our favorite!), fried chicken sandwiches, chicken salad, sweet potato fries, and onion rings. For kids, there are chicken breast tenders or "power packs" with yogurt, cheese sticks, goldfish crackers, and apple slices. Dessert options include lemon cupcakes, ice cream sandwiches, and seasonal pies. **L D S** $

New Orleans Square

TABLE SERVICE

BLUE BAYOU: The lure of this popular dining spot is as much the enchanting atmosphere as it is the menu. Occupying a terrace alongside the bayou in the Pirates of the Caribbean attraction, the restaurant appears perpetually moonlit—stars shine through Spanish moss draped languidly over the big, old live oaks. Off in the distance, an old settler rocks away on the porch of a tumbledown shack.

For lunch, choose from items such as pan-seared crab cakes, Cajun-spiced stuffed salmon, roasted chicken, beef short ribs, Royal Street seafood jambalaya, and New York roast. Vegetarians will be drawn to the portobello mushroom and couscous *maque choux* (a rich mix of peppers and corn). Of course, the venerable Monte Cristo sandwich (turkey, ham, and Swiss cheese fried in a battered egg bread) remains a favorite. For dessert, there's chocolate cake, pecan pie, and more.

The dinner menu features many of the lunch selections, plus the Bayou Surf & Turf combo —petite lobster tail paired with a broiled filet mignon. Kids' selections include steak, chicken breast, seared salmon, and Mickey's cheesy macaroni. Kids' meals are served with a beverage and side dish.

The busiest periods are from about noon to around 2 P.M. and from about 5 P.M. until 9 P.M. Reservations are suggested. **L D** **$$–$$$**

HOT TIP!

A gratuity is automatically added to the bill at some Disney restaurants. Examine the bill and tip accordingly.

CAFE ORLEANS: An authentic Cajun-Creole spot, the Cafe offers starters such as French onion soup and New Orleans gumbo. Among the entrées, look for salmon and spinach salad, blackened chicken sandwich, vegetable ragout, two versions of the Monte Cristo sandwich, and seafood and chicken gumbo crêpes. Dessert options include Mickey-shaped beignets and Bananas Foster crepes. Guests may dine inside or outside overlooking a gristmill on Tom Sawyer Island and the *Columbia* and the *Mark Twain* plying the Rivers of America. Reservations are suggested. **L D S** **$$–$$$**

FAST FOOD & SNACKS

FRENCH MARKET: Situated beside the old-time train depot in New Orleans Square, this eatery is a destination in its own right. On a pleasant day, nothing beats sitting on the open-air terrace, munching on baked chicken, salmon, roast beef, pasta, clam chowder served in a bowl made from a scooped-out loaf of bread, four-cheese pasta and vegetable gratin, or jambalaya, the house specialty. Kids' portions of baked chicken, roast beef, macaroni and cheese, and other pasta dishes are available. Dixieland jazz music is played periodically throughout the evening; the Royal Street Bachelors hold forth with such spirit that you could listen for hours. **L D S** **$–$$**

MINT JULEP BAR: Beside the New Orleans Square train station, this window-service bar serves Mickey-shaped beignets (topped with powdered sugar), hot chocolate, coffee, cappuccino, espresso, and iced coffee drinks. The (alcohol-free) mint juleps taste a bit like

lemonade spiked with mint syrup (definitely an acquired taste); happily, real lemonade is also on tap, as are other soft drinks. Enjoy your snack at one of the tables on the French Market's terrace. **B S** **$**

Happy Birthday, Disney Style

For starters, it's always a good idea to inform cast members when you are celebrating a special occasion, no matter where you are at the Disneyland Resort. But it also helps to plan ahead. Birthday cakes can be delivered to any full-service restaurant. They range in price from about $33 to $132 and can be ordered from 2 to 60 days in advance.

If you prefer a character-filled party at Disneyland, arrange a My Disneyland Birthday Party at Plaza Inn. Mickey and Minnie make a special appearance, as does the Plaza's own wacky baker/host, Pat E. Cake. In addition to cake, everyone in attendance gets a party hat and souvenir sipper cup. Cost is about $16 per person. Park admission is required. Reserve at least 5 days ahead.

Big Thunder Ranch Barbecue is the place to celebrate any and all occasions—cowboy style! The outdoor, family-style restaurant serves up plenty of entertainment and food to make for a super soirée.

The Paradise Pier Hotel's PCH Grill has birthday celebrations, too. The cost is about $5 per person (plus the meal) and includes party favors.

For details, to order a cake, or to make reservations at the aforementioned eateries, call 714-781-3463.

Finally, guests (of all ages) may enjoy a "bucketful of birthday magic" by purchasing a special Disney-themed bucket. Topped with a tiny birthday cake, buckets are filled with birthday treats. They cost about $20 (plus tax) and are available at many Disneyland restaurants that offer table service. Call 714-781-3463 for details.

ROYAL STREET VERANDA: Situated opposite Cafe Orleans, this little snack stand has bread bowls overflowing with creamy clam chowder, vegetable or steak gumbo (each with a bit of a slightly spicy kick); fritters that come with a dipping sauce; and a variety of beverages. Check out the wrought-iron balustrade above the Royal Street Veranda's small patio. The initials at the center are those of Roy and Walt Disney (this balcony belonged to an apartment that was being constructed for Walt himself). **L D S** $

Frontierland

TABLE SERVICE

BIG THUNDER RANCH BARBECUE: Yee-ha! This family-style dining experience invites guests to mark special occasions—birthdays, anniversaries, first-time visits to Disneyland, and more—with Western flair. The menu includes barbecue ribs and chicken with traditional sides, plus vegetarian and gluten-free items (upon request). Dessert is available for an additional cost. A popular choice is the family-style "chocolate chip cookie bake"—a fresh-baked cookie in a skillet, topped with vanilla ice cream and hot fudge. Reservations are recommended. **L D** $$

FAST FOOD & SNACKS

GOLDEN HORSESHOE: Head to this (dry) saloon for chicken nuggets, fish and chips, chili in a bread bowl, and chili cheese fries. Wash it down with a refreshing soft drink.

HOT TIP!

If you plan to celebrate a special event while at Disneyland (anniversary, birthday, honeymoon, engagement, etc.), tell reservationists ahead of time. They can help you make the occasion even more special. Call Disney Dining at 714-781-3463 for additional information and to make reservations.

Cap off your meal with an ice cream sundae. Seating is on a first-come, first-served basis. Disneyland purists may remember that the Golden Horseshoe Revue was one of the park's original 18 attractions and was the world's longest running stage show (July 17, 1955–October 12, 1986). **L D S** $

RANCHO DEL ZOCALO: Situated near the entrance to Big Thunder Mountain Railroad, this Frontierland eatery features south-of-the-border specialties. Several common Mexican dishes, including soft tacos and burritos, along with selections such as fire-grilled citrus chicken, carne asada, tortilla soup, tostada salad, and Mexican-inspired Caesar salad are sure to hit the spot. For dessert, there's flan, *tres leches* cake, and fresh tropical fruit. **L D S** $

RIVER BELLE TERRACE: The terrace, between the Golden Horseshoe Saloon and the Pirates of the Caribbean, offers one of the best views of the Rivers of America and of the passing throng—and the food is wholesome

PHOTO BY JILL SAFRO

B breakfast **L** lunch **D** dinner **S** snacks $ *under $15* $$ *$15–$29* $$$ *$30–$50* $$$$ *$51 and up*

GOOD MEALS, GREAT TIMES

and hearty. Walt Disney himself used to breakfast here most Sunday mornings. The menu features scrambled eggs, country-style potatoes, a fruit plate, and cinnamon rolls. Of the breakfast fare, the popularity prize goes to the Mickey Mouse pancakes—a large flapjack for the face, two small pancakes for the ears, a curve of pineapple for the mouth, a cherry for the nose, and berries for the eyes.

For lunch or dinner, the restaurant offers "signature sandwiches" (River Belle's Roast New York, Mississippi Turkey Breast, Tennessee BBQ Pork, and Vegetable Po' Boy), as well as entrées such as salads featuring New York roast, turkey breast, and Aunt Polly's Harvest Medley. Kids' meals (turkey or PB&J sandwiches) come with grapes, sliced apples, and soft drink. With its lovely interior, it's almost as pleasant to dine inside as it is to eat outside. **B L D** **$–$$**

SHIP TO SHORE MARKETPLACE: Nestled near the exit of the *Mark Twain* and *Columbia* riverboat attractions, this snack dispensary sells fresh fruit, corn on the cob, chimichangas, frozen lemonade, cold beverages, and hot chocolate. **S** **$**

STAGE DOOR CAFE: In the mood for one of Disneyland's famous hand-dipped corn dogs? Head here! This small fast-food stand, which adjoins the Golden Horseshoe Stage, also serves fish and chips, chicken nuggets, funnel cakes, and beverages. Grab a seat at a cafe table outside. **L D S** **$**

Fantasyland

FAST FOOD & SNACKS

EDELWEISS SNACKS: Next door to the Matterhorn, this chalet-style kiosk can supply a quick post-ride pick-me-up in the form of turkey legs, hot dogs, chimichangas, buttered or chili-lime corn on the cob, chips, and a choice of soft drinks (including a selection of frozen beverages). **S** **$**

TROUBADOUR TAVERN: Located within the Fantasyland Theatre (home of the Mickey and the Magical Map show), this spot dispenses bratwurst, baked potatoes with toppings, corn on the cob (served with hot butter or chili lime), frozen treats, and soft drinks. Breakfast pastries are served until 11 A.M. **B L S** **$**

VILLAGE HAUS: Near Pinocchio's Daring Journey, this house with its gables, pointy roof, and wavy-glass windows could easily have been relocated to Fantasyland from an alpine village. Inside, murals recount the story of Pinocchio. The menu features pastrami cheeseburgers, classic cheeseburgers, chicken sausage in a pretzel roll, pizza (cheese, pepperoni, or BLT flatbread), apple and cheddar salad, chocolate cupcakes, apple strudel, and soft drinks. A children's meal is available. **L D S** **$**

Mickey's Toontown

FAST FOOD & SNACKS

CLARABELLE'S: On Toon Square, adjacent to Pluto's Dog House, Clarabelle's specializes in "udderly" tasty frozen treats, Mickey Mouse crispie treats, plus sandwiches and salads. Wet your whistle with lemonade, root beer, milk, or other soft drinks. **S** **$**

Sweet Treats

One of the biggest treats in the park is the "Premium Viewing" package for Fantasmic! Guests enjoy a dessert box of pastries, fruit, and coffee, tea, and other beverages, plus they see Fantasmic! from the best possible vantage point at the water's edge. At about $59 per adult (kids pay $49), this is a super splurge. The 75 seats sell out quickly, so call 714-781-4000 up to 30 days in advance or sprint to the Guest Relations window at the entrance to the park (it's to the right of the turnstiles) and make your reservation first thing. Check-in time is 7 P.M. Seating is first-come, first-served.

Or make a beeline for Main Street, U.S.A., and the Jolly Holiday Bakery, the Gibson Girl Ice Cream Parlor, or the Candy Palace, which has tasty saltwater taffy. And by all means, sample a *churro* (fried dough rolled in cinnamon and sugar) from a food cart—it's quite popular.

DAISY'S DINER: This window serves up individual cheese and pepperoni pizzas (served with sliced apples). Cookies, milk, juice, sodas, and lemonade round out the menu. L D S $

GOOFY'S FREE-Z-TIME: The vacation trailer parked by Goofy's House is a dispenser of large frozen slurpy drinks. S $ (Seasonal)

PLUTO'S DOG HOUSE: Nestled between Clarabelle's and Daisy's Diner, this is the place to find a hot dog served with chips or sliced apples. Extras include cookies, Pluto's crispie treats, and soft drinks. The kids' meal comes with a turkey hot dog or mac and cheese with chips, and a soft drink. L D S $

Tomorrowland

FAST FOOD & SNACKS

TOMORROWLAND TERRACE: Near Star Traders, this is one of the park's largest dining areas. Breakfast items include scrambled eggs, French toast, breakfast burritos, and fruit plates. At lunch and dinner, choose from a menu that offers burgers (veggie, classic, or barbecue bacon burger: an other-worldly dish with bacon, cheese, an onion ring, and barbecue sauce), sandwiches (chicken breast with avocado salsa, roasted portobello and veggie, and grilled fish), or grilled chicken chopped salad. A children's menu is available, too. Dessert options include chocolate parfait, chocolate chip cookie, strawberry whole fruit bar, and carrot cake. B L D $–$$

REDD ROCKETT'S PIZZA PORT: Situated across from Innoventions, this food court overlooks the Moonliner and Cosmic Waves. Separate stations serve pasta, pizza, or salads, all prepared in an open display kitchen.

Menu choices include pizzas (cheese, pepperoni, veggie, and a daily special, by the slice

HOT TIP!
Well-balanced options are available throughout Disneyland—and children's meals are no exception. Kids' meals generally include a small entrée, side dish, and beverage, and come in kid-pleasing shapes and sizes. All meals come with a healthy side and a choice of lowfat milk, juice, or water. Toddler meals are available in some spots, too. If you don't spot a kids' menu, just ask—they're offered at many eateries.

or pie), Celestial Caesar Salad, Asian chicken salad, the Planetary Pizza Salad, Mars-inara (spaghetti and meatballs with tomato sauce), Terra Nova Tomato Basil Pasta, and Count-Down Chicken Fusilli. A beverage counter and cooler supply drinks. L D S $–$$

TOMORROWLAND FRUIT CART: Fruit may not sound very futuristic, but it is a healthy way to snack today. Stop here for apple slices with caramel dipping sauce, oranges, grapes, bananas, watermelon, pineapple spears, pickles, soft drinks, trail mix, and more. S $

A+ for Atmosphere

Disney's talent for creating a unique and memorable setting extends to the eateries throughout the park. For atmosphere, we pick the following:

New Orleans Square
The Blue Bayou restaurant, for its perpetual moon glow and grown-up atmosphere, and the French Market when the Royal Street Bachelors perform.

Main Street, U.S.A.
The Plaza Inn, for its antiques, charm, and front-porch seating.

Critter Country
Hungry Bear restaurant, for a wooded setting that lets you feel in the heart of things, yet curiously removed.

Frontierland
River Belle Terrace, for its pleasant views of the Rivers of America.

B breakfast **L** lunch **D** dinner **S** snacks $ *under $15* $$ *$15–$29* $$$ *$30–$50* $$$$ *$51 and up*

In Disney California Adventure

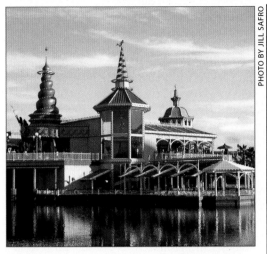

PHOTO BY JILL SAFRO

With a winery and an elegant bayside eatery, the tastes at Disney California Adventure are clearly grown-up. But several fast-food spots and snack stands supply theme park fare with an entertaining flair—retro Hollywood decor or a seaside boardwalk setting. Just remember: Don't gorge before experiencing thrill rides!

The full-service eateries here—including Ariel's Grotto, Carthay Circle Theatre, and Wine Country Trattoria—accept reservations. Call 714-781-3463 to book a table. For updates, visit *www.disneyland.com.*

Buena Vista Street

TABLE SERVICE

CARTHAY CIRCLE THEATRE: The original Carthay Circle Theatre was one of the best known and revered movie palaces in Hollywood history. It also happens to be where Walt Disney's *Snow White and the Seven Dwarfs* made its dazzling debut. The theatre has been painstakingly re-created here at Disney California Adventure. But don't go expecting to catch a flick—this version of Carthay Circle Theatre is actually a popular signature restaurant. Menu items such as roasted beet salad, warm artichoke tart, and grilled quail stuffed with prosciutto-wrapped peaches earn rave reviews. Reservations are recommended. **B L D $$$**

FAST FOOD & SNACKS

CLARABELLE'S HAND-SCOOPED ICE CREAM: Cones, shakes, and sundaes are the chilly treats served here. The lines are longest midday, when the energy-sapping sunlight is at its peak. **S $**

FIDDLER, FIFER, AND PRACTICAL CAFE: Named for everyone's favorite trio of little pigs, this cafe is a great spot to quell hunger pangs and enjoy a coffee drink, courtesy of Starbucks. **L D S $**

MORTIMER'S MARKET: Stop here for "the freshest fruit in town." In addition to produce, there are other healthy snacks and soft drinks from which to choose. FYI: The Mouse was almost named Mortimer. Lillian Disney talked her husband into naming him Mickey! **S $**

Hollywood Land

FAST FOOD & SNACKS

AWARD WIENERS: Hot and heaping cheese and chili dogs—with the occasional autograph request or two—are the specialties here. Sausages round out the menu. A nearby seating area provides plenty of shaded tables (by the Muppet*Vision 3-D attraction). **S $**

FAIRFAX MARKET: Inspired by the historic farmers market in Los Angeles, this stand serves up whole fresh fruits, sliced mango and watermelon, and strawberries with chocolate dipping sauce. Also on the menu? Fresh, cut vegetables with ranch dip, hummus, dill pickles, chips, and soft drinks. **L D S $**

SCHMOOZIES: Yogurt-and-fruit smoothies are the specialty of the house. For some, these chilly drinks are a meal unto themselves. Lattes, cappuccinos, and other coffees are also available. **S $**

STUDIO CATERING CO.: Dine like a movie star at this craft services-like catering truck. Choose from corn on the cob, chimichangas, turkey legs, soft drinks, and more. **L D S $**

Condor Flats

FAST FOOD & SNACKS

TASTE PILOTS' GRILL: The patties grilled at this establishment just may leave burger lovers on cloud nine. Expect items such as ribs, chicken breast nuggets, salad with grilled chicken, and onion rings to round out the lunch and dinner menu. For breakfast, look for selections such as egg white and spinach burrito, sausage breakfast burrito, oatmeal, cereal, fresh fruit, and more. `B L D S` $

Pacific Wharf

TABLE SERVICE

GHIRARDELLI SODA FOUNTAIN: San Francisco's famous sweet-maker now calls Disney California Adventure home. Stop by this soda fountain for a chocolaty treat, root beer float, or a malt. There's no better place to please a sweet tooth. (And there's always the possibility of a free sample.) The coffee is tops, too—both the hot and iced varieties. `S` $–$$

WINE COUNTRY TRATTORIA: Located on the lower level of the mission house at the Golden Vine Winery, this family-friendly spot offers creative Mediterranean fare that blends nicely with the international wine list. Favorites include "pasta your way," braised lamb shank, and sustainable fish with citrus pesto. Wines are available by the glass or the bottle (of course!). Wine flights with three tastings are also offered. There is a children's menu for the little ones.

Outdoor dining in the plaza features a fountain surrounded by herbs and flowers, conjuring images of Napa Valley. Inside, the dining room is reminiscent of a hacienda with plastered walls, terra cotta tiles, and arched doorways. Reservations are recommended.

World of Color picnic meals (to be enjoyed before or during the evening's fountain and light show) may be purchased and picked up at the Sonoma terrace. `L D S` $–$$$

FAST FOOD & SNACKS

ALFRESCO LOUNGE: One flight up from Wine Country Trattoria is an inviting lounge with a full bar and light appetizers. On the menu: Wine Country Shrimp served on polenta cake with lemon caper butter sauce; fried calamari; and beef tenderloin panini. Pair your food with red or white sangria, or a selection of wine flights from California or Italy. There is a full bar, and soft drinks are served. The Lounge offers guests a great view of Cars Land—which is exceptionally lovely at night. `L S` $$–$$$

COCINA CUCAMONGA MEXICAN GRILL: Tasty tortillas are the house specialties and serve as the foundation for most menu items. Among the choices are soft tacos, burritos, tamales, fire-grilled citrus chicken, carne asada, and chicken tamales. Kids' meals include a bean and cheese burrito, chicken taco, and chicken with rice. `L D` $–$$

LUCKY FORTUNE COOKERY: This walk-up eatery serves hearty Asian creations: beef, chicken, or tofu with vegetables, rice, and a choice of four sauces (Mandarin orange, spicy Korean, Thai coconut curry, or teriyaki). Sides include mango slices and steamed edamame. There's a special selection for children, too: teriyaki chicken and rice. `L D` $–$$

MENDOCINO TERRACE WINE TASTING: Take a break beside a hand-carved stone fountain and sip local varietals at this alfresco lounge at the Golden Vine Winery. Cheese platters complement the vino nicely. Included in each $15 platter are three types of cheese, grapes, olives, and crackers. Wines are available by the glass or bottle, and in sets of three sampling flights. Sparkling apple cider and other soft drinks round out the menu. `S` $$–$$$

PACIFIC WHARF CAFE: Guests at this extension of Boudin's display bakery have the opportunity to sample some of the country's finest sourdough bread (from a secret family recipe dating back to 1850). Hearty soups and salads are served up in thick bread bowls for lunch and dinner. Croissants and muffins are offered in the morning hours. `B L D S` $–$$

GOOD MEALS, GREAT TIMES

Paradise Pier

TABLE SERVICE

ARIEL'S GROTTO: A character-laden dining spot, Ariel's Grotto offers enchanting views of Paradise Pier's amusements and the water below (dinner is especially festive when the boardwalk is aglow with twinkling lights). What's more, Disney princesses arrive to mingle with diners at breakfast and lunch. Guests pay one price and select one item for each course. Expect all the usual breakfast favorites in the morning. For lunch and dinner, fish, salads, and pastas fill the menu. Specific menu items include herb-crusted chicken breast; spinach and ricotta agnolotti (stuffed pasta); cioppino with lobster, mussels, and shrimp; and pasta with Italian sausage. Meals start with an antipasti tower and include a basket of bread (whole grain and sourdough rolls), soft drinks, and dessert (lava cake, chocolate chip strips, s'more chocolate bites, and more). Reservations are recommended. **B L D $$$**

THE COVE BAR: This waterside, open-air lounge offers a light menu with items such as fish tacos, lobster nachos, spinach and artichoke dip, and more. A full bar is available. Guests may sit at the bar (provided they are 21 years old) or at nearby tables. **L D S $–$$**

FAST FOOD & SNACKS

BOARDWALK PIZZA AND PASTA: Near the water's edge, this buffeteria-style restaurant serves Italian dishes, including pizza by the slice, pasta with a choice of sauces, and salads. Meals may be enjoyed alfresco, on the shaded patio. Live entertainment from the Paradise Garden Bandstand is an added treat. **L D S $**

CORN DOG CASTLE: Juicy corn dogs, deep fried to a golden brown and served on a handy stick, reign supreme. **L D S $**

DON TOMÁS: Step up to this window to order turkey legs and hot dogs. Corn on the

HOT TIP!

In the mood for dinner and a show? Visit *www.disneyland.com* to order a picnic meal to enjoy while viewing World of Color. It's also possible to walk up and purchase a picnic meal at Sonoma Terrace in the Golden Vine Winery. Meals, which cost about $15 each, may be reserved up to 60 days in advance and must be redeemed for the designated show date and time.

For a bigger splurge, consider a World of Color Dinner Package at a table-service eatery. Call 714-781-DINE for information and to make reservations.

cob, chips, and beverages are also sold at this waterfront snack stand. **L D S $**

PARADISE GARDEN GRILL: True to its name, this spot specializes in grilled items, including marinated skewers of beef, chicken, or fish. The menu also includes Greek salad, strawberry brownie, and baklava. Kids choose from grilled chicken skewer or beef kabob, served with rice and fruit. **L D S $**

PARADISE ICE CREAM CO.: Refreshing soft-serve ice cream (chocolate, vanilla, and twist) helps guests cool off after a long day of fun in the sun. The "beachfront floats" are quite satisfying. **S $**

Cars Land

FAST FOOD & SNACKS

COZY CONE MOTEL: Sally's cozy motel has been converted to a quick-service eatery in the park's rendition of Radiator Springs. The menu was being tweaked at press time, but guests may find items such as hot dogs, ice cream cones, pop "cone," and chili "cone" carne. Beverages are served, too. **L D S $**

FILMORE'S TASTE-IN: Guests here fuel up on smoothies, plus other healthy snacks and soft drinks. It's the perfect place for a quick and refreshing pit stop. **S $**

FLO'S V8 CAFE: Inspired by classic roadside diners, Flo serves burgers, milkshakes, and root beer floats. The mac and cheese is a real crowd-pleaser. There is ample indoor and outdoor seating. **L D S $–$$**

In the Disneyland Resort Hotels

PHOTO BY JILL SAFRO

Disneyland Hotel

The diverse dining possibilities here range from grand to Goofy. For reservations or information, call 714-781-3463.

THE COFFEE HOUSE: Order bagels, muffins, pastries, fruit, yogurt, cold cereal, cookies, and coffee in this small shop. Sandwiches, salads, and fruit plates are available at lunchtime. As the name indicates, this place specializes in fresh-brewed coffee—with everything from a simple cup of decaf to a cafe mocha and ice-blended latte. Outside seating only. Expect long lines in the morning. **B L S** $

GOOFY'S KITCHEN: This whimsical dining room features popular meals and personal encounters with Goofy and other Disney characters. Service here is buffet style, so fill your plate as high and as often as you please. Just be sure to clean that plate!

Highlights at breakfast include Mickey Mouse-shaped waffles and made-to-order omelets. Dinner offers roasted strip steak,

pasta, chicken dishes, macaroni and cheese, pizzas (including peanut-butter-and-jelly pizza, a favorite with youngsters and Birnbaum editors alike), salads, breads, fruit, and desserts. Don't forget your camera—characters provide prime photo opportunities. Reservations are suggested (same-day reservations are not accepted, but you can put your name on the standby list). **B L D** $$–$$$

PHOTO BY KEITH GROSHANS

STEAKHOUSE 55: An upscale dining establishment, Steakhouse 55 is decorated with oak paneling and etched glass and has a nostalgic Hollywood motif featuring pictures of the matinee idols of yesteryear. But the real stars here are the steaks, all cooked to perfection. The menu also boasts a pistachio-crusted rack of lamb and seafood selections. Specialties of the house include a bone-in rib eye with the signature Steakhouse 55 rub, and lump crab cakes with remoulade. The impressive wine list touts several fine California vintages. Reservations are suggested. Menu selections are subject to change. **B D** $$$$

TANGAROA TERRACE: Visit this eatery and travel back in time. The retro-tiki design was inspired by the Tahitian Terrace restaurant— a longtime Adventureland staple. The fare at this casual counter-service restaurant, however, is decidedly modern. The breakfast menu includes an egg white, veggie and tofu bake; French toast with bacon and warm banana-caramel sauce; grilled cinnamon-spiced

---

HOT TIP!
You may encounter a very long line at The Coffee House in the morning. If so, head to Downtown Disney's Earl of Sandwich or La Brea Bakery for a quick breakfast or cup of coffee.

---

oatmeal cakes with island fruit compote; and a whole wheat breakfast wrap with scrambled eggs, ham, and avocado. Items available all day include Hawaiian cheeseburgers (with teriyaki sauce, bacon, and grilled pineapple); Asian chicken salad; and Kahlua pulled-pork flatbread. For dinner, consider miso-crusted salmon, teriyaki-glazed New York strip steak, or panko-crusted chicken. The kids' menu includes chicken breast nuggets, grilled salmon, and burgers. There is a "grab and go" selection, too. Choose from items such as a yogurt parfait with tropical fruit and house-made granola, tropical fresh fruit plate, pastries, sandwiches, and a variety of frozen treats. **B L D S** $–$$

Disney's Paradise Pier Hotel

The eatery here has all the bases covered—from creamy mushroom bisque to wood-fired pizza. And wait till you see what Mickey Mouse has cooked up for breakfast! For reservations at PCH Grill, call 714-781-3463.

HOT TIP!
Any full-service dining location at a Disneyland Resort hotel will validate your parking at that hotel; remember to get your parking pass stamped before you leave.

HOT TIP!
Napa Rose's adjoining lounge offers several of the restaurant's appetizers, as well as an impressive wine list.

DISNEY'S PCH GRILL: Besides the Surf's Up! Breakfast with Mickey & Friends (which offers a buffet meal), Disney's PCH Grill—the initials stand for Pacific Coast Highway—reflects classic California tastes. Family favorites are offered at the omelet station and kids' buffet, plus specialties that include breakfast flatbreads from the wood-burning oven, caramel banana French toast, grilled breast of chicken with roasted garlic sauce, and the signature chilaquiles with shredded beef, salsa verde, and queso fresco. Dinner is a character-free, à la carte affair. Reservations are suggested. **B L D** $$

Disney's Grand Californian Hotel & Spa

The restaurants here offer a taste of (and a twist on) California cuisine. For reservations, call 714-781-3463.

NAPA ROSE: This popular, nationally recognized, award-winning restaurant features a creative menu of market-fresh, wine country-inspired dishes flavored by fruits of the sea and vine (the eatery is named after California's most famous valley of vineyards). A striking, 20-foot, stained-glass window offers views of Disney California Adventure, while the open kitchen gives insight into California cooking.

The offerings evolve as new items are introduced, but favorites include pan-roasted scallops with a sauce of lobster and lemon

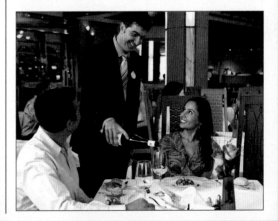

accented with vanilla; mushroom risotto; and braised Alaskan halibut. Slowly braised Angus beef short rib is a signature dish, but the Napa Rose best seller is the shared appetizer known as Seven Sparkling Sins. The dessert tray offers delectable creations from artisanal ice cream to a Wine Country Fuji apple crisp and Cordillera chocolate pave. The California wine list is one of the most extensive on-property. Reservations are suggested. **D** **$$$–$$$$**

HEARTHSTONE LOUNGE: Though primarily a drinking spot, this lounge offers appetizers and is open in the morning for early risers in search of coffee and the day's paper. Continental breakfast items—including specialty coffees—are also available. **B S** **$**

STORYTELLERS CAFE: It's hard to imagine a time before computers and television (especially for the youngest members of the group), when children were exposed to new cultures and histories only through the stories of others. This restaurant salutes tales set in the state of California, like "The Celebrated Jumping Frog of Calaveras County" and "Island of the Blue Dolphins," through murals that act as backdrops to the chefs at work in

the exhibition kitchen. In the morning, the stage is set for a festive, character-hosted buffet. Chip, Dale, and other Disney characters entertain guests, while the buffet offers a bounty of breakfast options, from pancakes and waffles to eggs, sausage, and a selection of fresh fruit. Lunch and dinner offer such pleasers as Nebraska corn chowder, spare ribs, flatbreads, pastas, steak, salads, seafood, and Sonoma braised chicken. Reservations are suggested. **B L D** **$$–$$$**

WHITE WATER SNACKS: The splish-splash of the waterfall and kids soaring down the slide at the Redwood pool set the mood for this ultra-casual dining spot. Open for breakfast, lunch, and dinner (though hours vary), the snack bar serves coffee, muffins, bagels, sweet rolls, French toast sticks, buttermilk biscuit egg sandwiches, Mickey waffles, oatmeal with berries and brown sugar, and breakfast burritos in the morning. Large salads, deli sandwiches, burgers, veggie burgers, hot dogs, personal pizzas, chicken or beef nachos, and grilled chicken are lunch and dinner options. Other items that may be offered: candy, crackers, whole fruit, yogurt, cereal, soft drinks, beer, and wine. **B L D S** **$**

HOT TIP!
If you don't have a reservation, expect a long wait at mealtimes. It is next to impossible to snag a table at a Disneyland Resort hotel or Downtown Disney eatery with any spontaneity. Don't get caught with your stomach growling—plan ahead! Restaurants may be booked up to 60 days in advance. Call 714-781-3463.

In Downtown Disney

CATAL RESTAURANT & UVA BAR: A sun-kissed balcony, outdoor tapas bar, and villa-style dining room set the Mediterranean mood at this casual but classy restaurant. The menu focuses on grilled seafood, chicken, and vegetables, infused with olive oil and citrus accents. With pastas and salads available, vegetarians have much to choose from here. The courtyard bar serves appetizers and cocktails. Reservations are suggested; 714-774-4442. B L D $$$

EARL OF SANDWICH: Here you will find a celebration of the history of the sandwich and the family credited with its creation. It features deli cuisine, with freshly prepared sandwiches and salads (request the the dressing on the side). Snacks and beverages are sold, too. B L D S $

ESPN ZONE: This spot serves up baskets of ballpark fare, plus items like grilled chops, ribs, wings, and salmon. If you want to get close to the action, you'll want to get a table (be prepared to place an order). Hard-core fans may want to ask about the leather easy chairs complete with sound systems and serving tables. If there's a big game on the schedule, arrive at least an hour early. L D S $$

HAAGEN-DAZS: The dessert specialist has ice cream, frozen yogurt, sorbet, and gelato—as well as baked goods and coffee. S $

HOUSE OF BLUES: Diners with a craving for Southern cookin' will find bliss at this Delta dive. With a menu set deep in the South, the eatery offers items such as Memphis-style ribs, voodoo shrimp, jambalaya, and tasty thin-crust pizzas. On Sundays, guests sing hallelujah for the all-you-can-eat Southern-style Gospel Brunch. Reservations are suggested; 714-778-2583 or 714-781-3463. B L D $$$

JAMBA JUICE: In the mood for a tropical smoothie? Perhaps one with protein or a berry blast? They've got that and more. S $

LA BREA BAKERY: Many offerings at this destination—breakfast treats, grilled panini sandwiches, and classic sandwiches—are built on La Brea's legendary, freshly made bread. Also available are salads (made with organic greens), soups, and turkey chili, plus coffees.

There is counter service and an outdoor, covered patio with table service. B L D S $–$$

NAPLES RISTORANTE E PIZZERIA: Dine inside or alfresco at this contemporary Italian trattoria. A large outdoor terrace provides perfect views of the Disney landscape, plus a peaceful and romantic setting for lunch or dinner. Pizzas are served in individual portions or *al metro* (one meter long and perfect for a hungry family to share). The menu also includes *piccoli piatti* (salads served tapas style), pastas, and seafood. Gluten-free pasta and other menu options are available. For reservations, call 714-776-6200. L D $$$

NAPOLINI: Adjacent to the popular Naples Ristorante e Pizzeria, this quick-serve spot also offers Italian fare, but on the simpler side than that served by its neighbor. L D $$

RAINFOREST CAFE: Greenery, misty waterfalls, tropical storms, mechanical animals, and several real-life creatures create a sometimes hectic, always colorful, atmosphere in this spot. The menu features sizable environmentally themed appetizers and entrées, including pastas, burgers, and sandwiches. Reservations, which are available up to one year in advance, are recommended; call 714-772-0413 at least two weeks ahead. B L D S $$–$$$

RALPH BRENNAN'S JAZZ KITCHEN: Sample some homestyle New Orleans specialties at this comfy cafe while listening to jazz. Gumbo, jambalaya, chicken, and fresh pasta dishes are house favorites. Reservations are suggested; 714-776-5200. L D S $$–$$$

TORTILLA JO'S: A colorful Mexican restaurant and open-air cantina, this spot offers culinary traditions including taquitos, quesadillas, handmade tortillas, made-to-order guacamole, and lime-marinated ceviches. Reservations are suggested; 714-535-5000. The adjacent Taqueria serves classic Mexican quick-service selections. L D S $$–$$$

WETZEL'S PRETZELS: Whether you prefer pretzels salty or sweet, Wetzel's can satisfy. Ambitious snackers enjoy the Sinful Cinnamon and the Cheese Meltdown. S $

Restaurant Roundup

There are more dining choices than ever before at the Disneyland Resort. We've picked our favorites, based on food quality, restaurant atmosphere, and overall value. Use these Birnbaum's Bests to help you decide where to grab a quick bite or have a hearty meal.

BEST RESTAURANTS FOR FAMILIES

TABLE SERVICE
Goofy's Kitchen ....Disneyland Hotel (p. 120)
Blue Bayou ....Disneyland Park (p. 112)
Storytellers Cafe ....Grand Californian Hotel (p. 122)
Rainforest Cafe...................................Downtown Disney (p. 123)

QUICK SERVICE
Royal Street Veranda ....Disneyland Park (p. 114)
Rancho del Zocalo ....Disneyland Park (p. 114)
Refreshment Corner ....Disneyland Park (p. 112)
Pacific Wharf Cafe.......... Disney California Adventure (p. 118)
Flo's V8 Cafe .... Disney California Adventure (p. 119)

BEST PIZZA

Naples Ristorante e Pizzeria
Downtown Disney (p. 123)

BEST COFFEE

Fiddler, Fifer, & Practical Cafe
Disney California Adventure
(p. 117)

BEST QUICK SERVICE

Flo's V8 Cafe
Disney California Adventure
(p. 119)

BEST CHARACTER MEAL

Goofy's Kitchen ....Disneyland Hotel (p. 120)

RUNNERS UP
PCH Grill...Paradise Pier Hotel (p. 121)
Plaza Inn ....Disneyland Park (p. 111)
Storytellers Cafe ....Grand Californian Hotel (p. 122)

BEST RESTAURANTS FOR ADULTS

Napa Rose .... Grand Californian Hotel (p. 121)
Steakhouse 55... Disneyland Hotel (p. 120)

RUNNERS UP
Carthay Circle Theatre........ Disney California Adventure (p. 117)
Ralph Brennan's Jazz Kitchen ....Downtown Disney (p. 123)
Wine Country Trattoria....... Disney California Adventure (p. 118)

BEST SNACKS

Jolly Holiday Bakery Cafe ....Disneyland Park (p. 110)
Tiki Juice Bar ....Disneyland Park (p. 112)

Entertainment
Disney Hotels

The Disneyland Resort has more to offer than thrill rides and characters. There's plenty to do at Disney's three hotels and in the Downtown Disney dining, shopping, and entertainment district. Whether you're seeking a break from the theme parks or a place to party the night away, the following options are sure to please.

Note: For additional information on evening theme park happenings, refer to the *Disneyland Park* and *Disney California Adventure* chapters of this book.

Lounges

DISNEYLAND HOTEL: The **Lounge at Steakhouse 55**, with its comfortable leather sofas, convenient conversation areas, and sophisticated decor, provides an intimate meeting place. **Trader Sam's**, named for the infamous "head" salesman at the Jungle Cruise and adjacent to Tangaroa Terrace, mixes drinks and snacks with a bit of Disney magic.

DISNEY'S GRAND CALIFORNIAN HOTEL: The lounge adjoining the elegant **Napa Rose** restaurant offers an extensive selection of wines by the glass and a soothing atmosphere. It's also possible to order a savory snack.

At the handsome **Hearthstone Lounge**, you can sip a cocktail or an after-dinner cordial opposite a roaring fireplace. If so inclined, you may enjoy your beverage on a comfy couch in the majestic lobby, where live piano music is always a possibility.

DISNEY'S PARADISE PIER HOTEL: The **Surfside Lounge** in the resort's lobby serves hot breakfast items in the morning and light fare (burgers, salads, sandwiches, snacks, and more) throughout the day.

Live Entertainment

DISNEY'S GRAND CALIFORNIAN HOTEL: As a tribute to the early 1900s storytelling tradition, entertainers tell tall tales in the hotel's main lobby throughout the day. A piano player adds to the ambience.

Fun & Games

DISNEYLAND HOTEL: Kids can steer small, remote-control Jungle Cruise boats by the hotel's lagoon. The beach's volleyball court is a hit, especially in the afternoon; the Game Arcade in the shopping enclave scores high points on evenings when the parks close early.

DISNEY'S PARADISE PIER HOTEL: Youngsters have a blast at this hotel's arcade, located off the main lobby.

Spa Services

DISNEY'S GRAND CALIFORNIAN HOTEL: A relaxing escape to a spa is as welcome a diversion as they come—especially when it is a visit to the world-class pampering palace known as **Mandara Spa**. Treatments here include all manner of massage, facials, body wraps, manicures, pedicures, and more. There are services specially tailored for couples and teens. A tea pavilion allows spa guests to enjoy a meditative, Zen Buddhist tea ceremony. For a complete list of services, go to their Website: *MandaraSpa.com*. To make an appointment, call 714-300-7350.

GOOD MEALS, GREAT TIMES

Downtown Disney

Easily accessed by foot (from the Disneyland Resort hotels or theme parks) or monorail (from Disneyland Park's Tomorrowland), this entertainment district offers escape from the hustle and bustle during the day, and a place to mix and mingle in the evening hours. Many Downtown Disney venues serve double (or triple) duty as dining and dancing (and sometimes shopping) spots.

Shops open early and don't close until late in the evening. Club performers generally hit the stage post-dinner and wrap past midnight.

Clubs & Concerts

HOUSE OF BLUES: Don't let the name of this jumping joint fool you—the lineup features a rousing mix of rock, R&B, hip-hop, reggae, and Latin music, along with a touch of the blues. Big-name bands and local acts are slotted to perform throughout the week. Call 714-778-2583 to learn the House's schedule during your visit. Ticket prices range from about $5 to $35, depending on the performer. Call Ticketmaster at 800-745-3000 or visit *www.ticketmaster.com* to buy tickets in advance, or stop by the club's box office the day of the performance.

RALPH BRENNAN'S JAZZ KITCHEN— FLAMBEUX'S JAZZ CLUB: The sounds of jazz set the tone for the relaxed atmosphere at this restaurant's lounge. Bands and singers entertain with live jazz every evening. A smooth soundtrack provides music when the stage is dark. Special tickets may be required for certain performances. Call 714-776-5200 to inquire about ticket reservations.

Lounges

CATAL RESTAURANT & UVA BAR: Designed to resemble the Art Nouveau style of a Paris metro station, this large wine and tapas bar tempts guests with the fruits of the vine and sea. Guests can drink under the stars at the outdoor bar or mingle indoors, and can select from the extensive wine list.

ESPN ZONE: Stop by the bar area of the Zone's Studio Grill for a tall one before heading upstairs to play arcade games at the Sports Arena. With large-screen TVs blaring from each section of the room, expect the joint to be jumping on big-game nights. If there is a big game you simply cannot miss, get there at least an hour (or more) before it begins.

MAGIC MUSHROOM BAR: Part of the lush Rainforest Cafe, this circular drinking hole is capped by a giant mushroom and serves up aptly named blended beverages, such as the Margarilla and the Tropical Toucan (nonalcoholic versions are also available). Don't be surprised if a tot takes over a neighboring stool—this establishment is a big family spot.

OUTDOOR PERFORMERS: Downtown Disney boasts an eclectic lineup of free, live musical entertainment. From calming classical to rousing rythym and blues, professional musicians create a party-like atmosphere on a daily basis. For up-to-the-minute entertainment schedules, text DTDNOW to DPARK (37275) to receive up to three text updates per week, or visit *www. disneyland.disney.go.com/downtown-disney/*.

GOOD MEALS, GREAT TIMES

Shopping

BLINK: This celebration of all that is denim features the latest wearable trends and accessories. While the merchandise does extend beyond the dungaree, the shop is proud of its denim-forward fashion: Denim experts are on hand to consult with shoppers and impart product wisdom.

BUILD-A-BEAR WORKSHOP: Create your own stuffed animal, as you "choose, stuff, stitch, fluff, name, and dress" your way through a series of bear-making stations. It's a "beary" special experience.

DISNEY PIN TRADERS: Do we really need to tell you what this spot specializes in? Didn't think so.

DISNEY VAULT 28: A chic boutique, this spot showcases trendy items and apparel for men and women, some inspired by Disney characters and films.

D STREET: A place where urban art-inspired products "intersect" with Disney design. This space showcases a mix of Disney-themed art created by local and underground artists. Also available are clothing, collectibles, and more.

ESPN ZONE STUDIO STORE: Sports fans will cheer for the ESPN, SportsCenter, and Monday Night Football-branded apparel and other stuff at this shop in ESPN Zone.

FOSSIL: Got the time? They do! Stop here for watches galore, plus fashionable leather goods, accessories, and jewelry.

HOUSE OF BLUES COMPANY STORE: A slew of spicy sauces lets you take a bit of this House back to your house. Home accessories and

House of Blues logo merchandise round out the options here.

THE LEGO STORE: Hundreds of the world's most famous building brick sets and products are for sale, along with hats, shirts, and other items. There's an indoor/outdoor play area, too.

LITTLE MISSMATCHED: Tired of trying to match up stray socks? This place is your dream come true. None of the socks here match! Also on the shelves are boots, flip-flops, jammies, dresses, and more. Most of the items are meant for young girls, but there are some selections for boys, babies, and grown-ups, too.

MARCELINE'S CONFECTIONERY: Named for Walt Disney's childhood hometown, this sweet-shop offers classic and contemporary candies and other treats.

QUIKSILVER: Surfer wear and accessories help guests dress the part of beachcomber.

RAINFOREST SHOP: Adjacent to the Rainforest Cafe, this shop offers plush animals, environmentally themed toys, Rainforest Cafe logo items, and snacks.

RIDEMAKERZ™: Build and customize your own radio-controlled vehicle at this supercharged, interactive store. Trick out real-world and concept cars: Ford Mustangs, Dodge Vipers, Chevy Corvettes, hot-rods, pick-up trucks, sports coupes, and much more.

SANUK: Retire those pinchy old shoes and replace them with cool and comfy footwear at Sanuk. In addition to "sidewalk surfers" for kids and grown-ups, this shop sells hats, hoodies, T-shirts, and more. FYI: *Sanuk* is the Thai word for fun. By the way, if we could wear Sanuks every day of the year, we would.

SEPHORA: A black-and-white motif provides a perfect backdrop for the colorful palette of products in this cosmetics mecca. Sephora's own line of makeup is complemented by a selection of popular beauty products and perfumes. It's possible to create personalized gift baskets, too.

SOMETHING SILVER: Perfect for celebrating a 25th anniversary, or just creating a look, the jewelry here is simple and stylish. Note that there are many lovely non-silver selections to choose from, too.

STUDIO DISNEY 365: Ready for your close-up? Come here for a Hollywood makeover and be turned into a star! Choose from five different "Studio Star Makeover and Transformation" packages, including hair, make-up, and wardrobe. Basic packages start at about $20–$80, plus tax. Reservations are recommended; 714-781-STYLE (7895). Makeovers are designed for guests ages 3 and up. All kids must be accompanied by an adult.

SUNGLASS ICON: Cool, custom-fit shades are the stock-in-trade at this shop. All the big-name designers are represented.

WORLD OF DISNEY: Shelves are stacked sky-high at this souvenir shopper's dream come true. Each overflowing room features a different theme and type of merchandise, from men's and women's apparel to watches and accessories, plus a lot in between. With areas dedicated to plush toys, dolls, home decor, DVDs, clothing, mugs, and collectibles, everyone is bound to find something here. The place is busy most evenings and on weekends—especially after the parks close.

WONDERGROUND GALLERY: Distinctive and eclectic, Wonderground is a work of art in and of itself. The contemporary venue showcases unique art collections and works from a new generation of artists, interpreted through different mediums, styles, and forms.

Fun & Games

AMC MOVIE THEATRES: Moviegoers enjoy wall-to-wall movie screens and comfy stadium seating at each of the 12 cinemas located inside this megaplex (including IMAX). Current releases are shown throughout the day, with special matinee and late-night screenings. The first showing of the day usually comes at a discount.

ESPN ZONE: This sports complex offers dining options and a lounge area, plus two distinct fun zones. In the Screening Room, sports fans can cheer their teams to victory, as games from around the world are televised on one central 16-foot screen and a dozen 42-inch monitors.

The Sports Arena challenges guests with sports-themed games that put your skills, strength, and smarts to the test. Game cards (necessary to play the arena's games) can be purchased in $5 increments.

Arrive early when a big game is scheduled.

HOT TIP!

Want to save a little money at Downtown Disney? Visit *www.disneyland.com* to see if there are any special offers available for the day you plan to visit.

Sports

Southern California's appealing combination of warm, sunny weather and invigorating ocean breezes has created a population of outdoors and exercise enthusiasts. Well-toned athletes flex their muscles on golf courses and tennis courts; atop surfboards, bicycles, and in-line skates; on hiking and jogging trails; or 15 feet underwater, mingling with schools of fish.

As part of Orange County, California, Anaheim is within easy distance of the county's 35,000-plus acres of parkland and several hundred miles of bike trails. Hiking paths and fishing streams crisscross 460,000 acres of mountain terrain in Cleveland National Forest. Just 15 miles south of Anaheim, prime Pacific Ocean beaches—perfect for basking in the sun or catching the ultimate wave—await the wayfarer. In fact, 42 miles of glistening sand and sleepy seaside communities are within an hour's drive of Anaheim.

Those who delight in spying on Mother Nature can catch glimpses of California's gray whales as they migrate to Mexico for the winter, or ospreys, blue herons, and swallows returning to the area in the spring. A team of Orange County's most entertaining creatures, hockey-playing Ducks, can be spotted from September through April (and later, if they make a run for the Stanley Cup). Even Angels have been sighted, gracing the bases at Angel Stadium, April through September (and possibly October).

No question, the sporting opportunities—in and around Anaheim—are quite bountiful.

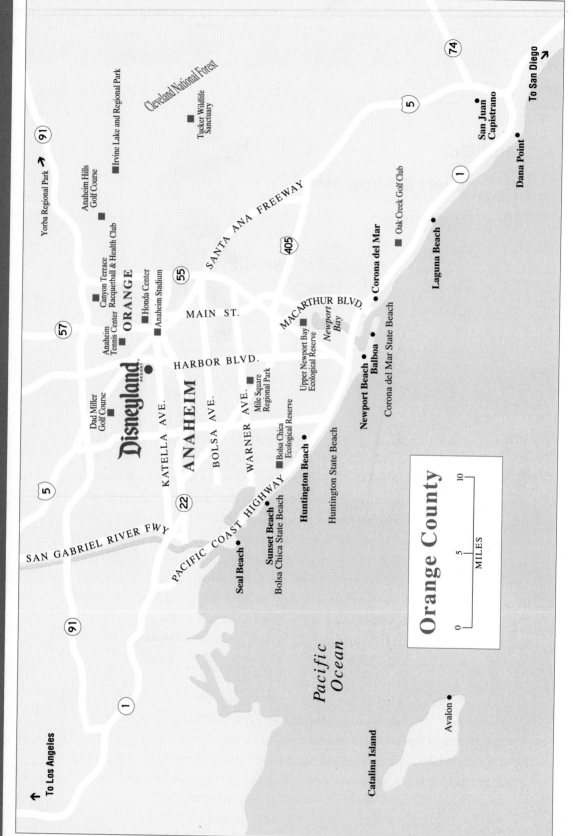

Orange County

MILES

0   5   10

Eye on the Ball

Golf

ANAHEIM HILLS GOLF COURSE: This challenging championship course is a hilly, par-71, 6,245-yard layout nestled in the valleys and slopes of the scenic Anaheim Hills. Greens fees (cart included) are $48 Monday through Thursday, $57 on Friday, and $66 on weekends and holidays. Guests ages 55 and older can play Monday through Thursday for $36 and Fridays for $41. Clubs can be rented for $30. Reservations are recommended (call seven days ahead for both weekend and weekday play). The course is open 365 days a year, dawn till dusk. 6501 E. Nohl Ranch Rd., Anaheim; 714-998-3041; *www.playanaheimgolf.com.*

DAD MILLER GOLF COURSE: "Dad" Miller made a hole-in-one on this course (on the 116-yard 11th hole) when he was 93 years old, and it's still a favorite with older guests, who appreciate the flat, walkable terrain and park-like setting. But if you're a tad on the younger side, don't let that keep you from playing here. This par-71, 6,025-yard golf course is one of the busiest in California—partly because of its convenient location in the northwest corner of the city, but also because it's just right for the strictly recreational golfer. The cost to play here is $27 Monday through Thursday, $35 on Friday, and $39 on Saturday, Sunday, and holidays. Guests 62 and older can play standby for $17 Monday through Friday. Golf carts cost about $24 for 18 holes, $15 for nine holes.

Reservations are suggested and may be made up to a week in advance. The course is open 365 days a year, dawn till dusk. 430 N. Gilbert St., Anaheim; 714-765-3481 (pro shop and reservations); *www.playanaheimgolf.com.*

HOT TIP!

To get additional information about these and other Orange County area golf courses and tournaments, visit *www.playocgolf.com.*

Tennis & Racquetball

ANAHEIM TENNIS CENTER: This public facility has all the perks of a private tennis club—an inviting clubhouse, a well-stocked pro shop, computerized practice machines, lockers, and showers. The staff will even try to pair you with a suitable partner, if you make your request in advance.

There are 12 fast, hard-surface courts, all lighted for night play. Singles and doubles rates range from about $5 to $8 per person, per hour (depending on time of day). Use of a ball machine is about $25 per hour; they are separated from the courts, but this area is still a good place to practice forehand and backhand strokes.

Playing hours begin at 7 A.M. and end at 10 P.M. Monday through Friday, and start at 7 A.M. and end at 6 P.M. weekends and holidays. Racquets are free for those taking lessons. Locker and shower facilities are free (you must supply towels). A half-hour private lesson with the resident pro costs about $38; call for rates for semiprivate or group lessons.

SPORTS

131

Reservations (which are bookable up to three days in advance for nonmembers) are suggested, especially for court times after 5 P.M. It's approximately three miles from the Disneyland resort. 975 S. State College Boulevard, Anaheim; 714-991-9090; *www.anaheimtenniscenter.com/about.aspx*.

CANYON TERRACE RACQUETBALL AND FITNESS CLUB: A real find for visitors, this facility has five air-conditioned racquetball courts and low court fees—$8 per person on weekends or before 4 P.M. Monday through Friday. After 4 P.M., it is $9 per person. The club rents racquets for $2 to $4 and offers its full-size weight room to nonmembers for $7. Towels may also be rented for a small fee. (All prices are subject to change.) There is a pro shop, too. Hours are 6 A.M. to 10 P.M. Monday through Thursday, 6 A.M. to 9 P.M. on Friday, 7 A.M. to 7 P.M. on Saturday, and 7 A.M. to 5 P.M. on Sunday. 100 N. Tustin Ave., Anaheim; 714-974-0280; *www.canyonterraceracquetball.com*.

Spectator Sports

BASEBALL

Los Angeles Angels of Anaheim (April–September): Angel Stadium of Anaheim, 2000 E. Gene Autry Way, Anaheim; call 714-634-2000 (info) or 714-663-9000 (tickets) *www.angelsbaseball.com*

Los Angeles Dodgers (April–September): Dodger Stadium, 1000 Elysian Park Ave., Los Angeles; 866-363-4377; *www.dodgers.com*

BASKETBALL

Los Angeles Clippers (October–April): Staples Center, 1111 S. Figueroa St., Los Angeles; 888-895-8662; *www.nba.com/clippers*

Los Angeles Lakers (October–April): Staples Center, 1111 S. Figueroa St., Los Angeles; 800-462-2849; *www.nba.com/lakers*

Los Angeles Sparks (May–October): Staples Center, 1111 S. Figueroa St., Los Angeles; 877-447-7275; *www.wnba.com/sparks*

HOCKEY

Los Angeles Kings (October–April): Staples Center, 1111 S. Figueroa St., Los Angeles; 800-745-3000 (Ticketmaster); *www.lakings.com*

Anaheim Ducks (October–April): Honda Center, 2695 E. Katella Ave., Anaheim; 877-945-3946 (info) or 800-745-3000 (Ticketmaster); *www.anaheimducks.com*

Surf & Sun

Beaches

Orange County's public beaches cover 42 miles of coastline—some dramatic, with high cliffs and crashing waves; others tranquil, with sheltered coves and tide pools. In summer, the water temperature averages 64 degrees but can get as high as 70; in winter, it's a nippy 57 to 60 degrees.

Beaches are open from around 6 A.M. to 10 P.M., with lifeguards on duty in the summer. Bicycles, in-line skates, and roller skates are available for rent in some locations. Access is free, but there is usually a fee to park. For additional beach information, go to the Surf and Sand section of *www.orangecounty.net*.

BALBOA/NEWPORT BEACH: The Balboa Peninsula juts into the Pacific Ocean, creating beaches—Newport on the mainland, Balboa on the peninsula—that are long and horseshoe-shaped, pleasant and sandy, and popular with families, surfers, and sightseers alike; *www.ocbeachinfo.com*.

The largest small-craft harbor in the world, Newport Harbor shelters more than 9,000 boats. For the best view, drive south along the peninsula on Newport Blvd. to Balboa Blvd.; turn right on Palm Street, and you'll find parking for the Balboa Pier and Fun Zone; *www.thebalboafunzone.com*.

HOT TIP!

For a scenic 45-minute walk, follow the harbor-hugging pathway around Balboa Island. For a mini-expedition, head to Little Balboa Island—it can be easily circumnavigated in about 20 minutes.

Throughout the fall and winter, the 1,000-acre Upper Newport Bay Nature Preserve and Ecological Reserve teems with great blue herons, ospreys, and many other winged creatures. The park's partially subterranean Muth Interpretive Center, at 2301 University Drive (at Irvine Avenue), has exhibits on bird life, the watershed, and the history of Newport Bay (closed Mondays).

During migratory season (October through March), the Newport Bay Conservancy leads free walking tours (once a month, on a Saturday), pointing out birds, as well as fossils, marsh plants, and fish. Every Saturday and Sunday morning, year-round, the conservancy also offers a 2-hour guided kayak tour of the Back Bay for $20 per person, ages 8 and above.

The reserve is open daily 7 A.M. to sunset. To obtain updated information about guided tours and various special events year-round, as well as directions to specific parts of the reserve, contact Newport Bay Conservancy: 949-923-2269 or *www.newportbay.org*.

CORONA DEL MAR STATE BEACH: Secluded Corona del Mar State Beach is a favorite for swimming and snorkeling; and the lookout point above the beach is a great place to watch the sun set. There are picnic tables, grills, fire rings, a snack bar, and showers. For information, visit *www.orangecounty.net* (Surf and Sand section) or call 949-644-3151.

HUNTINGTON BEACH: The self-proclaimed "Surf City, U.S.A." (and home to the International Surfing Museum) hosts competitions year-round (winter is best for wave height). Surfboards and wet suits may be rented or purchased; *www.surfcityusa.com*.

Huntington City Beach is a 3.5-mile stretch of sand fronting the town and is a popular place for swimming, bodysurfing, and beach volleyball. The pier provides an ideal spot for fishing and a good vantage point for observing the passing scene. For surf information, call 714-536-9303; *www.hbonline.com*.

Bolsa Chica Wetlands, 1,300 acres of Pacific Ocean marshland a mile north of Huntington Beach pier on Pacific Coast Highway, harbors fish and wetland birds. To get there, cross the bridge from the beach parking lot and follow a trail through the marsh; 714-846-1114; *www.bolsachica.org*.

LAGUNA BEACH: More than 20 different beaches and coves line this seven-mile coastline, popular with surfers, kayakers, body boarders, and snorkelers. Laguna is one of the best spots in Orange County to scuba dive, though you need a wet suit year-round.

Laguna Sea Sports (925 N. Coast Hwy.; 949-494-6965; *www.beachcitiesscuba.com*) offers full rentals, guided beach dives, classes, general information, and more; there's a pool on the premises, and it's only approximately one block from the beach. Main Beach (which is located in the middle of town) offers basketball and volleyball.

A short walk away, Heisler Park has picnic areas, beaches, cliff-top lookout points, and charcoal grills; stairs lead to tide pools. Serious hikers like to head for Crystal Cove State Park (*www.crystalcovestatepark.com*), Aliso and Wood Canyons Wilderness Park (*www. ocparks.com*), or Laguna Coast Wilderness Park. Watch the sun set from Laguna Art Museum or from Laguna Village; *www.lblg.org* or *www.lagunabeach.com*.

Fishing

In Orange County, you can cast for bass, catfish, and trout in tranquil lakes; troll the Pacific for bonitos, barracuda, halibut, and more; and scoop grunions (license required) off the beach.

FRESHWATER ANGLING: At Irvine Lake, a fishing license is not required, and there is no charge for catching fish, but there are restrictions on the type and amount of fish that can be caught. Gate fees are $24 for adults ($21 for guests 62 and older) and $11 for children 4 through 12; under 4, free; *www.irvinelake.net.*

Fishing poles, motorboats, rowboats, and pontoons may be rented, or you can launch your own craft for a $10 fee. A tackle shop and cafe are on-site. 4621 Santiago Canyon Rd., Silverado; 714-649-9111.

GRUNION ALERT: One place to try your hand—literally—at catching grunion (provided that you have a license) is at Bolsa Chica State Beach in March, June, July, and August, when the tiny fish come ashore to lay eggs in the sand and then head back out to sea on outgoing waves. (Grunion catching is illegal—with or without a license—in April and May.) They are quite slippery, and you are required to catch them with your hands; fortunately, they also shimmer in the moonlight so they're fairly easy to spot. The best time to go grunion fishing is about an hour or two after high tide on the second through fifth nights after a new or full moon. The park closes at 10 P.M.; gates close at 9 P.M. For additional information, visit *www.dfg.ca.gov* or *www.parks.ca.gov,* or call 714-846-3460.

SPORTFISHING: Fishing boats set out from Davey's Locker at Balboa Pavilion in Newport Beach (949-673-1434; *www. daveyslocker.com*), and from Dana Wharf Sportfishing at Dana Point Harbor (*www. danawharfsportfishing.com*; 800-979-3370). Reservations are suggested. Licenses, which are legally necessary for deep-sea sportfishing, are available at either location and cost about $14.50 per day.

Parks

IRVINE REGIONAL PARK: Located in Santiago Canyon, near Irvine Lake, this peaceful place has hiking and equestrian trails that wind through 477 hilly acres and centuries-old sycamores and oaks. The oldest county park in California, it offers bike trails, the Orange County Zoo, playgrounds, and a small waterfall, creek, and picnic facilities. Zoo admission is $2 for guests ages 3 and up. There is a $3 to $5 parking fee per vehicle year-round (The parking fee is usually $7–$10 on major holidays). 1 Irvine Park Rd., Orange; 714-973-6835; *www.ocparks.com/irvinepark.*

MILE SQUARE REGIONAL PARK: It's one square mile in area—hence the name. Besides five miles of winding bike trails, the park has a walking course, a nature area, and picnic areas and shelters. Bicycles may be rented here on weekends and holidays. 16801 Euclid Avenue, Fountain Valley; 714-973-6600; *www.ocparks.com/milesquare.*

TUCKER WILDLIFE SANCTUARY: This 12-acre sanctuary in the Santa Ana Mountains' Modjeska Canyon is an oasis of flora and fauna. Naturalists answer questions, and there are hiking trails, a small natural history museum, and a children's garden. A donation is suggested. 29322 Modjeska Canyon Rd., Modjeska Canyon; 714-649-2760; *www.tuckerwildlife.org.*

YORBA REGIONAL PARK: These 175 acres in the Santa Ana Canyon cradle four lakes, picnic areas, playgrounds, and hiking trails, equestrian activities, horseshoe pits, model sailboating, volleyball courts, baseball fields, and biking trails (bike rentals on weekends). Visitors can walk or ride a bicycle into the park without charge; parking a vehicle costs $3 to $5 ($7 on holidays). 7600 E. La Palma Avenue, Anaheim; 714-973-6615; *www.ocparks.com/parks/yorba.*

Index

Index

QUIKSILVER

15% off
your entire purchase

Subject to terms and conditions on reverse side.

Pack more magic into your Disney vacation with the *Disney Rewards*® Visa® Card and get amazing perks and dreamy rewards.*

Plus, get a

$50 Disney Gift Card

after first purchase with the credit card.

Apply today.

Visit **DisneyVisaOffer.com/Birnbaum** or call 1-800-440-3733 and mention key code 64CS01.

*See back for details.

Let's create some magic.℠

LA BREA BAKERY.

10% off
your final bill
(excluding alcohol)

Subject to terms and conditions on reverse side.

Wetzel's Pretzels

Free Pretzel
when you purchase two pretzels of equal or greater value

Subject to terms and conditions on reverse side.

---

60 Bonus Points

Purchase a $20 game card at ESPN Zone and recieve 60 Bonus Points—a $15 value.

Located in the Downtown Disney® District

Subject to terms and conditions on reverse side.

RIDEMAKERZ
BUILD YOUR RIDE®

10% off
your entire purchase

Build your own freewheel or radio-control toys and trucks at Ridemakerz™.

(See coupon code on reverse side)

Subject to terms and conditions on reverse side.

TERMS AND CONDITIONS

Coupon must be surrendered at time of purchase.

Not valid with any other sales, promotions, or offers. Cannot be used toward gift card purchase or toward durable goods.

For information, call 714-778-4274.

Limit one per coupon.

Photocopies will not be accepted.

Non-transferable, non-negotiable.

Employees please enter code DISNEYBG

Offer valid 1/1/14 through 12/31/14

TERMS AND CONDITIONS

Coupon must be surrendered at time of purchase.

Not valid with any other offers or discounts.

Limit one per coupon.

For information, call 714-535-5994.

Photocopies will not be accepted.

Non-transferable, non-negotiable.

Offer valid 1/1/14 through 12/31/14

TERMS AND CONDITIONS

Valid on full price merchandise in the Downtown Disney® store only and excludes alcohol.

Coupon must be surrendered at time of purchase.

Not valid with any other offers, discounts, or promotions.

For information, call 714-490-0233.

Photocopies will not be accepted.

Non-transferable, non-negotiable.

Offer valid 1/1/14 through 12/31/14

TERMS AND CONDITIONS

Redeemable at the Downtown Disney location in Anaheim, California.

Coupon cannot be combined with any other offer.

Reproductions of coupon not accepted in whole or in part.

Offer subject to change without notice.

Coupon Code: 90151

Offer valid 1/1/14 through 12/31/14

TERMS AND CONDITIONS

Present this coupon along with your game card to receive your free points. Game points must all be on one card. Coupon is valid on same day of game card purchase only. For every new game card purchase, there will be a $1 issuance fee. Game cards can be used on future visits; points expire two years from date of purchase. May not be combined with any other offers. No cash value. May not be resold. Limit one coupon per person, per visit, per day. For information, call 714-300-3776.

Photocopies are not accepted. Offer not valid on special events or during private parties.

Offer valid 1/1/14 through 12/31/14

Notes

Notes